Educating Adolescent Newcomers in the Superdiverse Midwest

BILINGUAL EDUCATION & BILINGUALISM

Series Editors: Nancy H. Hornberger, *University of Pennsylvania, USA* and Wayne E. Wright, *Purdue University, USA*

Bilingual Education and Bilingualism is an international, multidisciplinary series publishing research on the philosophy, politics, policy, provision and practice of language planning, Indigenous and minority language education, multilingualism, multiculturalism, biliteracy, bilingualism and bilingual education. The series aims to mirror current debates and discussions. New proposals for single-authored, multiple-authored, or edited books in the series are warmly welcomed, in any of the following categories or others authors may propose: overview or introductory texts; course readers or general reference texts; focus books on particular multilingual education program types; school-based case studies; national case studies; collected cases with a clear programmatic or conceptual theme; and professional education manuals.

All books in this series are externally peer-reviewed.

Full details of all the books in this series and of all our other publications can be found on http://www.multilingual-matters.com, or by writing to Multilingual Matters, St Nicholas House, 31–34 High Street, Bristol BS1 2AW, UK.

BILINGUAL EDUCATION & BILINGUALISM: 124

Educating Adolescent Newcomers in the Superdiverse Midwest

Multilingual Students in English-centric Contexts

Brian David Seilstad

MULTILINGUAL MATTERS
Bristol • Blue Ridge Summit

DOI https://doi.org/10.21832/SEILST7574

Library of Congress Cataloging in Publication Data
A catalog record for this book is available from the Library of Congress.
Names: Seilstad, Brian D., author.
Title: Educating Adolescent Newcomers in the Superdiverse Midwest:
  Multilingual Students in English-centric Contexts/Brian David Seilstad.
Description: Bristol, UK; Blue Ridge Summit, PA: Multilingual Matters,
  2021. | Series: Bilingual Education & Bilingualism: 124 | Includes
  bibliographical references. | Summary: "This book juxtaposes
  superdiversity with English-centricity in the US, set against
  long-standing challenges with migration and language policy recently
  underlined by Donald Trump's election. It explores the history,
  policies, and practices of a Central Ohio adolescent newcomer program
  seeking to provide an equitable education to its students"— Provided by publisher.
Identifiers: LCCN 2020048657 (print) | LCCN 2020048658 (ebook) | ISBN
  9781788927567 (paperback) | ISBN 9781788927574 (hardback) | ISBN
  9781788927581 (pdf) | ISBN 9781788927598 (epub) | ISBN 9781788927604
  (kindle edition)
Subjects: LCSH: Native language and education—Ohio. | Immigrant
  children—Education—Ohio. | English language—Study and
  teaching—Foreign speakers. | Multilingualism—Ohio.
Classification: LCC LC201.65.O5 S45 2021 (print) | LCC LC201.65.O5
  (ebook) | DDC 428.0071—dc23 LC record available at https://lccn.loc.gov/2020048657
LC ebook record available at https://lccn.loc.gov/2020048658

British Library Cataloguing in Publication Data
A catalogue entry for this book is available from the British Library.

ISBN-13: 978-1-78892-757-4 (hbk)
ISBN-13: 978-1-78892-756-7 (pbk)

Multilingual Matters
UK: St Nicholas House, 31–34 High Street, Bristol BS1 2AW, UK.
USA: NBN, Blue Ridge Summit, PA, USA.

Website: www.multilingual-matters.com
Twitter: Multi_Ling_Mat
Facebook: https://www.facebook.com/multilingualmatters
Blog: www.channelviewpublications.wordpress.com

Copyright © 2021 Brian David Seilstad.

All rights reserved. No part of this work may be reproduced in any form or by any means without permission in writing from the publisher.

The policy of Multilingual Matters/Channel View Publications is to use papers that are natural, renewable and recyclable products, made from wood grown in sustainable forests. In the manufacturing process of our books, and to further support our policy, preference is given to printers that have FSC and PEFC Chain of Custody certification. The FSC and/or PEFC logos will appear on those books where full certification has been granted to the printer concerned.

Typeset by Nova Techset Private Limited, Bengaluru and Chennai, India.

Contents

Tables and Figures	vii
Introduction	1
Preamble	1
The TALIME Study	3
The Journey to the TALIME Study	4
Overview of Chapters	8
1 Tensions Between Superdiversity and Translanguaging, English-centricity and 'Mainstream' in the Education of Adolescent Newcomers	**11**
Immigrants and Language Policy in US History	11
From the Right to Publically Funded Education for All to the Critical Search for Linguistically and Culturally Sustaining Program Models	12
Superdiversity as Practical Challenge and Relevant Theoretical Framework	14
Superdiversity and Language	17
Translanguaging as Key Framework for Sociolinguistic Description and Political Support	18
Ideological Challenges to Superdiversity and Translanguaging: The Symbolic Violence of English-centricity and 'Mainstream Schooling'	23
Language and Content Instruction for Adolescent Newcomers: Contexts, Elusive Clarity and Emerging Approaches for Equity	28
Learning and Teaching with Adolescent Newcomers	29
Language and Cultural Connections in Adolescent Newcomer School Contexts	30
The Challenge of Parallel or Non-parallel Education and Students with Limited or Interrupted Formal Education (SLIFE)	31
Possible Trajectories for Adolescent Newcomers	34
Development of Research about Newcomer Programs	39
Conclusion	43
2 An English-centric Program with Multilingual Margins	**45**
Ohio LEP and District ESL Programs as 'Flexible' Discourse in an English-centric Context	45

	Policy Enactments across Time: History of the Program, Profiles and Views on Bilingual Educational Approaches of Teachers, Administration and Bilingual Assistants	46

Policy Enactments across Time: History of the Program, Profiles and Views on Bilingual Educational Approaches of Teachers, Administration and Bilingual Assistants 46
Positive Yet Critical Teaching and Learning Practices 57
Linguistic Landscape 57
Teacher Talk 64
Instructional Materials 84
Assessment Practices 87
Conclusion 91

3 Students and Outcomes 92
 The Focal Students and Superdiverse Context 93
 A Year in a Day: The Patterns and Changes in the Lab Year 103
 Analysis of the Student Experience 108
 Case Studies 110
 English-centric Assessments and Results: Invisible, Dramatic and Debatable Growth 135
 Conclusion 139

4 Aspirations for Better Program Futures 141
 Overview 141
 Visions of Changes to Current and Future Programming 142
 Critical Reflections and Recommendations 148
 Challenges to Change 152
 Conclusion 157

Conclusion 158
 Summary of Central Findings and Recommendations 158
 Donald Trump and Anti-Immigrant Sociopolitics 159
 Coming Full Circle 162

Methodological Appendix 164
 Foundations for Research Questions: Before Method, Theory 164
 Research Rationale: Why the US? Why a Newcomer Program? Why Lab Students? 166
 Initial Research Questions and Methodology: What Did I Want to Know? Why is Ethnography Well Suited for the Inquiry? What Kinds of Ethnography? How Does it All Fit Together? 167
 Permission, Access and Consent/Assent 175
 Methodological Strengths Yet Several Issues to Address 175
 Corpus of Data 177
 Analysis: Or, How to Make Meaning 178
 On Writing 183

References 185

Index 204

Tables and Figures

Tables

Table 1.1	Summary of parallel/non-parallel and continuous/interrupted education	32
Table 2.1	List of key program actors	49
Table 3.1	List of students, their national origin and start and end dates in class	94
Table 3.2	General profiles of 'High, Mid and Low' students	110
Table 3.3	Student assessment data	137
Table A.1	List of teachers/instructional assistants involved in audio-video recordings	171
Table A.2	General research schedule	177
Table A.3	Corpus of data	178

Figures

Figure I.1	Tile of Ottoman calligraphy with the name of the Prophet Mohammed	2
Figure I.2	Similar Ottoman calligraphic style on Topkapi Palace in Istanbul, Turkey	2
Figure 1.1	Continuum of language understandings on cultural-historical fields	22
Figure 1.2	Interplay between superdiversity and translanguaging	23
Figure 1.3	Relationships between mainstream, parallel, non-parallel and no/little/interrupted schooling	32
Figure 1.4	Grade point average performance trajectories	37
Figure 2.1	'The Languages We Speak' sign	58
Figure 2.2	Image of 'I can learn English' sign	59
Figure 2.3	Image of school/district Positive Behavior Intervention and Supports (PBIS) motto	59
Figure 2.4	Image of Yuna with 'I want to be a singer' superimposed below	60
Figure 2.5	Samuel's text	61
Figure 2.6	'Hurts,' one of nearly 40 'Vocabulary Words of the Week'	61

Figure 2.7	The sole bi/multilingual sign documented in the 2016–2017 academic year	62
Figure 2.8	A wall hanging donated by the previous director of ESL	63
Figure 2.9	Ms Popov's home language test	79
Figure 2.10	Maria's home language writing section	79
Figure 2.11	Ms Popov's vocabulary building sheet	80
Figure 2.12	Home language test, original English version on the left, Arabic translation on the right: test on the left is Mohammed's, 9/10 correct; test on right is Salah's, 1/10 correct	90
Figure 3.1	Images from Ms Cabot's class in August/September, November/December and April/May of the 2016–2017 academic year	102
Figure 4.1	Current and envisioned future Lab structure	148
Figure C.1	Image from YES's mock 2016 election	160
Figure C.2	Sign Ms Cabot put up outside her classroom following the 2016 presidential election	160
Figure A.1	Library image from Transana	180
Figure A.2	Collections image from Transana	180
Figure A.3	Keywords image from Transana	181

Introduction

Preamble

Language and culture are inseparable, a languaculture (Agar, 1996), and this book focuses broadly on languacultural diversity with two concerns at its heart. First is the imperative to create a global society where people, especially refugees and migrants fleeing conflict or simply seeking a better or different life, have the legal right to migrate, are not hindered in that process and are even welcomed and assisted in their adaptation to new contexts. Central to this process is language learning, a focal concern of this book, and societal efforts to help people learn their new environment's dominant language(s) and develop the skills necessary to be independent, socially connected and successful in a new context. The second area is encouraging and supporting the learning of languages and cultures within a society. In most contexts, this means helping citizens or residents of a certain country or area to be aware and accepting of other languacultures. In the US context, the locus for this book, this is directly connected to challenging the centrality of English in order to create more space for people from other languacultures to live and thrive. In the US and other global contexts, this would include resisting language dominance, encouraging bi-/multilingual education or simply supporting new language communities. Put more simply, this book reflects a vision for humanity – a world where more people can and do communicate and connect, often across significant difference and not without certain difficulties, to create something new, unexpected and indeed beautiful.

As an illustration of this notion, I offer a type of Ottoman Arabic calligraphy that is a kind of mirror. The same word, the name of the Prophet Mohamed (Peace Be Upon Him) – starts from the right and left respectively and meets, embraces, in the middle (Figure I.1). That is the simple version of this vision; however, the example in Figure I.2 from Topkapi Palace in Istanbul more accurately represents its complexity.

There are manifold meanings embedded in these texts per se, and the analysis is far from straightforward. One is linguistic; proficient users of Arabic, myself included, can read both versions, but the second takes much more time and even then details may be missed or overlooked.

Figure I.1 Tile of Ottoman calligraphy with the name of the Prophet Mohammed

However, these are not simply words. There is a broad nexus of meanings to consider, including but not limited to the gold letters on green background, their placement on the Ottoman palace par excellence, Islam, Istanbul, power, borders, hybridity, consensus, conflict, the passage of time, and on and on. Not to be overlooked especially are the people – the architects and artisans – who created the image, selecting and rejecting materials, applying them with expert care and maintaining them over time. Moreover, my choice of these images over billions of others is both

Figure I.2 Similar Ottoman calligraphic style on Topkapi Palace in Istanbul, Turkey

suspect and subject to inquiry. In the end, a complete explanation of these meanings is an illusion; the best we can do is to attend carefully to these 'whispers of wind-voices,' as Truman Capote (1966) might say, and hold them in focus for a sustained moment.

The TALIME Study

This study, arising from a project entitled *Teaching and Learning in Multilingual Environments* (TALIME),[1] is about the experiences of newly arrived adolescent newcomers in Ohio considered by the state and district as 'Limited English Proficient' (LEP) and 'pre-functional,' meaning A1 learners in the Common European Framework of Reference (CEFR)[2] in terms of English language knowledge. In the urban Central Ohio district where this study is located, these learners are placed in a newcomer program, a specific institutional design responding to 'superdiverse' (Vertovec, 2007, 2016) demographic shifts, bringing together learners from dozens of different languacultural groups with manifold intersecting issues including immigration background, socioeconomic status, prior education and ability. These programs strive to help learners quickly acquire the English language and academic content knowledge necessary to transition to 'mainstream' schooling.

Using institutional ethnography and discourse analytic approaches to school- and classroom-based research at a local newcomer program called pseudonymously for this book 'Youth English Services' (YES), I followed one cohort of adolescent newcomer students across their coursework throughout the 2016–2017 academic year, and gathered ethnographic data – regular video-taping of classes, interviews and artifact collection – to explore first and foremost how the program understands and supports the students' languacultural backgrounds. This inquiry revealed the program's fundamentally and perhaps unsurprising English-centricity (Pacheco, 2016); however, the goal of the study was to positively explore the program's efforts to support its multilingual students and reveal areas of consensus that lead to encouraging student outcomes while also critically exposing the specific frictions and challenges that restrict student success. Key among these is how English-centric assessment practices lead the program to miss major patterns and problems in students' trajectories that are strongly related to their home language literacy and educational backgrounds. Thus, this book argues for reconsidering English-centric program policies and allocating resources to attend consistently and comprehensively to multilingual adolescent newcomers' home language literacy and prior educations so that the program can thoughtfully and humanely support all students.

The calligraphic images above will be used as a visual metaphor throughout the book to explore and explain YES's various outcomes and lessons. In due course, I hope to untangle and demonstrate aspects of this context and experience that are complicated and even deeply problematic while also showing elements of beauty and excitement emerging for the program and students. Primary among these is the interplay between, on the one hand, the English-centricity of Central Ohio and the focal program and, on the other hand, the multilingual abilities and realities of the students the focal program strives to serve. Put differently, this book explores the 'difficult loving care' deployed by the program, teachers and students to draw on knowledge from 'both sides of the line' that lead to educations and lives of dignity (García, 2020).

The Journey to the TALIME Study

When I came to The Ohio State University (OSU) in 2014 to begin my doctoral studies, I had over a decade of educational experience as a teacher, non-profit manager and educational administrator. My previous experiences included a nexus of interests and concerns around the teaching and learning of languages, specifically Greek, Latin, German, French, Arabic and English (Seilstad, 2012, 2014b), civic engagement through service-learning (Seilstad, 2014a; Seilstad & Meftah, 2016), and living in Morocco for six years and developing a certain focus on the Middle East and North Africa (Seilstad, 2015). Honestly, I assumed that some of these interests would have to be ignored or overlooked as I did not expect Central Ohio to have significant languacultural diversity, a prejudice I and perhaps others, American or otherwise, have about the Midwest.

However, almost immediately upon arriving in the city, I started to notice elements evocative or reminiscent of my experience in Morocco – women in hijabs in the grocery store, people speaking various languages in the parking lot, and many stores catering towards certain ethnic, linguistic or cultural groups along the road near where I lived. Wanting to be more involved, I Googled local refugee and other migrant support organizations, found one and filled out their volunteer application. A few weeks later, I received an email from the volunteer coordinator and soon found myself teaching citizenship classes to Bhutanese-Nepali senior citizens. At that time I had never heard of the ethnic conflicts that this population faced in Bhutan or their 20-year struggle in refugee camps in Eastern Nepal; however, I dedicated myself to learning the basics of the situation quickly. In December 2014, I became more involved with this agency by using my Arabic and French skills to support recently arrived adult refugees on their journey to learn English and find a job. This work evolved, with my writing a state grant for the agency to start a mentoring program to support middle and high school aged refugee youth. Engaging with academic research, during 2015–2016 I continued volunteering with the citizenship classes and initiated several smaller studies – one about Iraqi refugee narratives, one about the citizenship classes with Bhutanese-Nepalis (Seilstad, 2017, 2018) and one about workplace language among working adult refugees. These developed my own knowledge about the specific issues involved with refugee migration and adaptation to life in the US.

At the same time, my OSU coursework guided me to the focal program YES. Not being an Ohio native, I lacked first-hand knowledge about Ohio's approach to education and needed to learn about this context quickly; thus, I addressed this gap by conducting a small pilot study on OSU's First Educational Experience Program (FEEP), a course that requires any student considering an OSU education degree to take a class involving approximately 100 hours of fieldwork in schools around the area. In this project, I followed several FEEP students into different Central Ohio schools; two of the students had their placement at YES when it was at a different site and classified officially as a middle/high school. One of the FEEP students was in a class with a teacher, Ms Cabot, who ultimately became one of the focal teachers in this book. Thus, by chance I found a school and program that spoke directly to my interests of language learning, cultural complexity and migration.

In the summer of 2015, I met another teacher, Derek Braun,[3] at the refugee support agency, who happened to work at YES. Derek and I shared a number of characteristics including being multilingual (he in Spanish and Somali, I in the aforementioned languages), Returned Peace Corps Volunteers, and White males with a vision of languaculturally relevant and sustaining education for refugee and other migrant students. After a number of discussions, we agreed to collaborate on the TALIME research project, and I started the process to conduct research at YES and gained Institutional Research Board, school district and Mr Smith's (the school principal's) approval in October 2015. At this time, YES had undergone a dramatic shift from being an official middle and high school to a reclassification as a program and relocation to a different site. This change had followed more than 15 years of striving to work with newcomer populations more effectively. At the turn of the millennium and particularly through the rapid increase in Somali refugee resettlement, the school district recognized a need to develop new programming to work with newcomers, and started two Welcome Centers offering temporary English as a second language (ESL) services collocated at local schools that later consolidated into YES in 2006. This was designed to be a full middle and high school where students could study and graduate, but in February 2015 a state report found a number of problems with the school, including overcrowding, lack of student graduation and under-resourced classrooms. Thus, the state mandated that YES return to being a two-year program and be relocated to a different building, a former high school, starting in the Fall of 2015. In many ways, this program was starting over, and although I had not been involved in direct research at the former site, I felt disappointed that its full promise was not allowed to come to fruition. However, knowing that this transition would be critical and that, regardless of state policies, refugee and other migrant students would be arriving and in need of high-quality education, I initiated this study in November 2015 with Mr Braun and his 10th grade biology class. Throughout the rest of the year, a few colleagues and I collaborated on this project, leading to several conference presentations and publications (Seilstad & Kim, 2020; Seilstad et al., 2019).

The focal study for this book started in the summer of 2016. I wanted to research a group of first-year students who are high school aged, 15–21 years old, and relatively new to learning English. This age and English-language proficiency range had emerged for me as a particular population of concern, doing 'double the work' of having not only to learn English well enough to communicate but also to cope with the advanced academic demands and high-stakes tests that come in high school (Short & Fitzsimmons, 2007), in addition to navigating the cultural construction of adolescence as a transition period wracked by hormonal changes, social drama and age-specific issues (Lesko, 2012). These two factors may contribute to this group of students having a high dropout rate (Fry, 2005). For these reasons, I felt that researching a group of these students would be fruitful.

Coincidentally and conveniently, YES organized these students into cohorts called 'Lab' and 'Core', where the former, usually newly arrived students, are beginning English learners at approximately the A1 or A2 levels and the latter are more developed learners at A2 or B1. In the first Lab year, students shared, with slight variation, the same schedule and teachers to help facilitate sociocultural learning and group cohesion. My initial hope was that Mr Braun would be involved because he had been developing an approach to learning and teaching with this group that bridged bilingual education and TESOL immersion practices. For example, Mr Braun had designed a 'Bilingual Biomes' project during the last month of the academic year that asked the students not only to use their home language to help make meaning of the activity but also to make a PowerPoint and give a presentation in their home language to the class followed by an English translation (Seilstad & Kim, 2020; Seilstad et al., 2019). I felt that these efforts were exciting and innovative for the space and was eager to work with him.

However, the ethnographic reality of fieldwork in changing institutions came into play when, in midsummer 2016, Mr Braun was moved to another school's ESL sheltered site. Those who have done this type of research can appreciate the sense of panic that set in while I had to frantically find another group of teachers to work with. Thankfully, Mr Braun was able to make an introduction to several other teachers, Ms Cabot among them, who agreed to work with me and helped establish the relationships with the other focal teachers. Thus, by early August 2016, I had secured participation for regular video-recording of classroom activities, participant observation and interviews with the four key content area teachers – Ms Cabot for English, Ms Popov for social studies, Mr Shahiya for science and Mr Barre for mathematics – as well as broader institutional access.

Although students did take an 'Encore' class in art, music, gym/health or computers, the students did not remain a cohort in these classes so, for both methodological and practical reasons, I opted to focus on the content courses for regular, sustained video-recording of classroom activities and only observed the Encore classes a few times during the year. On the other hand, I was interested in another instructional context, the 'Reading Clinic,' an intensive English program for students identified by the Dominie assessment[4] as 'pre-K' in terms of reading and communicative ability in English. The Dominie is a face-to-face reading assessment where the students progress incrementally from an initial 'Show Me' activity with pictures to reading gradually more difficult books and answering questions until the student is unable to progress further. Then, the student's class level is assigned, from 'pre-K' and up, with each academic year divided into 'beginning,' 'middle' or 'end.' For example, a student might initially be assessed as 'pre-K' but progress through the year to 'mid-2nd.' As the Reading Clinic was a key intervention for select students led by the instructional assistant team that had many bilingual teachers, I did video-record these classes regularly throughout the year.

In considering the research project, I was influenced by Sierens and van Avermaet (2013) and wanted to conduct a study that commenced from the very beginning of the language learning experience, looked at a certain program context and design, was respectful and aware of relevant theory, resisted 'either-or' approaches and focused on what actually happens in the classroom (Sierens & van Avermaet, 2013: 209–210). For these reasons, I designed a focused study of the classroom that would connect to the broader Lab context, by observing and recording their language and content learning and social adaptation processes while also considering how these match up with various measures of their learning. I knew that this would not be a simple process, in that YES, by its superdiverse nature, enrolls new students throughout the year, has high student mobility and, for adolescent learners especially, would experience some drop outs. However, a goal of this research is to consider ways to ensure that students remain attached to the school and have the best chance to fulfill their educational potential.

To sum up, my work in this area is far from that of a disinterested observer. This school is moving through time and evolving. This was only the second year of its return to a two-year program rather than being a school where students could graduate. Now students should spend no more than two years at this school before transitioning to a 'sheltered site' at a mainstream school. These sites will themselves be fertile areas for future research, even though many issues there can be anticipated based on previous research (e.g. Bal, 2014; Trueba, 1988). Beyond these sites, the progression imagined for these students is attending all or almost-all mainstream classes, passing the required graduation tests, enrolling in post-secondary education, finding careers and developing self-affirming social identities, whether in the US or other transnational contexts (Anzaldúa, 2012; Bartlett, 2007; Orellana, 2016).

In broader terms, YES and this book illustrate how rapid demographic change impacts educational institutions and how the responses – from the institutions and their various actors – reflect histories and ideologies that create program practices supportive or constrictive of adolescent newcomers' learning. More generally, this book is about ensuring that schooling for these students is available, exciting, positive and progressive. All students, in the US or globally, deserve to enter school systems and receive an equitable education, but unfortunately this is not a reality for certain students, which the latter sections of this book will take up. Moreover, the election and administration of Donald Trump and other global leaders have made it clear that the demographic trends towards more multilingual, multicultural global societies are far less a natural progression than one molded by government policy towards refugees and other newcomers, economic development, employment possibilities and immigration law and enforcement. It is not a stretch of the imagination to see that certain members of American society and this administration would look at newcomer programs and determine that the easiest way to solve the educational issues therein would be to ensure that the students never arrive in the first place. This is not only an abrogation of what America and indeed humanity stand for but also a lost opportunity for educators to understand more fully how to create equitable educational possibilities in superdiverse contexts. Put differently, this book is founded on the hope and vision that diversity is good per se, which is supported by various data indicating that the US population is becoming more comfortable with diversity and even sees it as a strength, a hallmark of the nation (Cox *et al.*, 2011; Drake & Poushter, 2016). This book is part of this discussion, and my goal is on the one hand to advocate for these and other superdiverse contexts that welcome youth from around the world while, on the other hand, acknowledging that the work for teachers, administrators, staff and students is incredibly challenging, requiring at times critical yet constructive dialogue about the approaches being employed or considered.

Overview of Chapters

Following this Introduction, Chapter 1 reviews the background of newcomer programs and relevant pedagogies of language and content learning for adolescent newcomers. Newcomer programs emerge from the general struggles of various minoritized populations to ensure their rights to equitable educations as well as quite specific and rapid superdiverse demographic shifts. In newcomer programs, translanguaging frames the expected sociolinguistic practices and recommended pedagogical positions of the various actors. However, language ideologies filter these sociolinguistic, political and pedagogical realities and possibilities, particularly in newcomer programs where the power of students and their communities is relatively weaker than the educational institution.

Chapter 2 turns first to a description of YES within the relevant state standards, the program history, the school actors' trajectories and perspectives on supporting languaculturally diverse students and people as well as a general description of the research questions and methodology that are more fully elaborated in the Methodological Appendix. The chapter then moves to initial findings of the study that describe, on the one hand, the fundamental English-centricity of the space with, on the other hand, the various yet marginal multilingual practices that could be further recognized, formalized and expanded. This is accomplished through close analysis of the linguistic landscape, the common patterns involved with learning and teaching in this space, and some of the systematic challenges to engaging students' languacultural backgrounds.

Chapter 3 turns to the critical issue of the student outcomes by describing more fully the superdiverse context and the focal cohort. Then the chapter considers results from student assessments and aligns them with ethnographic case studies of students which illustrate some of the possibilities and difficulties of learning and teaching in this space. The key finding from this chapter is that YES's English-centricity creates a profound blind spot to the critical issue of home language literacy which then prevents the program from understanding or supporting all students efficiently, equitably or adequately.

Chapter 4, drawing primarily on the responses teachers, administrators, instructional assistants and students gave when asked what changes or improvements they might make to the structure of the program, addresses visions of program improvements which would challenge English-centricity and focus on understanding students' home language literacy and prior education as the primary consideration in program policies and practices. This underlines that the program is not a static institution but rather one with a dynamic future being shaped by external politics and policy, recommendations from multiple stakeholders and opportunities for principled change.

The Conclusion summarizes the central findings of the book and recommendations for program change while addressing the broader implications of the study and what it reveals about the challenges of providing equitable services to adolescent newcomers in the context of Central Ohio, around the US and globally. These emerging directions are potentially positive moves that envision and embrace an emerging identity for Central Ohio and the Midwest as a space with new and vibrant diversity being nurtured despite manifold pressures at the local, state, national and international levels. The final parts of the book – the references and especially the Methodological Appendix – give details regarding the previous scholarship and methods underlying the study.

Notes

(1) TALIME is an acronym of the Arabic word for 'education' or 'learning.'
(2) Ratings in the CEFR include the 'Basic User' levels at A1 and A2, 'Independent User' at B1 and B2 and 'Proficient User' at C1 and C2.
(3) All names in this book except for Mr Braun are pseudonyms.
(4) This and other types of assessment used in the program will be discussed more fully below.

1 Tensions Between Superdiversity and Translanguaging, English-centricity and 'Mainstream' in the Education of Adolescent Newcomers

Immigrants and Language Policy in US History

The United States, pre- and post-Independence, has had a long and tortured history with non-European, non-English speaking populations, especially those who had lived here for millennia as first peoples, who were brought here as enslaved people or who have come as immigrants. Throughout, educational language policies and practices have vacillated between efforts to eradicate, restrict, tolerate or support the languages people use in their private and public lives (Crawford, 2004: Ch. 3; García, 2008b: Ch. 8).

White European colonizers of the Americas imposed the 'full gamut of inhumanities' (Wiley, 2007: 91) on more than 12 million enslaved people by systematically and violently separating them from their home cultures and languages and forcing them to live either in compulsory ignorance or with only token levels of English-only education. The violence visited on the enslaved African populations is a deplorable situation which has marred social and educational life in the US up to the present day (Anderson, 2006; Haymes, 2001; Wiley, 2007: 91). Evidence of this policy of cultural eradication is that not one native African language survived the trans-Atlantic crossing and can be found spoken today in the United States. On the other hand, the traces and impacts of African languages and cultures do indeed survive in a wide variety of contexts, from African-American Vernacular English to hip-hop (e.g. Alim, 2006; Osumare, 2008).

The Native peoples, despite their diversity, educational practices and resources, suffered devastating losses at the hands of White European colonialists whose policies of genocide and forced/coerced integration ultimately led to forced migration onto reservations, many far removed from their native lands. Nevertheless, their descendants have fared somewhat better than enslaved peoples in terms of education and language, overcoming the 'civilizing' efforts of Native schooling to a point today where Indigenous language revitalization and maintenance is a reality, albeit an often tenuous one (Gaither, 2014; McCarty, 2007; Warren, 2014).

Immigrants come to the US for various reasons, ranging from temporary stays to pursue educational or economic opportunities to long-term residency and even citizenship. These transnational flows of people, money and ideas, while perhaps more pronounced today due to the greater ease of travel and telecommunications (Vertovec, 2009), have been occurring for centuries. After initial settlement and US Independence, European migration continued to dominate the 18th and 19th centuries of US history, creating significant blocks of German communities in the North, Spanish or French in the South and Chinese or Japanese in the West, especially in the coastal regions of California, Oregon and Washington. The 20th century brought many more groups from Northern, Central and Southern Europe, but the changes to the Immigration and Naturalization Services Act in 1965 expanded immigration opportunities to more communities from Asia, Africa and Latin America. However, educational policy for the many families and individuals from non-English speaking cultures has vacillated between tolerance and resistance, from early acceptance and promotion of bilingual schooling in the 18th and 19th centuries to backlashes brought on by the World Wars and more recent xenophobic political movements (García, 2008b).

From the Right to Publically Funded Education for All to the Critical Search for Linguistically and Culturally Sustaining Program Models

The rights guaranteed in the original US Constitution were limited to White landholding men but have gradually expanded to cover most citizens and even immigrants. While not directly a constitutional right, state-funded education developed from early mandates in Puritan Massachusetts (Teaford, 1970) to today's robust educational networks supporting students from pre-K through to advanced degrees. Although education for minoritized groups was often forbidden, suppressed or simply underfunded and neglected, the post-WWII era expanded access to equitable educational opportunities dramatically, with the Supreme Court's 1954 *Brown v Board of Education* decision, the Elementary and Secondary Education Act of 1965 and the Bilingual Education Act of 1968. Critical for immigrants from non-English speaking cultures, the Supreme Court's 1974 *Lau v Nichols* decision demanded that students from these cultures should not be subjected to English-only education but should rather be provided with adequate linguistic support for their learning. More specifically, the Supreme Court's 1981 *Castañeda v Pickard* decision demanded that programs serving students in this category:

(1) must be based on (a) a sound educational theory that is (b) supported by some qualified experts;
(2) must be provided with sufficient resources and personnel to be implemented effectively; and
(3) after a trial period, students must actually be learning English and, to some extent, subject matter content (de Jong, 2011: Ch. 6; Haas & Gort, 2009).

While a positive step in many ways, this decision does not mandate the language(s) of instruction, leaving the states and local school districts to set language policy. This leeway has perpetuated a debate between those who promote bilingual education for all students (e.g. García, 2008a: 389; García *et al.*, 2008) and those who argue that all educational efforts should be made to support the acquisition of English with little or no institutional concern for the home language (e.g. Porter, 1996, 1998).

As a result, some research on bilingual education has been confusing, often for methodological reasons. For example, a common unit of analysis in studies of bilingual or English-only program models has been English language acquisition, whereas home language development is rarely measured and, if it is, generally focuses on Spanish (e.g. Greene, 1998). Moreover, clearly separating pedagogical approaches and their specificities for comparison has been difficult, leading to results that promote a certain aporia about which programs are most successful (Rossell & Baker, 1996). In contrast, more careful studies have demonstrated that some form of bilingual education is consistently better for both English and home language development (Baker, 2011: Ch. 12; Collier & Thomas, 2004; Greene, 1998; Sparrow *et al.*, 2014; Rolstad, 2005; Umansky & Reardon, 2014; Valentino & Reardon, 2015).

On the other hand, this growing academic consensus around bilingual programming has generally focused on elementary and middle school children, where longitudinal studies can compare students in two or more different types of bilingual or immersion programs and investigate their results across time (Slavin *et al.*, 2011; Umansky & Reardon, 2014; Valentino & Reardon, 2015). Even in two-way dual-language programming, which exhibits the fastest and most advanced acquisition of two languages by, ideally, equally mixing students from different home languages (e.g. Spanish-English), it still takes approximately six years for both groups to match or exceed the language and academic proficiencies of their native-speaking grade-level peers (Collier & Thomas, 2009: 25–28). However, what is remarkable is that this equal proficiency is in two languages, lending credibility to arguments for bilingual programming.

However, this emphasis on language of instruction should not ignore culture. Although language and culture are virtually inseparable – a languaculture (Agar, 1996) – some scholars have focused on culture and argued that culturally relevant and sustaining approaches help students, especially those from minoritized groups, feel comfortable and empowered in educational contexts (Ladson-Billings, 2009; Paris, 2012). This field has many different dimensions and applications ranging from teacher training to math education (May & Sleeter, 2010), but one of the connections to bilingual education is whether the approach is 'weak' or 'strong' (Baker, 2011). 'Weak' approaches are those that reduce culture to specific objects such as food, music or clothing which can be used temporarily in the classroom, whereas 'strong' approaches understand culture as dynamic and interwoven into all parts of life (McDermott, 1999; Street, 1993). In schools and classrooms, this places a deeper onus on educators to integrate cultural knowledge and engagement into every aspect of instruction. This is especially important when the race, ethnicity or linguistic background of the teacher differs from that of the students, but it must be underlined that, while having shared cultural connections between teachers and students is likely to be beneficial, it is not a strict determinant of whether equitable and culturally sustaining education can occur (Cherng & Halpin, 2016; Ladson-Billings, 1995, 2009). However, for bilingual students it is clear that, in order to have culturally sustaining education, their native, home or community languages cannot somehow be separated or divorced from culture (Gutiérrez, 2008; Macedo & Bartolomé, 2014; Orellana, 2016).

Superdiversity as Practical Challenge and Relevant Theoretical Framework

Thus, bilingual programs, especially two-way dual-language immersion, show the most promise for supporting languaculturally minoritized groups, provided that they align with grade-level academic achievement, develop bilingualism and biliteracy and develop sociocultural competence (E. Howard *et al.*, 2018). However, in the US it remains a reality that English acquisition is the overriding policy goal of the national government as well as of most states and districts. Perhaps part of the challenge is that some of the most compelling results of bilingual program models are relatively recent (Umansky & Reardon, 2014) or even that robust findings and their implications are still being processed by policy makers and educators (August & Shanahan, 2006).

However, there are other barriers to bilingual education beyond the political disputes and lack of research clarity. One of the most significant is the increasing 'superdiversity' (Vertovec, 2007) that many school districts face today, where the languacultural diversity goes far beyond one or two major named language groups such as Spanish or other large world languages – Arabic, French, German, Japanese, Mandarin and

Russian – profiled by the Center for Applied Linguistics (CAL) Dual Language Program Directory (CAL, 2016), but rather includes many more heritage languages that are often neglected in school programming (CAL, 2013). Moreover, superdiversity extends beyond language and ethnicity and includes many additional variables such as 'differential immigration statuses and their concomitant entitlements and restrictions of rights, divergent labour market experiences, discrete gender and age profiles, patterns of spatial distribution, and mixed local area responses by service providers and residents' (Vertovec, 2007: 1025). These index connections and challenges to 'governmentality' (Budach & Saint-Georges, 2017: 66–69), particularly in the forms of various social institutions that, either by law or disposition, serve people across superdiverse contexts (e.g. King & Carson, 2016).

More importantly, these factors are interwoven, and it is the quality of these intersections that must be understood. Thus, Blommaert focuses on superdiversity's 'mobility, complexity, and unpredictability' (Blommaert, 2013a: 6), which can be reformulated as 'spread, speed, and scale' (Meissner & Vertovec, 2015: 546). For example, Arnaut *et al.* (2016) describe the Dutch city of Ostend as having residents from 17 distinct ethnic groups of mainly European origin in 1990 and nearly 100 from virtually every continent in 2011. This development is perhaps similar to the US, where the number of immigrants increased by 70% from 1995 to 2014 compared to a 20% increase in the population born in the US. In addition, according to a report by the National Academies of Sciences, Engineering, and Medicine (2017: 3), 'Geographic settlement patterns have changed since the 1990s, with immigrants increasingly moving to states and communities that historically had few immigrants.'

The popular media has chronicled these changes in different ways helpful to understanding superdiverse shifts. For example, *USA Today*'s 'The Changing of America' project has a 'Mapping Diversity Interactive' that draws on the diversity index, which gives a number from 0 to 100 representing the probability that two people chosen at random in a given region will be from different ethnic groups. In this index, 0 indicates no diversity and 100 total diversity – a theoretical limit in which every person in a region was ethnically distinct. In the US in 1980 this number was 34, in 2010 it was 55 and in 2020 it is predicted to be 58. In the focal Ohio county for this book, these numbers were 28, 50 and 53, respectively, quite similar to the national trends but less diverse than other areas such as New York, Florida, Texas or California and more diverse than areas such as Montana or North Dakota. More interestingly perhaps for the Ohio county is the 2020 racial breakdown, where 11% of the total is 'Other' (i.e. not White or Black), and the Hispanic share of the total is only 6%. Compared to the national numbers of 17% in the 'Other' category and 18% Hispanic share, this indicates some of the significant interethnic diversity of this Ohio county (Overberg, 2014).

In addition to the diversity index, the *Washington Post* recently analyzed demographic trends from 2000 to 2014 (D. Keating & Karklis, 2016) and explored four types: those that had low diversity in 2000 and did not change by 2014; those with low diversity in 2000 and big changes in 2014; those with high diversity in 2000 and little change in that diversity in 2014; and those with high diversity in 2000 and even bigger increases in 2014. These trends vary widely across geographic areas, leading to a patchwork of change or stability across the US, in the Midwest and particularly in a state such as Ohio. The general trend is that many urban areas such as this book's focal Ohio county have been highly diverse since 2000 and continue to become more diverse. Moreover, this particular county is surrounded by areas to the north and east that have had rapid increases in diversity, and areas to the south and west that have not been particularly diverse and have not changed much since 2000. These data highlight some of the interesting dynamics around migration patterns and how areas that are quite close geographically might have very different demographic profiles and trends.

Another useful tool is the *New York Times*' 'Immigration Explorer' (Bloch & Gebeloff, 2009), which documents the settlement patterns of foreign-born groups across the US. In broad terms, this tool demonstrates the changes in the US resulting from the 1965 immigration reforms that have been referred to as 'The Browning of America' (Montanaro, 2016; Segura, 2012), indexing the visible nature of the demographic change that is often perceived as a threat to White hegemony. At the national level, this tool shows how many urban areas and particularly Florida or states along the US–Mexico border have large foreign-born populations from Latin America. The Ohio situation is similar yet distinct in that, in 1950, the largest foreign-born population in Ohio counties were people from Western Europe, Russia and Eastern Europe. However, in 1980 and 2000, these shifted to people of primarily Asian or Middle Eastern backgrounds.

These factors are reflected in the perspectives of various actors at the pseudonymous 'Youth English Services' (YES) program. Ms Sharp, one of the program's most senior members, provides a historical and personal perspective on the superdiverse shifts that happened in her over 40-year career in the district. During the 1980s, Ms Sharp became part of a growing cohort of English-language educators focused on refugees and other migrants, particularly with the Cambodian population that was increasing at that time. After enrolling in a special program at OSU focused on this population and various pedagogies designed to support them, she was a founding member of a nascent ESL program when the most recent shift happened in the late 1990s.

> **Mrs Sharp:** Actually what happened with the Welcome Center was that we in that particular year or actually the year before I would say about '97 we started getting Somali students. In Spring, I

> remember we had one family. The next year we had more families, and the following year I had 116 students and 65 of them were Somali. Same thing they were coming very rapidly and a lot of them were secondary migration. But some came directly here. So it was a growing community. (Ms Sharp, personal communication, April 27, 2017)

These trends continued, leading to the program shifts described briefly above and elaborated more fully in Chapter 2, and can be juxtaposed with a conversation I had with Mr Samuelson, one of the current program's counselors, who has a key role in planning the schedule before the start of school and then making shifts throughout the year.

Brian: What's your expectation [for next year]? What is your top end in that you're planning for in terms of [new students]
Mr Samuelson: I think 800 at least. I'm thinking if we grow just like we did this year with the 400 who will be back, we could be at 800 [by the end of the year]. I don't know what we could handle ... I don't know how many kids are going to leave. You don't know how many are really going to give, with Trump in the office and things are changing. You don't know, you can't bet, you can't prepare. You just know that they're coming. How many, I don't know. (Mr Samuelson, personal communication, June 5, 2017)

Thus, these demographic shifts in Ohio and particularly the focal county for this book, while part of broader demographic trends in the US, meet the specific conditions of superdiversity. Diversity has been highly mobile, happening rapidly in the last 20 years, complex in that it is not dominated by one or two ethnic groups, and unpredictable in that future shifts are certainly not foregone conclusions but rather highly dependent on other factors such as the economy, national immigration policies and local support of migrants. Moreover, this ethnic diversity intersects with other issues such as migration status (Meissner & Vertovec, 2015), local histories and policies promoting or counteracting segregation (A. Williams & Emamdjomeh, 2018) or, the focus of this book, language (Arnaut *et al.*, 2016), which impacts the educational sphere directly. As Kreck (2014) points out, some states have seen their linguistic diversity increase 600%, straining teachers and systems accustomed to a small number of students in need of languacultural support, not hundreds or thousands.

Superdiversity and Language

A significant challenge when considering language and its relationship to superdiversity is the distinction between two ways of thinking about language. The first is named or 'capital' L- language such as 'English' which is '*real* as an ideological artifact because people believe it exists', whereas regular l- language is 'language as observable social action – the specific forms people effectively use in communicative practice' (Blommaert, 2016a: 6). In turn, Silverstein (1972, 2014) described this difference as 'language' and 'speech' communities in which the former is 'a social group, generally a primary reference group, the members of which are, by degrees, oriented to a denotational norm, however much within its compass they recognize situated variation' (2014: 4) and the latter 'organizes people by how they engage in and interpret such context-bound (inherently indexical) communication, seeming therein to reference social norms for discursively mediated social interaction, whether carried on through the medium of one denotational code or many' (2014: 5).

This distinction is similar to those made about discourse (Gee, 2015) or culture (McDermott, 1999; Street, 1993), and Blommaert describes the relationship between capital L- and regular l- language as being 'laminated', where language use consists 'of *practices* joined, organized, and structured by *beliefs about practices*' (Blommaert, 2016a: 4, italics in original). The latter here forms the broad field of *language ideology* and the former that of *register* (Agha, 1999; Blommaert, 2016a). Different registers are deployed in different chronotopes – space-time arrangements that 'produce specific kinds of person, actions, meaning, and value' (Blommaert, 2015: 109). These insights have broadened sociolinguistic studies dramatically from simply counting, for example, how many capital L- languages are spoken in a specific area to subtle analyses of how language use indexes a range of concerns including social status, gender, ability, region and education.

Superdiversity, therefore, has important sociological and sociolinguistic implications for both practice and theory. However, it should not be construed as a new social phenomenon; certainly there have been previous moments in human history that would meet Blommaert's criteria of mobility, complexity and unpredictability. However, superdiversity's three Ps of power, politics and policy (Meissner & Vertovec, 2015: 546) provide a potent link to a second key theoretical framework for this book, translanguaging.

Translanguaging as Key Framework for Sociolinguistic Description and Political Support

In the broader environment in the US where the state can no longer force students into English-only schooling, debate over the most appropriate way to support linguistically or culturally minoritized groups has continued. As mentioned above, researchers focused on this issue have struggled on occasion to conduct studies that have comparable, replicable and relevant results, but the overarching principle has pointed educators towards stances of 'understanding and caring' for all students and especially those with different languages and cultures from the mainstream (Faltis & Hudelson, 1997). Through this stance, educators are encouraged to understand the school experience from the perspective of the students and, wherever possible, to adapt instruction and activities appropriately to help learners engage with the material, feel excited and push to produce their best possible work and selves.

However, a key challenge in this area related to superdiversity is how sociolinguists describe the language practices of people, especially those with bi- or multilingual abilities. The central issue is rooted in the capital L- or monoglossic language ideologies which include beliefs promoting the use of one national language to the exclusion of all others, arguing that there are pure or more correct versions of national languages or asserting that bi/multilingual people have separate mental spaces for each specific language they know (García, 2008b). This perspective has been pervasive throughout phases of American educational history, especially those that encouraged migrants to forgo the use of their home languages and assimilate completely to English. Thankfully, this position has been challenged and has largely lost its credibility in educational life, replaced by views that see the home language and culture as a resource for learning, a fund of knowledge; however, there are still profound tensions over the ultimate goal of learning in US education largely being assimilation to the English language as mode of expression and American culture as way of life (Faltis, 2010; Gonzalez *et al.*, 1992).

Embedded in this broader discussion are sociolinguistic descriptions of bi/multilingual language use that have struggled with the monoglossic ideology, often creating inaccurate or subtly deficit-oriented perspectives. Among these is the description of how bi/multilingual people engage in 'code-switching' between two or more languages. This descriptor, even when used to compliment or empower bi/multilingual people in a variety of contexts (e.g. Gort, 2012; Gulzar, 2010), describes the bi/multilingual mind as somehow different from the monolingual mind. However, what has emerged from neurolinguistics is not that there is a physical difference between the bi/multilingual or monolingual minds but that some distinctions exist in how these regions work under monolingual or bi/multilingual conditions. Evidence here points to somewhat more activity (e.g. increased blood oxygenation levels) when bi/multilingual abilities are engaged (Kovelman *et al.*, 2008), leading to notions of the 'bilingual advantage' in terms of improved general cognitive ability or reducing the risk of dementia over the lifespan (Bialystok, 2009; Neuroskeptic, 2015; Paap *et al.*, 2015).

These neurolinguistic issues intersect with fields such as applied linguistics or sociolinguistics through the apparent contradiction of the many social, national or named languages in the world interacting constantly across time and context against a reality that 'the myriad linguistic features mastered by bilinguals (phonemes, words, constructions, rules, etc.) occupy a single, undifferentiated cognitive terrain that is not fenced off into anything like the two areas suggested by the two socially named languages' (Otheguy *et al.*, 2018: 2). However, these theoretical issues about language are hardly obvious or settled (MacSwan, 2017; Otheguy *et al.*, 2015, 2018) in that they engage not only cognitive issues but also the historical and lived realities of phenomena such as nationalism, colonialism or racism (Alim *et al.*, 2016; Makoni & Pennycook, 2006; Pennycook, 2006) which establish hierarchical relationships between named languages. Although it is possible to argue that other phenomena such as globalization with the spread of English as a world, international or lingua franca or urban multilingualism and an increased awareness and acceptance of linguistic diversity in various forms may mitigate these factors (Alim, 2006; Farr, 2011; Kachru, 1990; King & Carson, 2016; McKay, 2010; Pennycook & Otsuji, 2015b), it remains a significant experience for many that their languages and cultures have been decimated over time or face constant negative pressure across multiple contexts.

Schools and classroom pedagogy are strongly implicated here in terms of arguments about how teachers should allow or promote the use of certain languages in educational spaces, with some insisting on a defined language at all times (e.g. English in an immersion program) or certain languages at certain times (e.g. Spanish and English time separated in a bilingual program). However, these have also been challenged, pointing out that restricting language use in this way, at least as part of educational environments, may be counterproductive (e.g. Auerbach, 1993; Cummins, 2007).

To resist this monolingual bias and the restriction of language use in educational spaces, an influential and relatively new theoretical perspective has emerged in *translanguaging*, a term coined by Cen Williams but appropriated and expanded, perhaps most notably by Ofelia García (García & Li Wei, 2014). Translanguaging has two main elements. The first is a more accurate sociolinguistic description of human languaging, especially for bi/multilinguals, that incorporates and transcends terms such as code-switching. The core of this argument is that translanguaging is simply what bi/multilingual people do as part of their everyday lives or, as Gort (2015) drawing on Auer (1984) describes it, 'doing being bilingual.' Seen in this way, the language(s) that bi/multilingual people use in their everyday lives are non-trivial aspects of their existence and deeply embedded in their personhood and core identity. Thus, educational activities ranging from language policies to individual teacher practices that restrict language use are not simply pedagogical debates but epistemological and ontological, threatening the knowledge and personhood of bi/multilinguals. Flowing from this is the second element, a necessary political movement to destabilize these national notions of language that often restrict or oppress people, especially experienced or emergent bi/multilingual migrants who might not (yet) know the national languages of their country of (current) residence.

From the sociolinguistic perspective, translanguaging counters the underlying vision of the bi/multilingual mind as divided or segmented with certain languages being 'switched' on or off, with the notion of a coherent *linguistic repertoire* that is deployed by people 'without regard for watchful adherence to the socially and politically defined boundaries of named (and usually national and state) languages' (Otheguy *et al.*, 2015). This repertoire has at least three dimensions – individual, social and multimodal – that people use to make meaning of and interact with the world, especially but not exclusively in educational contexts (Busch, 2012, 2017; French & de Courcy, 2016; Gutiérrez & Rogoff, 2003; Kachru, 1982; Nichols & Snowden, 2016; Rymes, 2010, 2014). The most fundamental level of the repertoire is individual in that each person draws on the linguistic resources they have developed over their lifetime, which may involve multiple named/national languages at varying levels of proficiency. Indeed, even people who may consider themselves monolingual have in fact a broad linguistic repertoire in that every named/national language includes vocabulary that has been incorporated over time as well as neologisms, in addition to the multiple registers necessary for different social situations (cf. Agha, 1999; Blommaert, 2017). Beyond the individual, the social dimension of the available environment – a classmate, dictionary or instructional assistant – contributes to the individual's repertoire as people draw on their shared linguistic repertoires to make meaning. For example, students who share a language background in closely related named/national languages such as Spanish or Portuguese might draw upon their repertoire in collaboration; moreover, even students who come from different named/national languages might find interesting and surprising commonalities (e.g. between Nepali/Arabic or Somali/English). Finally, a new feature of the technological and internet-connected world contributing to one's linguistic repertoire is the multimodal dimension that uses internet- and computer-based tools to help people learn and make meaning together (J. Choi & Yi, 2016; Jewitt, 2013; Yi & Angay-Crowder, 2016). For example, language tools such as Google Translate can augment, in real time, one's linguistic repertoire or contribute to an expansion of the repertoire over time with programs such as Duolingo (www.duolingo.com) or Babbel (www.babbel.com).

Translanguaging has been influential, particularly in sociolinguistic work in education (e.g. Canagarajah, 2011; Creese & Blackledge, 2010; García *et al.*, 2016), but its most significant impact is perhaps political. The prefix 'trans-' creates linkages to other movements such as transculturalism, transgender, transsexual or transnationalism (e.g. Blackburn, 2002; Orellana, 2016; Vertovec, 2009) which envision a world accepting, understanding and supporting all humanity, specifically by rejecting dualisms, binaries or compartmentalization.

> 'Trans' suggests a movement *beyond* borders, a transcendence or transformation of things that were being held apart, or artificially constructed as separate and distinct. This is not the same as hybridity, which presumes an even and presumably equitable blend of different forms. Nor is

it the erasure of difference. Rather, it is about questioning the ontologies that hold things apart. It involves the resolution of dialectic tensions and the emergence of something new – something that we perhaps cannot even imagine. (Orellana, 2016: 91, italics in original)

This view of the world intersects with the reality that, while much positive change has occurred to affirm and support the humanity of all people, significant challenges remain, not only in the day-to-day work in spaces such as schools but also with the broader discussions about the kind of world envisioned through a 'trans' perspective. Indeed, these notions constitute a continuum represented by Figure 1.1 with monolingual understandings on one side and translanguaging on the other, with bilingual/multilingual in the center within parentheses to mark these as social constructions in addition to linking them together. All these are placed on a field of cultural-historical struggle in the hope that these movements can provide 'new opportunities for multilinguals' (Leonet *et al.*, 2017: 218) connected to a range of other concerns such as open borders, a just distribution of income and wealth, and civil rights (e.g. Bregman, 2016; Hayter, 2004; Oliver & Shapiro, 2006; Piketty, 2014; Riley, 2008).

Thus, superdiversity and translanguaging create a broad framework for this book. Superdiversity specifically addresses sociological elements of rapid change in terms of mobility, complexity and unpredictability and links well with the sociolinguistic perspective of translanguaging, especially for bi/multilingual communities. Perhaps most importantly, however, both perspectives balance science and politics through 'ethnographic openness and a keen awareness of hegemonic dynamics' (Arnaut, 2016: 53). Figure 1.2 demonstrates this interplay between the two theories.

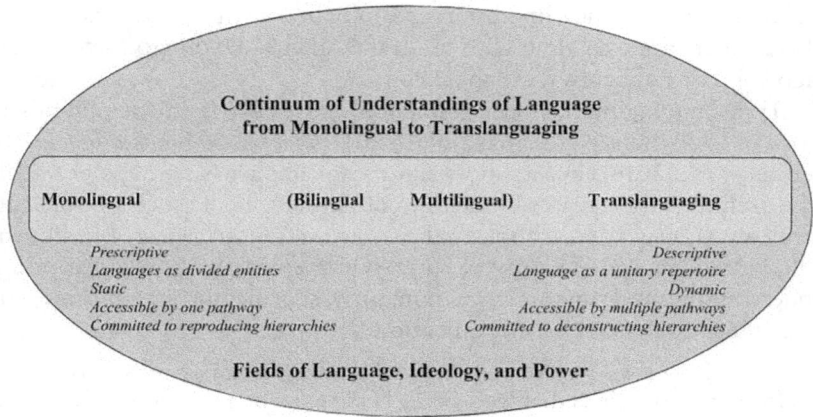

Figure 1.1 Continuum of language understandings on cultural-historical fields

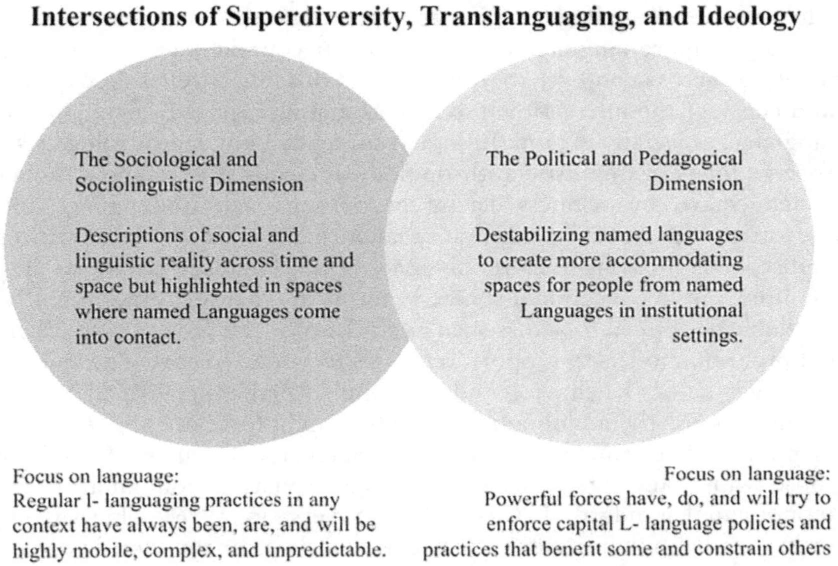

Intersections of Superdiversity, Translanguaging, and Ideology

The Sociological and Sociolinguistic Dimension

Descriptions of social and linguistic reality across time and space but highlighted in spaces where named Languages come into contact.

The Political and Pedagogical Dimension

Destabilizing named languages to create more accommodating spaces for people from named Languages in institutional settings.

Focus on language:
Regular l- languaging practices in any context have always been, are, and will be highly mobile, complex, and unpredictable.

Focus on language:
Powerful forces have, do, and will try to enforce capital L- language policies and practices that benefit some and constrain others

Figure 1.2 Interplay between superdiversity and translanguaging

Ideological Challenges to Superdiversity and Translanguaging: The Symbolic Violence of English-centricity and 'Mainstream Schooling'

> Because we have to follow a regular high school schedule, that presumes a whole lot of stuff that we can't presume. (Ms Cabot, personal communication, June 29, 2017)

Although superdiversity and translanguaging are powerful theories framing this book and the education of adolescent newcomers, how they are taken up in different contexts depends on many factors, among which are ideologies that individuals or groups share and the relative power they have to enact policies or practices related to these ideologies. This section describes two ideologies – English-centricity and 'mainstream' schooling – that challenge or complicate the issues and recommendations raised by superdiversity and translanguaging and introduce the possibility for a range of oppressive practices to emerge that impose symbolic and even real violence on those with relatively less power.

An important set of ideologies for this book are those related to language. Due to the fact that everybody is a de facto expert on language, Woolard and Schieffelin (1994: 55) note, 'There is as much cultural variation in ideas about speech as there is in speech forms themselves. Notions of how communication works as a social process, and to what purpose, are culturally variable and need to be discovered rather than simply assumed.' More specifically, studies in linguistic anthropology of education privilege language in use, foreground the participants' point of view, explore language use in particular contexts, assume shifting identities across context, analyze patterns of semiotic cues across time and consider the interactional dynamics among capital L- or regular l-language, especially in bi/multilingual contexts. Language ideology, as a specific focus of linguistic anthropology, includes studies about 'belief systems shared by members of a group – ones that apply to language' and the 'often-implicit construals that speakers make of particular instances of discourse' (Wortham, 2001: 254–256). These language ideologies then manifest in the educational sphere in terms of what identities might be available or applied to actors such as students or the provision of different program models to support, regulate, reproduce or ritualize student (or other actors') behavior and learning (Wortham, 2001: 254). For example, strongly monolingual ideologies might force certain behaviors or policies that can create feelings of inadequacy or frustration among those whose language varieties are seen as deviating from an arbitrary monolingual standard (de Costa, 2016; Silverstein, 1996). Alternatively or in parallel, bi/multilinguals may consciously or unconsciously deploy a number of behaviors or strategies to resist or redefine these monolingual standards (de Costa, 2016; Farr & Song, 2011; Razfar & Rumenapp, 2012; Spotti, 2011).

In this book's context, a key language ideology is 'English-centricity', which underlines that English, whether its learning or use, is centric to a space although many of the people in the space may be bi/multilingual.

> English is the medium of instruction due to not only official language policy, but through the dominance of English as the language of verbal exchanges, the curriculum, instructional materials, and classroom resources like textbooks or storybooks. I use English-centric rather than *English-only* with an understanding that students and teachers in these environments are often multilingual, and thus, the negotiated and constructed contexts in which they participate reflect aspects of this multilingualism. (Pacheco, 2016, italics in original)

English-centricity as an ideology is a product of historical and cultural forces as well as daily practices. Moreover, it is important to underline that the 'English' meant here is only one variety of the many forms of English used historically or in the world today (Clark, 2013; Halliday, 2003; Kachru, 1990; Lippi-Green, 2011). Specifically, this type is often called Mainstream American English (MAE), which is closely related to pronunciation structures in the Midwest of the US and prominent across many American media forms. However, there are many other varieties of English in the US or globally, distinct in terms of pronunciation styles, vocabulary or grammatical structures. These styles are often closely related to regional or racial groups such as the accents prevalent in the South or Northeast, the broader dialect of African-American Vernacular

English or, beyond the US borders, the many ways in which English is adapted and integrated with local languages such as Singapore's Singlish.

Critically, MAE indexes many aspects of Whiteness and White privilege and the power of certain groups to create, maintain and demand adherence to certain language types. In schools MAE is even further elaborated, with distinctions made between everyday discourse and academic language. This creates additional challenges, particularly for English language learners (ELLs; Arias & Faltis, 2013), but is salient in that the program, while accommodating of students' language development and home languages, is oriented towards teaching the academic language considered necessary for success in school and certain, generally white-collar, careers, and not necessarily the language of everyday talk.

A second ideological field relates to the notion of 'mainstream' education and related terms such as 'general education,' 'normal' and 'regular,' that index the fact that most nations today have a national or quasi-national curriculum and educational spaces designed for students who were born and raised in that country, speak the official or quasi-official national languages, lack significant mental or physical impairments and conform to a society's subtle yet powerful notions of gender, race, sexuality and so on. Throughout the mainstream educational environment, minimum standards for learning outcomes are debated and codified through processes that seek to balance personal, political and educational aspirations that map, however loosely, to knowledge, skills and attitudes deemed important in a society's past, present and future (Gutmann, 1999; Stone, 2011). Some of these can be positioned within discourses of 'continuity' in that they reinforce bodies of past knowledge and argue for present relevance. For example, the teaching of Greek and Latin may fall into this category in that although the languages are themselves 'dead,' many feel that learning them still has important cognitive and social value. In contrast, discourses of 'progress' or 'innovation' orient towards the future based on present assessment of future needs. Today, the push for learning computer languages is an example. Throughout, those that argue for both continuity or progress often do so by pointing out discrepancies in student performance along various lines (e.g. test scores, college acceptance rates, etc.) in comparison to other groups and that their form of educational reforms are necessary to right the national ship.

In the US, for most of the past hundred years, these 'mainstream' skills have focused on literacy, mathematics and scientific reasoning, but there is wide variety in other areas such as understandings of religion, history, civic engagement and the arts. A critical point here is that the mainstream standards and corresponding curricula are not neutral or static but rather usually created by those with significant political or economic power. When these standards have been established, the maintenance and reproduction of the mainstream environment remains the target and is rarely deeply questioned, challenged or changed, resulting in what Bourdieu called a 'cultural arbitrary' that is represented, defended and reproduced through 'pedagogic action' by 'pedagogic authorities' (Bourdieu & Passeron, 1990). Those who do not fit easily or neatly into the mainstream environment may be subject, at a minimum, to 'symbolic violence,' 'the imposition of a cultural arbitrary by an arbitrary power' (Bourdieu & Passeron, 1990: 5). In the US educational system, many have pointed out one element of the 'cultural arbitrary,' and the proof for its durability through reproduction is the organization of schooling into content-specific classrooms, time schedules and testing, almost entirely in English, mirroring the work demands of the late 19th or early 20th centuries' industrialized economy (Davidson, 2012, 2017). Indeed, observers of this phenomenon comment that 'the fundamental aspects of learning institutions remain remarkably familiar and have done so for something like two hundred years or more' to the point that a student from the 19th century transported to a 21st century classroom in many schools would fit right in with the general structure even if many elements such as cell phones, online learning or certain aspects of collaborative, task-based pedagogies may be jarring (Davidson *et al.*, 2009: 8). Thus, the cultural arbitrary and symbolic violence are powerful and create distinct boundaries and consequences; for example, any educational actor who tried to speak exclusively in Spanish in an English class or study English in a science class would receive the 'symbolic violence' of a failing grade or possibly other sanctions.

However, this view of the cultural arbitrary and symbolic violence must be tempered by the fact that any society has multiple cultural patterns that exist simultaneously, sometimes in conflict and sometimes in parallel. Thus, although 'mainstream' relates to the notion of integration in society, it is more accurate that people, whether they are aware of it or not, are never fully 'integrated' into a 'society' because integration is not a 'single process but a multiple one in which several very different forms of "integration" need to be achieved, into numerous specific social *milieux* and niches, each organized and characterized by their own sociocultural normative codes' (Blommaert, 2016b: 3, italics in original). However, those who grow up in the mainstream may be quite unaware that their own individual efforts are part of and unconsciously in sync with this much broader and powerful cultural arbitrary. To illustrate this, Sensoy and DiAngelo (2011: Ch. 2) use the metaphor of a fish in water to describe how a cultural arbitrary can be so thoroughly encompassing that those either born in or having spent long periods in the water begin to forget about the powerful energy of the currents themselves. These currents only becomes palpable when, for some reason, the current changes, or the individual fish tries to swim in the opposite direction or is plucked out and placed in some other water that may be quite different in terms of temperature, salinity, speed of current or the types of other fish. Depending on the severity of the changes, the fish might be able to adapt; however, if there are significant changes in one or more areas, the result may be death.

This is not so different for humans; indeed, most people would not survive being transported suddenly from their homes to a desert for an extended period. In the human social world these shifts are often more subtle and the risk of actual death less pronounced, but there remain serious risks and challenges when a person moves from one current to another, whether permanently or only temporarily.

Thus, the political nature of these relationships between education, language, ideology, power and symbolic violence raises again the point addressed earlier that many groups have had to struggle mightily, over not only symbolic but also actual violence, to gain access to the mainstream environment. In the US, these movements have included the educational inclusion of African-Americans, Native Americans, women and the disabled in mainstream schooling. However, once access has been established, then a broader struggle for control of the mainstream and the ability to create legitimate educational currents within or in parallel to the mainstream emerges, all with the ultimate goal of helping students meet or exceed those minimum educational standards which then confer an educational credential certifying that the student has acquired the requisite knowledge.

A relevant example here is the interplay between the Common Core curriculum (www.corestandards.org) and the Seal of Biliteracy (www.sealofbiliteracy.org), both of which have gained prominence and some controversy over the last decade. The Common Core, whether in full or adapted form, fundamentally represents the US English-language 'mainstream' curriculum, and Ohio has created its own learning standards largely in parallel with this. From the perspective of newcomer students, the codification of these standards is helpful as a relatively clear guide to learning goals; however, the standards are certainly not tailored to the newcomer students' home languages and prior knowledge. On the other hand, a possible rectification relevant to newcomer students is the Seal of Biliteracy, which confers an additional credential to the high school diploma certifying that the student has not only met the graduation requirements but also has advanced proficiency in one or more languages in addition to English. These two initiatives demonstrate the intense power of the 'mainstream' curriculum to codify national intended learning outcomes that largely reflect dominant groups and, in turn, critical efforts to shift some focus from these goals to support new or historically minoritized communities.

To summarize, this book is framed by, on the one hand, the demographic, sociolinguistic and pedagogical realities of superdiversity and translanguaging that argue for more sophisticated and equitable approaches to teaching and learning, particularly for adolescent newcomers. On the other hand, ideologies of English-centricity and mainstream schooling with their attendant policies and practices complicate and even frustrate efforts to develop systems and approaches with the greatest probability of helping learners adapt and thrive.

Language and Content Instruction for Adolescent Newcomers: Contexts, Elusive Clarity and Emerging Approaches for Equity

As mentioned above, many areas of the US have been experiencing superdiverse shifts in their populations in the last 20 years. In the educational field, these changes often occur more rapidly than the educational infrastructure can adapt. For example, although Central Ohio has several large capital L- languacultural communities such as Spanish, Somali, Nepali, French or Arabic-speaking populations that could, theoretically, have enough speakers to justify bilingual programming, there are 80 or more other home languages such as Masalit, Wolof, Fulani, Zomi or others whose population would be a theoretical, logistical and pedagogical challenge to traditional bilingual approaches. However, the provision of bilingual options for these students is depressingly rare, especially for adolescents, leaving them with immersion ESL environments and approaches. Indeed, Lewis and Gray (2016) point out that although 62% of public school districts have high school English learners, only 11% of these offer some mode of bilingual education; moreover, only 31% report having a paraprofessional who speaks the students' home language.

In addition to the language of instruction, adolescent migrant students – a relatively small but still significant population (NCES, 2016; Waggoner, 1999: 38) – face considerable educational pressures, particularly the compressed time frame for the acquisition of language and content required for college and career. However, adolescent migrants as ELLs do not benefit from the same level of academic clarity as those in the elementary bilingual program have received. Some research focused on secondary students in bilingual programs has concluded that migrant students, even newcomers, have more opportunities to have their language and cultures understood and validated (Faltis & Hudelson, 1997: Ch. 6; Vazquez, 2013). However, these results are not yet overwhelming or conclusive, and some recent evidence, including European examples, adds weight to the argument that immersion approaches, with adequate languacultural support, are more effective for newcomer adolescents (Macías *et al.*, 2013; OECD, 2015).

Moreover, each educational context may produce different results in that many of these studies show that some regions of the world are more committed to bi/multilingualism than others. For example, newcomers in Europe may benefit from the possibility of inclusion in a broader multilingual society (Cenoz *et al.*, 2014; King & Carson, 2016; McHugh & Sugarman, 2015; McHugh *et al.*, 2015; Muller & Beardsmore, 2004; Smyth *et al.*, 2009) committed, at least in principle if not in practice, to education in the home, national and international language (García, 2008b: 9). However, in the US it cannot be ignored that English maintains dominance across manifold domains including popular culture, politics and schooling (Gándara & Hopkins, 2010; Tse, 2001). On the other hand, the US picture is more complex in that some areas are highly multilingual such as Texas, Florida, New York or California, but their language policies in education diverge significantly. Texas, for example, has maintained commitments to bilingual education, whereas Arizona, Massachusetts and California became infamous for their anti-bilingual education bills, which California and Massachusetts have only recently repealed. In contrast, many states, especially in the Midwest, South or Northwest, despite some familiarity with languacultural diversity, are not as accustomed or prepared to work effectively with these demographic changes. For example, on the one hand, Ohio was the first state to have a bilingual education law in 1839 designed particularly for its then sizable German minority, and many states in the region had similar programs catering for their European populations. On the other hand, there also existed repressive educational forms against, for example, Chinese immigrants and Native Americans. Moreover, the 1900s and its World Wars ended many bilingual programs, and today Ohio does not mandate bilingual education for any population (Faltis & Hudelson, 1997: 1–15; Ohio Department of Education, 2014). Since the 1960s, bilingual programs have experienced a resurgence, especially in the traditional migrant areas mentioned above, and some states such as Minnesota are catching on quickly, establishing policies and programs designed to capitalize and build upon migrants' bilingual abilities (Schultz & Vana, 2008; C. Williams, 2015). Despite these movements, the CAL Dual Language Program directory only lists eight bilingual programs in Ohio, with Spanish, French and Chinese offered.

Learning and Teaching with Adolescent Newcomers

The reality, especially for teachers of ELL adolescent newcomers, is that it is very likely that they will encounter a student who is linguistically and culturally different from them and may justifiably ask the question, 'What should I do/think/be in this situation?' The response to this question is likely to map closely to the monolingual to translanguaging continuum above. That is, a teacher with a monolingual perspective may draw on different pedagogical practices when various inevitable situations arise. For example, when students speak in their home language, a monolingually oriented teacher might ask or insist that the students speak only English in the classroom or remind them that such disturbances are disrespectful and distracting to the lesson. On the other hand, a teacher on the other end of the continuum might respond by getting closer to the students, asking them to repeat what they said and trying to understand by drawing on the teacher's own linguistic repertoire. This teacher might use Google Translate, another student or a bilingual paraprofessional if necessary to connect what the students said to the material the teacher is trying to teach that day. Throughout, this teacher would be open to modifying the lesson plan to follow a new line of thinking.

This approach has been most explicitly developed recently in García et al.'s (2016) 'Translanguaging Pedagogy', built on García's work defining translanguaging as a theoretical construct (García, 2008b; Otheguy et al., 2015) with significant implications for education (García & Li Wei, 2014). The pedagogy starts by helping teachers to understand the *translanguaging corriente*, the natural flow of students' bilingualism through the classroom, and proposes a series of *dynamic translanguaging progressions*, a flexible model that looks holistically at bilingual students' language performances in specific classroom tasks from different perspectives at different times. This, however, requires a *translanguaging stance*, a philosophical, ideological or belief system that understands and supports bilingual students' different languaging practices and repertoires as working together, not separately. Then the teacher engages with *design*, strategically planning lessons to work within the translanguaging corriente by supporting complex content and texts, developing language practices for academic purposes, creating space for bilingual practices and ways of knowing, and supporting socio-emotional development and bilingual identities. Finally, the teacher is open to *shifts* by maintaining a flexible stance to respond to unplanned moment-by-moment events that happen in the translanguaging corriente.

These insights emerge from a broader field of scholars and teachers working in and researching both ESL and bi/multilingual contexts, thinking about how to work with linguistically and culturally diverse students effectively in different areas such as computer technology and the arts across the lifespan (Arias & Faltis, 2013; Chappell & Faltis, 2013; DeVillar & Faltis, 1991; García et al., 2008). These insights dovetail with other scholars such as Collier and Thomas (2004, 2009, 2014; Thomas & Collier, 2012), and are critically located in the broader struggle to decenter or contest the hegemony of English or other named/national languages in order to understand, value and engage the skills bi/multilingual people, students and communities have throughout the educational system (Baker, 2011; Crawford, 2004; Cummins, 2000; Gándara & Hopkins, 2010; García, 2008a, 2008b; García & Sylvan, 2011).

Language and Cultural Connections in Adolescent Newcomer School Contexts

Although a relatively rare intervention (Lewis & Gray, 2016), newcomer programs are part of this broader infrastructure of ways to help newly arrived students meet the demands of the mainstream environment. Because many newcomers and their communities often lack political power and robust community organization initially, these standards may seem immutable and frustrating. However, the newcomer should be aware that the mainstream itself has shifted considerably through the intervention and political pressure of previous immigrant groups and that the very existence of a newcomer program is the result of many decades of work to promote inclusion of all students in the mainstream educational environment. In addition, newcomers may not be aware that newcomer programs are being scrutinized and that changes will inevitably be made to further reorient the program and even the mainstream towards better pathways for inclusion.

However, adolescents also find themselves in a US context without any clarity about effective program models, in addition to a lack of bilingual programming that would most likely serve them best. As a National Academies of Sciences, Engineering, and Medicine (2017: 316) report summarizes, 'Overall, research examining instructional practices with ELs in secondary school is less reliable than that for ELs in elementary school.' The result here is that a number of 'promising practices' might be recommended, such as focusing on writing and academic English, integrating content and language, developing analytical abilities, using explicit instruction, having extended discussions and creating regular peer-assisted, small-group instructional support, but the lack of empirical rigor and questioning of the monolingual English program model is difficult in light of the more robust research at the elementary level.

Even more troubling are the Pew Research Center studies by Richard Fry showing that the average dropout rate for recent arrivals is 16.4%, with a large disparity between those arriving with continuous schooling (9.9%), and 70.9% for recently arrivals with interrupted schooling – a significant population in newcomer programs serving refugees and other migrants. On the other hand, there is great variance in this 70% average, from over 80% for Mexico and several other Central American nations down to around 30% for Asian arrivals and approximately 18% for migrants from Africa (Fry, 2005). Even the Central and South American numbers vary widely from, for example, 20% for Columbians up to the aforementioned 82.9% for Mexico (Fry, 2014). Thus, although recent trends seem to be improving for certain groups, unlocking some of these broader questions is key to ensuring educational equity.

The Challenge of Parallel or Non-parallel Education and Students with Limited or Interrupted Formal Education (SLIFE)

Adolescent newcomer programs, whether they are conscious of it or not, respond to superdiverse shifts that trouble the existing educational infrastructure. As a result, policy makers starting as early as the 1970s conceived of newcomer programs which have been defined as 'specialized academic environments that serve newly arrived, immigrant ELLs for a limited period of time' (Constantino & Lavadenz, 1993; Short & Boyson, 2012: vii). Individual programs may have additional criteria for identifying a student as a 'newcomer' for placement in these programs, such as time in the US, home language or English literacy, income, and documentation of prior educational experiences, including whether the student has experienced parallel/non-parallel, continuous/interrupted education in relationship to

Table 1.1 Summary of parallel/non-parallel and continuous/interrupted education

	Continuous	Interrupted
Parallel	More or less the same curriculum as the US and attended school to grade level	More or less the same curriculum as the US but is not at grade level for either (1) being held back or (2) being out of school
Non-parallel	Different curriculum from the US but attended school to grade level	Different curriculum and not at grade level

'mainstream' schooling (Table 1.1; Custodio, 2010; Custodio & O'Loughlin, 2017; Faltis & Coulter, 2007: 51–61; Short & Boyson, 2012: 11–13). Recalling the metaphor of the fish, newcomer students come to the US transported from a vast array of different mainstream 'currents.' These educational currents and their students can be described as representing parallel or non-parallel and limited or interrupted formal schooling. Figure 1.3 represents the relationships between these situations.

Parallel education refers to when a student attended an educational system with roughly the same curriculum as in the US. Continuous or interrupted education, mentioned briefly above, refers to whether the students have been attending school regularly and on grade level prior to coming to the US. For example, a student with parallel-continuous

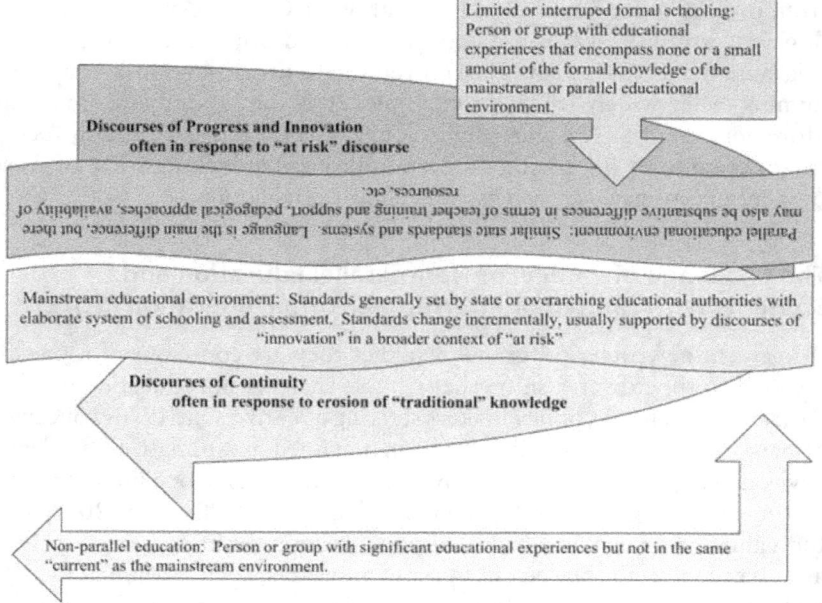

Figure 1.3 Relationships between mainstream, parallel, non-parallel and no/little/interrupted schooling

education, represented in the slightly darker current above, would have attended a school for four to six days a week for most of the calendar year with courses in language arts, science, math, social studies and some elective courses taught by qualified teachers; thus, the main difference between that system and the US is language, not content. These students would take some time to adapt to the mainstream environment, but the similarity between the systems would speed up the process.

Non-parallel education, represented in the light current at the bottom, refers to when a student does attend school regularly but the curriculum is vastly different from the US public system. A good example of this might be traditional Islamic education, where a student's primary years would mainly be devoted to memorizing the Quran and then the secondary[1] years to learning related Islamic texts and applying that knowledge to various cases. Thus, if these students came to the US, they might be quite well educated and linguistically talented, but simply have different language and content knowledge which would take some time to adapt to the mainstream environment. On the other hand, SLIFE status, represented in the section at the top, can happen for many reasons before coming to the US. These might include the necessity to seek shelter or migrate during times of crisis; many refugees have experienced interrupted education as a result of war. Alternatively, SLIFEs may not have moved but simply stayed out of school because of local instability, lack of schools or cultural attitudes towards education based on gender, ability, race, caste or socio-economic status. This is not to argue that these students lack intelligence or even 'education' in the sense of learning new skills throughout life; indeed, many of these students acquire vast knowledge, including how to protect and care for flocks of animals, how to negotiate confusing and oppressive legal and political systems or how to learn languages quickly in a survival environment. However, due to the fact that these are generally not skills that map easily onto a national school curriculum, SLIFEs or students with non-parallel educations often take the longest to adapt and tend to pose the greatest challenge to the mainstream educational system and educators.

Despite this wide variety, newcomer programs must welcome all students across this spectrum and respond to these issues while having a primary goal of English or other national language learning. At the same time, they also exist to partially shelter newcomer students from mainstream environments where they may suffer from the well-attested phenomenon of direct or indirect othering, neglect, violence or deficit perspectives from mainstream students, staff or teachers (Bal, 2014; del Carmen Salazar, 2008; Stewart, 2014; Trueba, 1988). This is a delicate balance for a school system to maintain between, on the one hand, providing linguistically rich environments with access to target language speaking peers and, on the other hand, ensuring that those target language speaking peer environments do not harm the newcomers.

Possible Trajectories for Adolescent Newcomers

Research on immigrant students' trajectories takes multiple forms and has often focused on the 'segmented assimilation' that points out that the immigrant experience is highly moderated by a number of factors including prior education, legal status, economic opportunity and so on (Portes, 2007; Portes & Rumbaut, 2001). This book's focus on the YES program and adolescent newcomer program research in general is concerned with broader issues about educational achievement and socioeconomic prosperity. As discussed above, migrants as ELLs face manifold challenges when arriving in the US, from overt racism and discrimination to subtle forms of exclusion, including the extent to which their home languages are incorporated into their school experiences, which will be further explored below. A fundamental difficulty here is that these groups, with rare exceptions, come to the US with little economic capital with which to defend or promote themselves. Moreover, although these groups might have significant cultural or social capital in their communities (Yosso, 2005), converting this to economic capital in a new context is slow and difficult, often taking generations to achieve (Bourdieu, 1986). In terms of education, the concerns and perspectives of these groups can and do exert some influence over the mainstream, but because the competing interests of educational professionals and the state are often quite consolidated, quick and significant change is unlikely to occur (Gutmann, 1999).

Many (but certainly not all) refugees or other migrants – YES's and most adolescent newcomer programs' primary students – come to the US with little more than the clothes on their backs and a few suitcases of belongings. Although these groups may share similar experiences at the level of fleeing conflict and seeking stability, at a practical level they have often quite disparate experiences and trajectories. The resettlement of official United Nations High Commissioner for Refugees (UNHCR) refugees is often considered a last step in resolving a refugee crisis, only after efforts to repatriate refugees to their country of origin or integrate them within their current host countries fail. Thus, official refugees who have gone through the resettlement process have often lived in a refugee camp or as urban refugees for long periods and passed through a relatively orderly process of application, screening, acceptance and reception, granting them authorized status and some economic capital provided by the receiving country and international bodies. When refugees arrive, although they might have some vague intentions to return to their original home countries, these options are constrained and most refugees face long-term residence and eventual citizenship in the country of resettlement – indeed, this may be the first country to offer these refugees legal status. The students in the program, particularly those with origins in Bhutan or Nepal, Syria, Iraq or Somalia, generally arrive with this status.

On the other hand, other migrants, particularly the unauthorized, do not have this support and often live in significant fear of deportation. Although they might live with family members who have resided in the US for many years, the legal and political uncertainty involved in their status is significant. Moreover, these migrants may have considerable economic motivations – to support family at home, to pay off a loan to a coyote or to make enough money quickly to return to their home country. In addition, they may have passed through quite difficult and harrowing experiences, especially crossing the US–Mexico border. For the youth in these situations, especially those from Mexico or Central and South America, this might include extended stays in juvenile detention centers with questionable standards before being either deported or released to a family member while waiting adjudication of their asylum or other claims to protected status.

An important issue related to these two trajectories is the students' and their communities' experience of transnationalism or 'sustained cross-border relationships, patterns of exchange, affiliations and social formations spanning nation-states' (Vertovec, 2009: 2). Although generalizations here are difficult and many exceptions exist, it can be said that official refugees' experience of transnationalism is perhaps more linear as they likely face long-term residence, citizenship and acculturation to many aspects of US life, whereas migrants, especially the unauthorized, have more developed transnational notions, including lifespans and aspirations to live and maintain connections that may or may not be officially authorized in two or more nation-states across the lifespan. This view is commensurate with translanguaging's disregard for named or national borders, which partially manifests in how refugees and migrants use technology to maintain closer connections to their home countries, friends and families, perhaps dampening the frustration that these factors might bring.

However, beyond these distinctions, many refugees and migrants share similar experiences in the US, such as living in low-income areas with poor housing standards (Subedi, 2013), working in low-wage jobs often for large multinational corporations (Gee *et al.*, 1996) and going to under-resourced schools that further neglect their backgrounds. These issues are intertwined with historical inequalities in the US ranging from segregation to the funding of public schools based on property taxes, and connect to broader socioeconomic or sociopolitical forces such as neoliberalism or neocolonialism.

YES and newcomer programs more generally were designed to be a counterweight to these experiences, and the goal of this research and book is to learn more about how it has wrestled with the factors discussed above, particularly in the case of older adolescents. Although all the grades represented in the program – from the middle school's 6th–8th graders to the high school's 'Lab' for first year or beginning ELLs or 'Core' for second year or intermediate students – would be worthy of focus, I wanted to follow a Lab group because, as mentioned above, this is a group that presents a significant educational challenge in general, as Mr Smith, the school principal made clear to me in an interview on November 17, 2016: 'If you come here and you learn no English, you're already fifteen years old, you're way behind the eight ball. Then, that bulls eye is right on your chest.' This is especially true for students who come to the US with interrupted educations. Fry (2005) argues that the labor market is the strongest pull factor for recently arrived adolescent youth with educational challenges before arrival, especially males; he points out that schools have a great responsibility to attract and convince these students to stay in school, for both their own and societal benefit, even if their original intention was to come to the US to work in the formal or informal economies.

> School dropout rates are an important basic indicator of youth well-being. Nearly four times as many foreign-born youths as native-born youths are out of school. Youths who do not complete high school have greatly restricted opportunities in post-secondary education and their employment rates and earnings are significantly below those of youths who do finish high school. On average, the prospects of foreign-born youths are clearly diminished by their difficulties in finishing high school. (Fry, 2005: 15)

At a more fine-grained level, Suárez-Orozco *et al.* (2010) researched approximately 400 newcomer students between the ages of nine and 14 or 'just at the cusp of adolescence' in a number of different school contexts. Their study used quantitative methods combined with case studies to identify five trajectories based on the outcome of academic performance – low, improving, precipitous decline, slow decline and high – and considered a number of factors impacting these trajectories, including school characteristics, family characteristics, academic engagement, academic English proficiency, psychological symptoms, age and gender. Figure 1.4 shows the relationship between these types. Overall, they concluded that: students attending highly segregated schools were likely to be among the lower profiles; families with two adults in the household were more likely to be on the high end; students reporting strong high school engagement were more likely to be on the high end; students with strong English ability were more likely to be on the high end; students with psychological issues tended to be in the middle or on the low ends; and being female was more likely to put a student on the higher end. Interestingly for this study, being older had different effects in that slightly older but not overage students had stronger likelihood of being on the high end, whereas overage students or those with three or more school moves were more likely to be on the low end.

These insights dovetail in part with the work of Short and Boyson (2004, 2012) on adolescent newcomer programs. Short (2016) conceptualized the

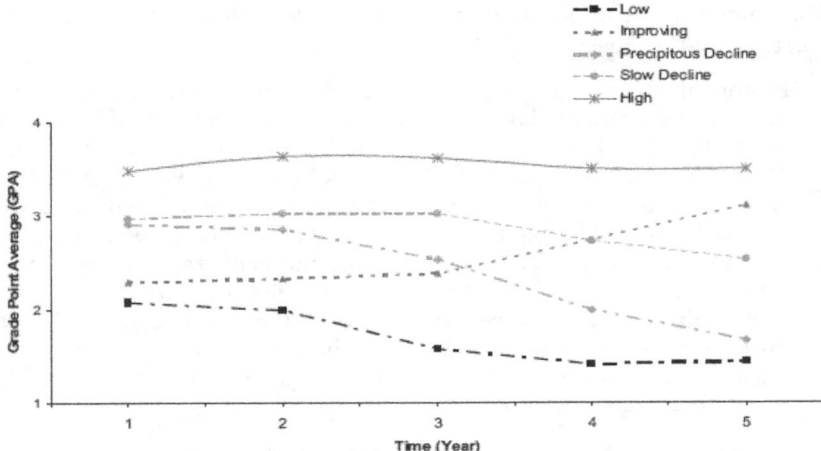

Figure 1.4 Grade point average performance trajectories
Source: Suárez-Orozco et al. (2010: 608).

relationship between English literacy development (as an indicator of overall academic performance), home language literacy and parallel, 'partial' or SLIFE school experiences. Overall, Short theorized three main groups of students: (1) those who come with home language literacy and 'grade-level content knowledge'; (2) those who have home language literacy but may not have grade-level content knowledge; and (3) those lacking both (Short, 2016: 8).

Focusing more on the home and target languages, scholars of early childhood students engaged in bilingual learning have identified three groups: (1) advanced bilinguals – those who have, at an early age, reached high proficiency in both the home and target languages (although the borders between these distinctions break down in many specific situations); (2) home or target language dominant – those who show particular strength in either the home or target language; and (3) emergent bilinguals – those who are still developing in both the home and target language (Páez et al., 2007).

Connecting this to the broader socioeconomic picture, the US educational system's success or failure in working with foreign-born youth is directly linked to either social uplift or the perpetuation/creation of classes of people who may be financially poor due to un- or underemployment. This is not to argue that individuals with less income or wealth are somehow deficient (cf. Bomer et al., 2008; Payne, 2005); however, financial poverty is a significant life stressor and is often linked to challenging situations with health, education and even the legal system. In the broader global context of widening income, wealth and social divergence and in the absence of broad socioeconomic policies to address these inequalities, education is one of the few levers remaining to counteract these disturbing trends, a point that inequality and wealth economist Thomas Piketty (2014) argues:

> Historical experience suggests that the principal mechanism for convergence at the international as well as the domestic level is the diffusion of knowledge. In other words, the poor catch up with the rich to the extent that they achieve the same level of technological know-how, skill, and education, not by becoming the property of the wealthy. The diffusion of knowledge is not like manna from heaven: it is often hastened by international openness and trade (autarky does not encourage technological transfer). Above all, knowledge diffusion depends on a country's ability to mobilize financing as well as institutions that encourage large-scale investment in education and training of the population while guaranteeing a stable legal framework that various economic actors can reliably count on. (Piketty, 2014: 136–137)

In the context of a newcomer program with global students who are at or near the age of adulthood, receiving, welcoming and steering these students towards positive and progressive educational possibilities is essential. This is particularly important because these adolescents have much more agency than, for example, elementary age students, and can vote with their feet and choose to stay in school or not. Thus, attracting and retaining these students is essential not only for public schools but for the general welfare. However, with a 70% dropout rate for SLIFEs, clearly something is not working well, and Fry (2005: Part VII) adds, 'Approaches other than traditional high school retention programs may be needed to address the skill-development needs of these youths.'

Thus, newcomer programs are designed to improve outcomes and trajectories for adolescent newcomers. The general goal is to guide these students towards the same goals as 'mainstream' students, which are frequently positioned as 'college and career,' although other 'Cs' such as citizenship are sometimes promoted as well (Common Core, 2018; Herczog *et al.*, 2011; National Council for the Social Studies, 2013). In turn, schools guide students away from dropping out or turning towards socially adverse behaviors such as criminality. However, with adolescent newcomers there are certain probabilities that Fry and others predict; for example, a male student with interrupted education would be more likely to drop out for work whereas another student with continuous education might struggle in the program but would be more likely to graduate high school. Indeed, Fry puts the dropout rate for this group at only 9.9% compared to the aforementioned 70% for students with prior difficulties.

These numbers may be commensurate with YES, as reflected in the perspective of Mr Smith, the school principal and also director of ESL for the entire school district:

Brian: What's your guesstimate of kids who come into the program pre-functional, and then make it all the way to graduation [in four, five, or six years]?

Mr Smith: If I had to guess, and I bet I'm pretty close, less than 20%. 15–20%. (Mr Smith, personal communication, November 17, 2016)

Despite this pessimistic outlook for adolescent newcomers generally or at the local program level, it must be underlined that these outcomes are not deterministic but rather probabilistic, reflective of the current overarching educational, political and socioeconomic factors as well as the personal circumstances of any adolescent youth. A change in any variable could have dramatic effects in other areas; thus, researchers and writers must be aware of how they approach the analysis, interpretation and communication of continuous, rather than binary, data and where dominant biases or narratives threaten deeper and potentially more accurate discussions of the outcomes (Silver, 2015, 2017).

Therefore, this book's focus on a group of Lab students in a newcomer program engages a group of students who represent a general cross-section of these issues as well as exploring a specific system of teachers and related supports that have been working with this population for nearly 20 years. This study provides a window into the day-to-day activities, offering some deeper, evidence-based explanations about why 70% of students with nonparallel and/or no/little/interrupted education might drop out, in addition to broader conclusions about other student groups and educational processes.

Development of Research about Newcomer Programs

Research about newcomer programs started with the first synthesis by Chang (1990), describing the 'newcomer program phenomenon' in California and the 'demographic challenge' of this rapid increase in diversity. The response, newcomer programs, had existed as early as 1969 in San Francisco, but the Chang report emphasized that these were 'not a product of a coherent statewide educational policy' but were rather '*ad hoc* responses to demographic changes in their localities' (Chang, 1990: 11, italics in original). This report shed light on these programs by telephoning 50 districts to see if they were operating newcomer programs and then following up with 17 of them with a survey, interviews and site visits. The results highlighted that these programs aimed to create a 'safe haven' for students, to 'build bridges' to American society, to offer robust social services, to work closely with parents and to accommodate student mobility and needs (Chang, 1990: 17–28). On the other hand, the practical challenges of the program structure included appropriate intake and placement systems, location, language of instruction and exit policies. Language of instruction is a specific issue in that these newcomer programs did strive to use the home language as much as possible, even in direct instruction, but the difficulty of working with languages beyond Spanish, the low numbers of certain languages and the shortage of bilingual teachers made bilingual instruction difficult if not impossible in some areas, leading to a preference for ESL methods (Chang, 1990: 29–49). Following this report, several other synthesis pieces emerged (Constantino & Lavadenz, 1993; Friedlander, 1991; Munoz & Clavijo, 2000; Schnur, 1999), which led to reviews of existing research on newcomer programs or pedagogies (Bajaj & Bartlett, 2017; Center for School and District Improvement, 2004; Francis *et al.*, 2006), surveys about work with newcomers in geographical areas such as Canada, Europe, Australia, Rural America or California (Gunderson, 2002; Kreck, 2014; Matthews, 2008; McHugh & Sugarman, 2015) and advice for starting a newcomer program (Custodio, 2010; Kennedy, 2007). These types of program guidance include shorter profiles by Hersi and Watkinson (2012), Hones (2007) and Schnur (1999) and are generally focused on one (Huseman, 2016; Kolodner, 2017; Munoz & Clavijo, 2000; Sylvan, 2013; Vazquez, 2013) or a smaller group of newcomer schools (Pascopella, 2011).

However, the work of Deborah Short and Beverly Boyson at CAL is seminal to newcomer program research and continued from the early 2000s until 2014 (Boyson *et al.*, 2002; CAL, 2014; Short, 2002; Short & Boyson, 2004, 2012). This work started with a national survey of 115 newcomer programs in 29 states from 1996 to 2001. This survey was accompanied by phone interviews to learn more about overall program design as well as what literacy strategies were being used to transition newcomer students to other programs (Short & Boyson, 2004: 9–12). In addition, case studies of three 'well-established programs' were carried out, involving site visits, classroom observation, interviews with administrators, teachers and students, and document analysis (Short & Boyson, 2004: 79–140). One of these programs was a bilingual program, one was an ESL/bilingual with home language literacy classes and the other was ESL with home language literacy. In addition, the research was linked to a national conference on elementary and secondary newcomer educators to, in part, share the research results and also explore new areas of inquiry (Boyson *et al.*, 2002).

This was the first phase of CAL's research, and a second phase started in 2008 with a new survey focused on secondary programs. The need for additional research was pressing, with the impact of the testing requirements of No Child Left Behind bringing ELLs more into the spotlight, as well as the results of the anti-bilingual education laws in California, Arizona and Massachusetts. This second phase took place from 2009 to 2011 and the survey resulted in a database of 63 programs (many of the first 115 had closed due to the economic recessions in 2001 and 2008). They also conducted case studies of 10 well-established and diverse programs with documented student growth. The methods in these case studies included interviews, focus groups, observations and a review of documents. The results of this work were published in 2012; in addition, CAL maintains a searchable online database of the program surveys.

Short and Boyson's work revealed the variety of features newcomer programs have to address regarding issues of language and cultural adaptation. One of the largest overarching issues is the language of instruction. Some newcomer programs are part of bilingual or ESL departments, which have quite different goals for student teaching and learning. Beyond this essential division, there are manifold details involved in the administration of these programs. This starts with program placement, which may be made at a central office or within the program itself; this assessment may also include measures of math or other subject knowledge. Assessments are generally only in English or another national language but may include some Spanish or other languages if appropriate assessment tools are available. In addition, the students may be exempt from state testing requirements but not usually for more than two years. Within the program, there will be assessments for special education available, and there should also be tests for gifted abilities. The program may offer elective programming, computer-assisted language learning, access to some mainstream classes, fieldtrips or tutoring. In-class instruction may be one teacher, co-teaching, or a teacher and paraprofessional, often bilingual. The teachers should be certified in their content area and should also have TESOL or bilingual endorsements. The program may also offer programs such as cultural orientation, wrap-around social services and after-school/weekend/summer programs. After completing the program, the student may 'graduate' into an ESL, mainstream or bilingual program or even complete high school within the program. Throughout, although the overarching program type and language policy may vary, it is rare that a program would completely neglect or marginalize the home language (Short & Boyson, 2012: 14–28).

Beyond Short and Boyson's work, a number of focused studies began in the late 1990s and have continued to the present to hone in on one or a small range of research questions, often tightly aligned with an aspect of social or educational theory such as identity, agency or positioning. These studies focus primarily on the US, Canada and Europe where newcomer programs are more common. Starting this trend, Hertzberg (1998) conducted an ethnographic investigation of the local construction of 'success' in a newcomer program through classroom-based participant observation, document analysis, observation of the school environment and interviews with students, teachers and administrators. Following this, many studies have emerged investigating specific issues such as theorizing communities of commitment (Ancess, 2003), name-calling and name-claiming of newcomer youth (Allen, 2007), homework practices (Bang, 2011), teacher perceptions and politics (Fleuret *et al.*, 2013; Hersi & Watkinson, 2012), students' use of linguistic social capital (Straubhaar, 2014) and reflections from program graduates (Scully, 2016). In addition, aspects relevant to newcomer programming have been explored such as the teaching of social studies (Y. Choi, 2013; Taylor, 2013), art education (Gulla,

2015), types of support students have needed and received (Mendenhall et al., 2017), Latino students (Matas, 2012), critical sociolinguistics (Mijares & Relaño Pastor, 2011), early program transitions (Rivera, 2009), a teacher's community-building efforts (Roxas, 2011), a vocational training program (Salerno & Kibler, 2015) and feelings of social exclusion (Steinbach, 2010).

An important body of work has emerged around the Internationals Network for Public Schools, one of the most prominent and well documented networks of newcomer schools in the US today (cf. Ancess, 2003). In 2021, this network has 28 schools in New York City and State, Virginia, Maryland, California, Minnesota and Kentucky (Internationals Network for Public Schools, n.d.). Work here includes profile pieces such as the film *I Learn America* (Dissard & Peng, 2013) and the narrative journalism book, *The New Kids* (Hauser, 2012). Moreover, studies on the Internationals Network have generated important theoretical concepts such as the notion of 'dynamic plurilingual education' as both an analytical and an evaluative tool for newcomer and bilingual programs (García & Sylvan, 2011). Dovetailing here is the research of Lesley Bartlett, who has been focused on newcomer programming and specifically the Internationals Network for much of the past 10 years. The approach of these schools has recently been synthesized as a 'critical transnational curriculum' with four main tenets: (1) using diversity as a learning opportunity; (2) engaging translanguaging; (3) promoting civic engagement as curriculum; and (4) cultivating multidirectional aspirations (Bajaj & Bartlett, 2017).

The Internationals Network is one of the few newcomer programs that has had a sustained research focus drawing on both qualitative and quantitative methods that speak to important policy outcomes. Fine et al.'s (2005) study about the Internationals Network included qualitative work similar to the synthesis pieces, using focus group methodology to describe how these schools develop a transcultural community, intellectual home and global citizenship skills. The quantitative analysis, the majority of the report, looked at dropout, graduation and discharge rates across three of the network's schools located in New York City. Using descriptive statistics, the report presents evidence that the Internationals Network students have higher graduation rates (88.7% for a seven-year graduation rate versus 69.2%) and lower dropout rates (11.3% at Year 7 versus 30.8%) than their New York City peers and also, drawing on the post-graduation narratives, do well in college and career. This report has been quite influential and is the source of the robust claims made by the Internationals Network for having found a model that works well for newcomer students (cf. Yip, 2013).

Finally, Bang (2011) used hierarchical multiple regression through a survey given to 192 students with a response rate of 97% to investigate homework practices by newcomer immigrant students at a school in the Internationals Network in New York City. This survey analyzed the students' homework completion rate as the dependent variable and considered a variety of independent variables such as gender, behavioral and cognitive engagement, learning styles, family conflict and school homework support. The study concluded that individual characteristics were the most crucial factors but that the family and school environment, especially those with low perception of conflict, led to higher completion. The study's implications focused on ensuring that teachers create an engaging classroom experience but also on systematic approaches like after-school homework programs or parent outreach that can improve homework completion in newcomer environments.

Conclusion

Thus, newcomer programs address a real educational need in the US and globally – how, in superdiverse contexts and conditions, to equitably and efficiently educate adolescent newcomers, build on their languacultural backgrounds through translanguaging and prepare them as quickly as possible for the world of college, career and citizenship. However, these programs have developed as ad hoc solutions rather than as a coherent approach, with a great deal of variability due to the historical and ideological contexts. This leaves newcomer programming open to a number of questions and criticisms.

The first issue is one that has plagued education for generations – segregation. Although newcomer programs are designed to temporarily house students in a sheltered educational environment so they can catch up with their similarly aged target language speaking peers, it remains a valid question as to whether these programs represent 'salvation' or 'segregated oblivion' for students (Feinberg, 2000). That is, by separating students from the mainstream environment, even temporarily, are these programs denying students the chance to participate meaningfully in educational programs with their English-speaking peers and have legitimate pathways to graduation and post-secondary education (Fine *et al.*, 2005: 71; US Department of Justice & US Department of Education, n.d.; Yip, 2013)?

The second point is language learning and whether these programs understand and support the processes involved in language and content learning and the challenge of transitioning students to mainstream environments (August, 2002). One essential question remains as to which program model would be best: bilingual or content-based ESL (García & Bartlett, 2007; Sylvan, 2013; Vazquez, 2013)? However, perhaps this question needs still fine-tuning to focus on the specific types of students who would benefit from these divergent approaches. Perhaps 'home language dominant' students who are literate in their home language and with many years of formal schooling would do well in the ESL-focused environment, whereas those without home language literacy or education would benefit most from a bilingual approach (Páez *et al.*, 2007).

Beyond language, the third point raises the issue that migrant adolescent lives are filled with psychological, emotional and social needs that require a nexus of institutional support (McBrien, 2005; McDonnell & Hill, n.d.). Untangling and assessing these strands is essential because the current research on adolescent outcomes points to highly segmented assimilation with this population's experiences in schools (Portes, 2007; Waters *et al.*, 2010). Specifically, scholars have identified four types of adolescent students from the achievement data: high achievers, low achievers, precipitous decliners and slow decliners (Suárez-Orozco *et al.*, 2008, 2010). All schools and especially newcomer programs need to be aware of these potentialities and have programs and interventions in place to anticipate and address these types of students.

Finally, at a broader level, newcomer programs are part of the conversation about the kind of America envisioned for refugees and other migrants (Salomone, 2010). Is this one where adolescent newcomers arrive and have ample access to educational experiences and opportunities that support and develop their previous knowledge, or will they encounter limited programs that lead to diminished opportunities because of a lack of a high-quality education?

Note

(1) I have used the terms 'primary' and 'secondary' here to provide a loose connection to the US system. However, Islamic education is less tied to one's time in a certain sequence of grades (e.g. six years of primary education) and more to one's mastery of the target material (Moore, 2006; Wagner, 1994). Although Islamic educational programming does have certain progressions under the guidance of their instructors, precocious students can go more quickly and vice versa.

2 An English-centric Program with Multilingual Margins

Chapter 1 described the tensions at the core of this book. On the one hand are the demographic reality and challenge posed by superdiversity and the pedagogical and political possibilities opened up through translanguaging. On the other hand are the constraining forces of English-centricity and mainstream education which often inflict symbolic violence on minoritized populations such as refugees or other migrants. Recalling this book's calligraphic metaphor, this chapter will look through the lens of Ohio in general and the pseudonymous 'Youth English Services' (YES) program in particular to illustrate, on the one hand, YES's fundamental English-centricity which reflects the basic goal of the program and Ohio to teach English quickly and effectively to this population of students. On the other hand, this chapter will describe some of the multilingual approaches and affordances that, however inconsistent and unofficial, refract YES's superdiverse context and translanguaging approaches. This detailed description will highlight the program's background and practices through the lens of the central research question regarding the program's support of students' languacultural backgrounds. This description relies on critical (Blommaert & Bulcaen, 2000; Fairclough, 1992; Rogers, 2011) yet positive (T. Bartlett, 2009; Macgilchrist, 2016; Martin, 2004) discourse analysis as a framework to understand this English-centric yet multilingual context.

Ohio LEP and District ESL Programs as 'Flexible' Discourse in an English-centric Context

> School districts have the flexibility to decide on the education approach that best meets the needs of their LEP students and leads to the timely acquisition of the level of English proficiency the students need to succeed in school. (Ohio Department of Education, 2014)

The Ohio Department of Education identifies students with the label 'Limited English Proficient' (LEP), which immediately indexes a deficit approach to these learners that was present in the No Child Left Behind Act's shift from a bilingual to an English-acquisition approach (Crawford, 2004; García *et al.*, 2008). As mentioned previously, terms such as emergent or experienced bilinguals would more appropriate. Nevertheless, the Department, responding to the appropriate legal requirements, cites the *Lau v Nichols* decision and offers school districts 'flexibility' to meet the standards of *Lau* through five possible programs:

- bilingual education;
- the immersion approach;
- pull-out English as a second language (ESL) classes;
- in-class or inclusion instruction;
- individual tutoring. (Ohio Department of Education, 2014)

These are positioned as relatively equal options; however, what stands out here is that the state, following the legal precedents discussed above, does not mandate what the language of instruction should be for any population nor present relevant research about these program models. This contrasts with other states or districts that require bilingual education for languacultural communities with enough student numbers to create a classroom or school environment where the home language is balanced with English.

Although this flexibility could be used to develop bilingual programs, in the focal district this is generally not the case. The district does have three elementary bilingual schools for Spanish, French and Chinese, a globally oriented high school, and a number of charter schools with various languacultural communities dominating (e.g. Somali), but the stated programming of the ESL department lists pull-out or push-in approaches using small-group English literacy interventions with bilingual assistants in parallel with specialized ESL programs and 'mainstream' classes. The district has both sheltered sites and separate sites for ESL support, with the latter being YES. Critically, YES's sole mention of bilingual supports is the role of the bilingual assistants; no specific bilingual or home language courses are mentioned although these are developing.

Thus, this overarching discourse of 'flexibility' frames the program possibilities as relatively equal options, but, as much of this chapter will demonstrate, the lived reality is an English-centric environment and practices. However, this 'ideological' flexibility does create critical 'implementational' spaces (Hornberger, 2005; Johnson & Freeman, 2010) that support the students' languacultural backgrounds and can be the foundation for more progressive ideological reform.

Policy Enactments across Time: History of the Program, Profiles and Views on Bilingual Educational Approaches of Teachers, Administration and Bilingual Assistants

> If you look closely at language-focused discrimination, you will find that it is not language per se that is relevant; instead we need to understand the individual's beliefs about language and following from those beliefs, institutional practices. (Johnson & Freeman, 2010: 14)

As mentioned previously, the ESL program evolved from a relatively small group of educators and students in the late 1990s to a large program serving nearly 7000 students across the district and nearly 800 students per year at YES. As a result, the program has gone through a number of phases from the initial design of the Welcome Centers in the early 2000s, to the creation of a separate high school in 2009, to reclassification as a program in 2015. The key themes of this time emerge from the interviews in the following way: rapid implementation, consolidation and reorientation.

At the end of the 1990s, a relatively small cadre of ESL educators – Ms Sharp among them as well as the previous (to Mr Smith) ESL director and the previous (to Ms Johnston and Ms Lincoln) assistant principal of YES – recognized the need for more focused programming for newcomers and proposed a district task force to work on this issue and make recommendations. The superintendent approved, and the group began planning and even visited other newcomer programs around the nation. At the end, the group made recommendations, focusing on the creation of specialized middle/high school Welcome Centers and improvements to in-school ESL support for elementary students. To the task force's surprise, all their recommendations were adopted by the district, setting off a rapid implementation phase. As Ms Sharp said, 'Yes, it was very intense. We spend a lot of weekends and nights working on it' (Personal communication, April 27, 2017). A key part of the challenge was that the program had to hire and train staff very quickly, and some of the narratives people relate about their trajectories to the program illustrate how the urgency of this time created unexpected pathways into a career working with adolescent newcomers, for example: Mr Smith told his story of being essentially hired off his front lawn after meeting a friend who was acquainted with the previous director; Ms Cabot discussed being gradually moved to the program through a supportive principal, drawing on her training as an English language arts teacher; Ms Popov explained how she was quickly hired based on her Russian, English and Spanish backgrounds after getting her teaching credentials certified; and Mr Barre and Mr Shahiya both benefitted from new programs to help Somalis with appropriate content knowledge to gain a teaching credential quickly.

Although these individual trajectories may have felt haphazard or even providential to the actors, the programs were coordinated and based on the task force's recommendations and research about what structures and practices were likely to support adolescent newcomers. Despite this broad coordination, much of the practice at that time reflected, as one retired teacher who had been in the program at the beginning said on February 7, 2017, that 'We were just doing what felt right.' That is, the various actors were drawing on their previous experiences to support this new community of adolescent newcomers. However, it was clear from the beginning that the program needed more focused support than that offered in the mainstream. Thus, one key feature of this time was the rapid hiring of bilingual instructional assistants and teachers from a number of migrant categories. The former group were hired as hourly staff to assist certified teachers and the latter group benefitted from specialized teacher training programs designed to help these teachers transition their previous educational or professional experience to a teaching credential. Thus, by the mid- to late 2000s, the program was relatively well resourced in terms of teachers and staff with the requisite experience and languacultural backgrounds to work with adolescent newcomers. Table 2.1 gives a summary of these teachers and other key program actors in this book.

In addition, the program continued to evolve to address the emerging needs of the community. For example, Ms Sharp discussed a specialized program for older adolescents:

> **Ms Sharp:** For students who were older, somewhat older like 17 to 22 years old. We realized that they weren't going to be able to get the credits that they needed with English and time, so we started that, well, most of them, unless they came with credits from their country showing their credits and transcripts. So we developed a program where they had intensive English with half a day, where the other half of the day they were in a career track, getting some training at the career center. The goal was to pass the GED and even if they didn't, what we were thinking is that your junior year, the second year they place you in a job, and I think some of them were placed in a job, and even if they didn't pass the GED, the employers kept them anyway because they were good workers. (Ms Sharp, personal communication, April 27, 2017)

Thus, this early rapid implementation period built on the task force's previous experiences, their research and visits to other sites, and developed a set of programming options and a cadre of professionals with broad languacultural experience to serve this population.

However, the program continued to evolve and, in the mid–late 2000s, consolidated the Welcome Centers to become a full 6–12 diploma-granting school, further elaborating the system of support, including teachers with content area/TESOL training, bilingual assistants, social services (counselors, nurses), special education and specialized interventions such as the 'Reading Clinic.' This version of the program achieved some notoriety and was featured several times in the local media and even in academic work about the newcomer phenomenon. However, bilingual programming was not included nor, as the former assistant principal told me, really considered due to the complexity of serving such a diverse student body. Thus, many of the themes around this time that emerged from the interviews indicated a certain satisfaction with working in this environment, the challenge of evolving to meet emerging students' needs and generally, as Ms Cabot stated, 'being left alone' by the district and state to

An English-centric Program with Multilingual Margins   49

Table 2.1 List of key program actors

Name	Role	Gender	Ethnicity	Time in program	Linguistic repertoire
Mr Smith	School principal	Male	African-American	15 years	English
Ms Johnston	Assistant principal	Female	African-American	5 years	English
Ms Lincoln	Assistant principal	Female	African-American	2 years	English
Ms Sharp	Reading Clinic coordinator	Female	African-American	25 years	English
Mr Samuelson	School counselor	Male	White American	3 years	English and Spanish
Ms Cabot	English teacher	Female	White American	15 years	English, some learning of Latin, German, French and Spanish
Mr Barre	Math teacher	Male	Somali-American	16 years	English and Somali with advanced proficiency in Italian
Mr Shahiya	Science teacher	Male	Somali-American	16 years	English, Somali, Arabic
Ms Popov	Social studies teacher	Female	Russian-American	17 years	English, Russian, Spanish
Ms Grey	Reading Clinic assistant	Female	African-American	3 years	English
Ms Son	Reading Clinic assistant	Female	Cambodian-American	3 years	English, Cambodian
Mr Dahal	Reading Clinic assistant	Male	Bhutanese-Nepali American	3 years	English, Nepali, Hindi, Dzongkha
Ms Ilich	Reading Clinic assistant	Female	Serbian-American	5 years	English, Serbian
Ms Lee	Reading Clinic assistant	Female	Chinese-American	10 years	English, some Mandarin Chinese
Mr Adisa	Reading Clinic assistant	Male	Ethiopian-American	20 years	English, Amharic
Ms Abadi	Reading Clinic assistant	Female	Iraqi-American	10 years	English, Arabic
Ms Tucek	English teacher (long-term substitute for Ms Cabot)	Female	White American	2 months	English, some French learning

work with this population. However, this time was not without critical change. For example, Ms Cabot described how the program would initially track students by their English reading level, putting students into 'low-intermediate-advanced' cohorts, only to discover that, in the second year of the 'Core' program described above, when the students were recombined and started their state-mandated four-year cohort, these distinctions were only exacerbated. Thus, Ms Cabot and the program identified a central problem with school tracking mechanisms that has long been the focus of academic research and criticism (e.g. Gee, 2000; Kanno & Kangas, 2014). The current 'Lab' approach, combining all 'pre-functional' learners (i.e. generally students below a 3rd grade English reading level), reflects a shift towards more inclusive programming.

Despite this work, the program encountered the challenge of the state's demand for students in its high schools to graduate in four years. A state audit of the program in Spring 2015 revealed a number of perceived shortcomings in addition to the low graduation rate, such as overcrowded classes, and forced the school to move buildings in Summer 2015 and revert to program status in Fall 2015. This was not uncontroversial, with some pointing to the program's broader context and the challenge of supporting refugee and other migrant students as well as some encouraging results, as assistant principal Ms Johnston underlined when I asked her about Mr Smith's statistic of only 15–20% graduating from the school.

Ms Johnston: Well … we actually were up to 75% … The last one we have, I want to say we're at 77% … We were able to graduate 77% of the kids based on a four-year cohort … That's why we were all confused like, 'Our graduation rate's better than 50% percent of the high schools in the district,' and we actually did a breakdown comparison of our scores, by subject, by grade level compared to the shelter sites and we outperformed every sheltered site in the district. (Personal communication, March 27, 2017)

In checking the state data for the school, unfortunately Ms Johnston's assertion is hard to warrant in that the reported graduation rate for the school was as low as 14% for a four-year cohort; however, in the last year before reclassification, the school did register a 68% graduation rate for the five-year cohort. This points out the difficult nature of working with tracking and interpreting data about educational program 'effectiveness,' as Mr Smith emphasizes in response to my question about the school's effectiveness and graduation rates:

Mr Smith: That's what we're doing now. I mean because now with the ESSA [Every Student Succeeds Act] laws, we have to track, monitor that more … That's pretty much why we became a program, ODE [Ohio Department of Education] stepped in and said, 'Hey, wait a minute. You got nine hundred kids here, you've got kids that have six, seven years here.' Over the five years we had a, over a four-year period you had a cohort of in every year, 1, 2, 3, 4 years you should had a cohort total of three hundred and fifty graduate in four years based on the cohort and age while you only had eighty or ninety. You know what I'm saying? ... One year they had like a, they went from a 12% graduation rate to a 67% graduation rate. But what you got to remember is this, of the, I think they had 51 or 61 graduate. I can't remember the exact number ... when it was a school, but you got to remember, I think it was like 31 of them were the kids from the non-grads class that had come through. They did all the course work but never passed the OGT [Ohio Graduation Test]. Then, they come back with Ms [a specialized bilingual assistant] to pass the OGT. With some intense tutoring everyday, they pass the OGT pieces. Then, of course, that was the year that a majority of them did really well over there with that intense one-on-one combined with a few that did come through with the right cohort, that shot that number up. That one year ... I'm not trying to knock anybody ... but you have to look at the details. You have to take a look at that graduation rate number. That was just for that one year, but for the most part it's in four years you should have had, I'm going to go low. You should have had two hundred graduate in the four years. Well, you only had eighty. You see, so, it was being tracked. (Mr Smith, personal communication, November 17, 2016)

Thus, for these reasons, debatable or not, the school was returned to program status but maintained the separate-site model where students can study English intensively for one or two years and then matriculate to a sheltered site in a mainstream program. Despite this shift, the overall structure of the program remained largely the same, as assistant principal Ms Lincoln, who joined the school in 2015, points out.

Ms Lincoln: Well, to be honest with you, I know that they see this place as a program, but with me being in the schools that I've been in, still runs as a school ... It has bell schedules like a school, kids get in trouble, we have to have a conference with the parents, they have lunches like a regular school, the only thing that's different ... kids had to go to their home high school for the sports, and that's the same way for our program, so as far as this place being different from a regular school, in my opinion, it's not. (Personal communication, April 17, 2016)

Therefore, despite the change in program status and physical site, a certain amount of consistency remained but additional opportunities for reorientation remain.

The wide range of individuals in the current staff and program can be partially explained by their previous experiences and bilingual abilities. The administration, the director Mr Smith and assistants Ms Johnston and Ms Lincoln all started in the district in the mid-2000s and gradually moved to an administrative role, particularly through the district's one-year administrative training program. Although none of these administrators is bilingual, they have developed ad hoc understandings of language acquisition through, in the case of Mr Smith, a TESOL endorsement, and in the case of Ms Johnston and Ms Lincoln, their current PhD/EdD programming. That said, their understandings, particularly of bilingualism, may be less robust, leading to an English-centric position, as exemplified by the following statements:

Mr Smith: We got to get them first in English because this is where they're going to be, we need to them ready. In my opinion, you really have to focus on the English ... though in the future is probably leading to learning and teaching in his language because if he can count to 10 in his language, there's a merit to that. (Personal communication, November 17, 2016)

Ms Johnston: It's only because this is this age to be honest with you, I don't want to turn on, I don't want to have to make them (the students) turn on two lights, because you think about it, if you're in a living room and you want to turn on the light in the kitchen you can't reach both of them. (Personal communication, March 29, 2017)

Ms Lincoln, a relative newcomer to the program, might be more accommodating of bilingual approaches but is still developing her knowledge of this field.

Ms Lincoln: Well to be honest with you, if that was me, if it was me I would want to know how to speak my own language well, I would want to know the academic piece of English, well since English is my language, I would want to know the academic piece of my own language, and I think that that would, if they have the academic piece of English and the academic piece of their own language, then maybe they could transfer their language to the English language piece and they that make them stronger as a student. (Personal communication, April 17, 2016)

The teachers themselves are more distinct in terms of both ethnicity and bilingualism. As demonstrated above, the focal teachers for this study are highly diverse, and these same patterns would have been repeated with virtually any other cohort I might have worked with. As might be expected, the attitudes towards bilingualism represent this continuum as well.

Mr Shahiya: I think bilingual should be like an assistant and understanding doing that way. I think the main lesson, instructional medium should be English. (Personal communication, December 20, 2016)

Mr Barre: It's [bilingual education] not bad, is just a good idea. I heard that also in California but exactly I've never tried. But to educate them [the students] in a language then what is the problem is when they're going to learn the language, the English, so they when they are going to learn if they're just taught everything in Somali? Also, they need to learn English as a language. What I understand, the way they [other teachers using bilingual strategies] do it, those who are using, I don't believe that they do in the whole content in their own language. They try to interpret or translate. Like, decimals we doing this, add and subtract it. They're going to explain in their own language what it means addition, what it means subtraction. But the instruction is just still in English. (Personal communication, December 20, 2016)

Ms Cabot: I don't understand why we can't create a heritage Spanish class, get these kids working on their reading skills, in their native language. (Personal communication, October 28, 2016)

Ms Popov: I like using their language ... when the people are with different languages in the same class, it enriches them. They learn from each other and like this interaction. (Ms Popov, personal communication, November 22, 2016)

Mr Shahiya and Mr Barre express an opinion that might be commensurate with Mr Smith above – that bilingual approaches might be useful, but within the goal of learning English. Ms Cabot's view may be more radical, orienting towards support and development of the home language as a goal per se, and Ms Popov's view perhaps straddles the two, seeking to use the home language in interaction to help students learn (English) from each other. These perspectives will be more critically interrogated with actual classroom data later in this chapter.

The last key group are the bilingual assistants who work most directly with the students in the Reading Clinic but who in previous years had been in-class assistants. The coordinator of this group, Ms Sharp, despite not being bilingual herself, has potentially the longest experience of anybody in the program, and an affirming orientation to languacultural supports for the students. For example, during the weekly meeting for this group, Ms Sharp would often start by sharing books or other resources that might be useful during the small-group Reading Clinic sessions. These ranged from the many early childhood books such as *The Seasons of Arnold's Apple Tree*, whose art and nature themes were thought to be easily understood by the students, to more explicitly bilingual or languaculturally affirming books such as *The Swirling Hijab*, a bilingual Arabic-English book, or *One Day We Had to Run*, which reflects refugee experiences. That said, some of the bilingual assistants expressed a certain unease about how to engage the home language in their small groups, particularly when students are sent to them based on their English reading level, not their language background, as an interview with Ms Ilich demonstrates. Ms Ilich has a strong background in science education and was also taking a TESOL endorsement class with a research component, which she references below when I ask her about bilingual classes and using the students' home languages more systematically in instruction.

Ms Ilich: That's a great question and I wish you could give me the answer because I am thinking of it as well [chuckles]. I am thinking of writing my research project based on using the L1, and thinking of the way how to utilize it and that's something – again I don't have the good answer. I Google things for instance what I do in my class, I find some articles, I find some websites that can translate articles from one language to another, from English and my kids love them. They love them and I give them those in both languages. They want to take it home, most of the time we keep all the work in school. But I thought, the kids can take this home, they really want, they love to see something great in their life. I ask them do you feel they are learning. Especially these kind of students of course because my students will say, 'I know this in my language.' Once they read in their language … I would print in all their languages. Because I have small groups, I would print in Arabic, I give them both two versions English and their language, and ask them first, 'Why don't you read first in your language?' Read in your language, and then for the first maybe do only their language second and then they can compare, they can highlight, they can underline the words, especially Spanish because there's so many common words they are going to find English very simple. They'll figure out, 'Oh this is this. Acrobat is acrobat.' A zillion words, and then at the end we only read in English. Once they maybe going to spend two or three days looking at it, it depends how long that article is, but the final day will be in English. It's not like they are going to get mixed. They will just use it, maybe some translate some of them not. Some of them don't even, there are a few students. There are some students who don't read nor write in their language and that's all right … In that situation I have one student actually. She would just use English, she would like, 'Can I use English word?' Maybe use a dictionary, maybe some words she can look in dictionary. Again [she speaks Kinyarwanda], I can't find it in the dictionary that's the only one I couldn't find here in the building. I have dictionaries, but I could not find a dictionary.

Brian: They exist but I mean. Because in Rwanda the whole national curriculum is in Kinyarwanda, I mean that there are resources out there in the world but there you know we'd have to go kind of get them ... but like when I think about the answer to your question like you know for bilingual resources for students that I might, my main concern is you know the kids who are not literate in their home language, they have a big challenge to do that transfer.

Ms Ilich: That's a good point, I agree actually another student who is even less because she told me she speaks Fulani and when I gave her, I'm sorry Swahili, I'm mixing up, Swahili. I gave her the dictionary and then the kids are telling me 'Miss she couldn't' because this was another activity, they gave him something and they were supposed to look for the words in their language, like use the dictionary, it's also practice because that's the only accommodation they can get during the state testing so I want them to have that skill, and she couldn't use the dictionary but she was using I didn't even know, and then students were telling her, but she cannot read or write. I agree, that's a challenge. (Ms Ilich, personal communication, March 3, 2017)

This section shows how Ms Ilich, who is bilingual in Serbian and English but does not generally share an individual linguistic repertoire with the majority of her students, has a translanguaging stance and design for supporting her students' home language but struggles with the superdiversity of her class. Many of the other instructional assistants expressed a similar stance and wrestled with, in some cases, their own monolingual backgrounds or a mismatch between their bi/multilingual linguistic repertoires and the students', but generally supported various methods to draw on the students' languacultural backgrounds. However, Ms Ilich's unease with her own approach in the context of the English-centric school indexes the broader struggle of bilingual paraprofessionals to have their skills and perspectives validated (and compensated) in school environments throughout the US and internationally (Cable, 2004; Ernst-Slavit & Wenger, 2006; Gao & Shum, 2010; Thorstensson Dávila, 2018; Wenger *et al.*, 2004). As with the teachers, this stance will be more critically evaluated with the actual classroom behavior later in this chapter.

Thus, this history of the program and profiles of the administration, teachers and bilingual assistants are important to highlight the narratives of evolution, growth and change that manifest specifically in the actors' varying perspectives about the best methods to support the students and their communities. This is partly reflected in the program's outreach to parents and community groups, particularly under superdiverse conditions. Ms Sharp, for example, discussed on multiple occasions how, when the ESL department was small, she would make home visits that gave her an insight into the conditions of students' lives and created a direct connection between the home and school. However, as the superdiverse shifts occurred, this became less feasible, leading her to lament this loss. In turn, Mr Smith as the ESL director, throughout the research years was exploring various ways to improve these connections. One regular means was the program's 'Community Council', composed of school counselors, administration, key teachers and a number of community representatives, including a few from the languacultural community organizations themselves. More specifically, he reached out to a number of community groups representing the district's primary languacultural groups – Spanish, Somali, Arabic, Nepali and Francophone – and attempted to hold meetings both at the ESL office and at community centers. However, he told me that the initial efforts were difficult in attracting caregivers or community groups to these meetings. At the end of the research, Mr Smith said that he felt that this aspect of the program's work was still in development but had the goal of having regular, sustained conversations with community groups. This demonstrates, in part, the ongoing challenges for programs working with superdiverse groups; despite many positive intentions, working out the details of these initiatives remains complicated.

However, after nearly 20 years of program development, Mr Samuelson raises the cyclical, political and unstable contexts the program exists within:

> Mr Samuelson: I think that's one of the negatives of being a program, that the leadership higher up, for budget reasons, for whatever reason, politics, I don't even know. It would be hard to get behind the scenes and to know. Just speculation, I guess, is that they just left the director like what you're saying, 'You've got to figure it out.' Figuring out what's best for the kids and figuring out what's best for the school district, it doesn't match. (Personal communication, June 5, 2017)

This perspective of uncertainty and frustration with the district policy or leadership emerged across multiple issues and contexts including issues such as: (1) the allocation of teachers based on the initial enrollment at the program when it is well known that the student numbers would likely double or triple over the year; (2) following this point, difficulties in creating the school schedule (e.g. multiple sections with low initial class sizes where new students would be added or fewer sections with higher class sizes where new students would be placed into new empty sections) and subsequent district directives to modify the schedule; or (3) related to the overarching issue, the ability to quickly hire new teachers or substitutes as enrollment increases. These various pressures add a level of uncertainty and frustration that, from time to time, led the experienced teachers such as Ms Cabot to wax nostalgic about the early days when the program was growing and was largely 'left alone' by the district authorities.

Positive Yet Critical Teaching and Learning Practices

> All human language behaviors are political and … the role of sociolinguistic research should be to understand how this political nature of language is reproduced through social interactions. (Flores, 2014)

> When we have done this, I feel we will give less praise and blame to particular superintendents, commandants, wardens, and abbots, and tend more to understand the social problems and issues in total institutions by appealing to the underlying structural design common to them all. (Goffman, 1961: 124)

This initial sketch of the program has relied primarily on interviews with the program actors to describe its foundational history, personalities and perspectives. The remaining sections of this chapter will describe how these elements emerge in institutional and pedagogic practices. Throughout, this section will warrant the fundamental English-centricity of the space but also an array of multilingual practices, however marginal, that create possibilities for more robust support of the students' linguacultural backgrounds.

Linguistic Landscape

> My interest is to try to understand instances of language when it is being used, not abstracted for pure analysis but grounded in actions which take place in the material world of day-to-day life. (Scollon, 2013: 185)

As mentioned above, language studies include a broad range of semiotic understandings. Linguistic landscape studies are part of this trend, seeking to understand the role of the various signs, often written (Backhaus, 2006; Ben-Rafael *et al.*, 2006; Blommaert, 2013a, 2016c) but not exclusively (Pennycook & Otsuji, 2015a), that manifest in public and private spaces, including schools (Brown, 2012; Gorter, 2017). This field, in turn, connects with language ideologies in understanding and questioning the role of power – who has the power to place signs, what beliefs or ideologies underlie these placements, and how these placements are perceived and reacted to by the people who experience them (Jane-Francis & Foncha, 2014; Moriarty, 2012). Thus, in general, linguistic landscape studies connect to the fields of literacy studies and discourse analysis to consider how the lived semiotic environment is filtered through people's senses, perception and cognition (Bloome & Enciso, 2006; E. Keating, 2015; Scollon & Scollon, 2003).

YES, just like any school, is replete with signs available for recognition and interpretation, from the official sign for the program, placed on a kind of billboard approximately 10 feet above the ground juxtaposed with the crumbling ground-level sign of the former school building, to the entrance of the school with the district motto, various direction/exit signs and,

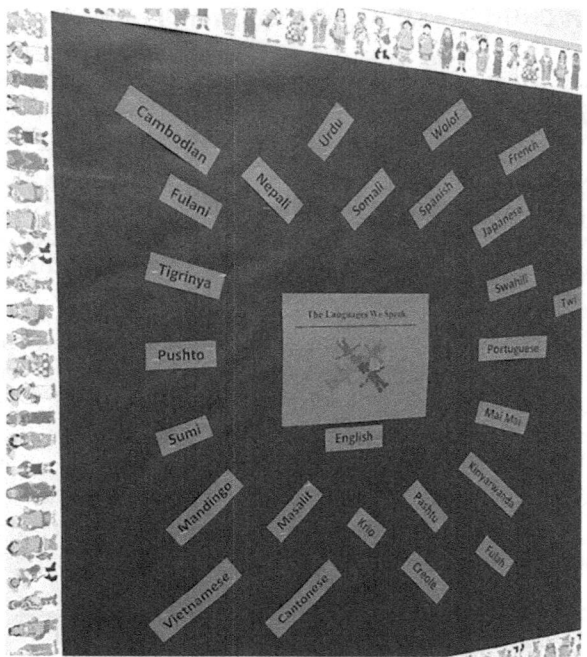

Figure 2.1 'The Languages We Speak' sign

again, the remnants of the previous school's colors, sports mascot and motivational phrases. Moreover, the semiotic environment of the program, particularly in the public hallways, was not static but evolved throughout the year as I was able to photograph about 140 different signs, including those that existed at the beginning of the year and those that appeared later.

These 140 signs demonstrate, in sum, the argument regarding English-centricity with multilingual margins, perhaps best exemplified by the image in Figure 2.1. This bulletin board is placed somewhat conspicuously across the hall from the main office. The central 'The Languages We Speak' with 'English' below and the radiating 25 languages, in addition to the border with various images of people, represents an essential aspect of the program, languacultural diversity, while pointing to the centrality of English in the overall scheme, emphasized by the sign in Figure 2.2.

In turn, Figure 2.3 ('The [blank] Way' obscures the school name) demonstrates the importance of student behavior and the Positive Behavior Interventions and Supports (PBIS) program that the school, district and state has embraced (Knoster & Drogan, 2016).

One of the first changes during the year was the addition of images and statements related to October's College and Career month. A student intern at the school was tasked with putting up a number of signs around

Figure 2.2 Image of 'I can learn English' sign

the school with this theme. These generally were arranged with a focal word or phrase in the center – How to Succeed, Careers, Go To College, Make Goals, College, College-Career-Service – and then related images radiating out. Although many of these signs can be read as promoting American educational institutions (e.g. local/regional colleges) and jobs

Figure 2.3 Image of school/district Positive Behavior Intervention and Supports (PBIS) motto

Figure 2.4 Image of Yuna with 'I want to be a singer' superimposed below

(medical, construction or service industries), there were a few places where languacultural connections were more visible or non-traditional work promoted, such as Figure 2.4's image of Yuna, a Muslim Malaysian female musician.

In addition, the intern incorporated student work into the College-Career-Service bulletin board, attaching short statements such as this text in Figure 2.5 from Samuel,[1] a student who was briefly in the focal classroom before being moved to the Core section. The blurry text reads:

> Since I was a little child, I always wanted to be a business man after finishing my study. In Haiti, my father was a rich man so now In U.S.A., I will follow the steps of my father. I know with my will, I will succeed. But I've to go to school everyday, first. Or if I cannot be a businessman, I can be a doctor.

Beyond this first shift, many signs announced various events and cultural days throughout the year. These included school-internal events such as staff versus students sporting events or fundraisers, local attractions, a photography exhibition of Bhutanese-Nepali refugees by a local artist/advocate, seasonal changes, national events or holidays. Many of these images strove to represent the students and their backgrounds in a manner similar to Yuna above.

In addition to extracurricular events, individual classes placed a variety of signs in the hallways broadcasting their academic work. This was most prominent with the art and technology classes but also included the

An English-centric Program with Multilingual Margins   61

Figure 2.5 Samuel's text

math and science classes. For example, Mr Shahiya had the focal students create 'Gallon Bots' that visually demonstrated the relationship between cups, pints, quarts and gallons, as well as art created with an X–Y activity which, when completed properly, created pictures of various animals.

One of the most significant groups of signs were the roughly 40 'School-Wide Vocabulary Words of the Week' that were placed on walls throughout the school, particularly down the academic wings of the building. These signs, printed in black and white on 8.5 × 11" paper, had a focal English word with a corresponding definition in English and several pictures demonstrating the definition. For example, Figure 2.6 shows the sign for 'Hurts: To feel pain in part of your body' and the three images demonstrating this verb, one with a person on crutches and two images of back and head pain.

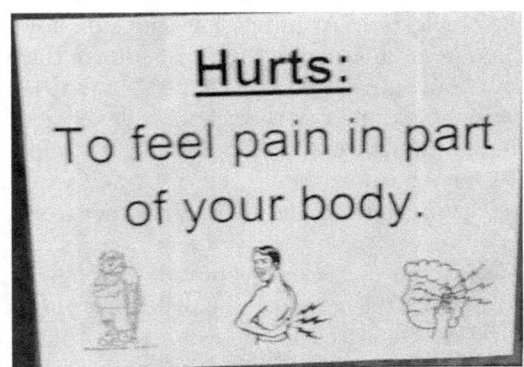

Figure 2.6 'Hurts,' one of nearly 40 'Vocabulary Words of the Week'

Figure 2.7 The sole bi/multilingual sign documented in the 2016–2017 academic year

These various signs clearly demonstrate the English-centric nature of the space. In fact, the only bi/multilingual sign I documented was Figure 2.7, placed at the library entrance. This paucity of bi/multilingual signage for a space with adolescent newcomers and with a multilingual staff who would easily be able to create, either individually or with students, a number of bi/multilingual signs is startling. On the one hand, this is a positive sign and would be legible in the home languages of many of the students; on the other hand, there are generally no German or Chinese speakers in the school, and there is no Nepali or Arabic script, two of the five dominant languages of the school.

The final sign is a kind of outlier and bridge to a critical discussion of English-centricity. In one of the halls in the center of the school, the fabric wall hanging in Figure 2.8 was placed. This art piece clearly contrasts with the rest of the wall hangings and was loaned out of the previous ESL director's collection. Although I am not sure how all the various actors in the school read this image, Mr Adisa, one of the bilingual assistants, told me in a conversation on April 4, 2017 that he felt that this wall hanging in the broader context of the school indexed a kind of 'cultural clash' in the school or maybe even in American society in general, in that some Americans have been so convinced of 'American exceptionalism' that they can barely understand that there is another world outside of the United States.

These various printed signs clearly point to the English-centric nature of the space but reference the bi/multilingual character of the student body as well. This was also reflected in the more verbal signs of the school announcements at the beginning of the day. These announcements were delivered primarily in English by assistant principals Ms Johnston or Ms

An English-centric Program with Multilingual Margins 63

Figure 2.8 A wall hanging donated by the previous director of ESL

Lincoln and were intended to convey essential school information to students, teachers and staff, reinforce the rules of the school and wish the school body a pleasant day. However, at one point in the school year, Valentine's day 2017, the administration, PBIS team and bilingual assistants collaborated to create a short announcement, delivered on YouTube, about the candy gram sale in English, Spanish, Arabic, French, Nepali and Somali, the five primary languages of the school and district. This is certainly positive but, like the image above, a relative outlier.

However, it is important to remember the trajectory of the school, in that this was only the second year in the new building and the previous building had had a much more languaculturally affirming linguistic landscape. It is possible that the collective trauma of being downgraded from a school to a program was difficult and significant work remains to be done to reclaim that languaculturally affirming identity, as Ms Johnston makes clear.

Ms Johnston: [This building] is not home yet. Not home especially for those of us like you say, like the way we felt like it was home. They said it almost felt like we had built a home away from home for the kids … because this is all they've [the students] ever seen. For them, this is really interesting, it's almost like a home away from home. If you won't have built an atmosphere where they can be themselves, and even if like they love it, but for us we've known the old school. This is still kind of disjointed. It's still kind of [makes 'eeeeew' sound]

Brian: Like you don't see the other languages on the wall yet, you don't see the big maps, you don't see the library. It's getting there, the library's [taking over a larger space]. That's going to be huge but it was going to, I feel like we got to refurbish that courtyard and there is a lot of things

Ms Johnston: There's a lot of things that just make this school this school. The courtyard should have their languages all over it ... Then what, the maps, I want the maps back. I mean the flags. I want those flags hanging through this building, that's a dream of mine. I want to hang outside of my office ... I said, 'Let's just bring it back.' To bring back that feeling of belonging. Even when new kids come, help them go up and put their pin in.
(Personal communication, March 27, 2017)

This evidence clearly warrants the argument that the linguistic landscape is broadly English-centric, but both the outliers of the languaculturally affirming signs and the bi/multilingual texts must be seen less as static end points for the program than as beginning points on a new trajectory which, if the English-centric, mainstream or American exceptionalism trends can be overcome without provoking an internal culture class, can lead to a return and even an expansion of the former program's affirming linguistic landscape. At the time of writing, this process has already partially come to fruition in that the inner courtyard was totally refurbished in Summer 2017, and the school has worked with local groups, particularly the mentoring program at the refugee support agency, to create many beautiful murals representing the school community.

Teacher Talk

This section focuses on the degree to which the teachers and Reading Clinic assistants draw on the students' languacultural backgrounds to help them make meaning of their English-centric learning tasks. As has already been shown, the four focal teachers and instructional assistants display various attitudes towards this issue, with the English-centric position being the default. This section, in partial contrast, will draw on the classroom video, participant observation and artifact data to consider three issues relevant to the classroom context itself: (1) teacher talk that either curtails or supports the home languaculture; (2) learning materials in the form of curricula or handouts given to students; and (3) the use of computer-based learning platforms. These practices will demonstrate the English-centricity but also a range of multilingual practices at the margins which, if recognized and elaborated further, could better support the students' home languages and translanguaging practices.

The data corpus had approximately 145 hours of video-recordings. The transcription of the classroom talk had a number of foci with a primary one being the teacher talk whether at teacher–class or teacher–student levels (Bloome, 1989). Nearly all of this talk was in English and directed towards the various English or content-learning tasks in which the students were engaged. During this talk, the teachers used a range of techniques that can be understood broadly as attempts to provide 'comprehensible input' (Krashen, 1985) or 'language which learners process for meaning and which contains something to be learned, that is, linguistic data slightly above their current level' (Ortega, 2008: 59). This theoretical construct is a key part of second language acquisition (SLA) theory and has been appropriated or developed in a number of pedagogies, including the influential SIOP Model (Echevarria *et al.*, 2017). Indeed, SIOP is an influential pedagogy at YES in which teachers such as Ms Cabot have received specialized training. Generally, 'Comprehensible input' is the fundamental goal of SIOP's eight pedagogical aspects from lesson preparation to assessment, which have been both summarized and elaborated across a number of publications (Echevarria *et al.*, 2017; Short *et al.*, 2010; Vogt & Echevarria, 2007). More specifically, SIOP encourages the use of verbal techniques such as restating, repeating or speaking slowly, paralinguistic cues such as demonstrations or gestures, and audio-visual supports such as pictures, objects or graphic organizers. A key question with SIOP and SLA is how much home language support to use while focusing on target language and content acquisition. SIOP encourages, for example, home language use to clarify topics as needed or more robust efforts to engage the students' home languages and cultures.

Notwithstanding these broader issues with SIOP, debates in SLA or bilingual education, the teachers worked to ensure comprehensible input by following a general pattern that included (1) some kind of direct instruction, (2) student work and (3) evaluation of the work. This is commensurate with the patterns in educational discourse that have been studied for many years, starting with Mehan's (1985) discussion of the Initiation-Reply-Evaluation (IRE) pattern. For example, a teacher might introduce an activity or target concept, talk about that relatively slowly, repeat phrases several times, refer to a handout projected on the wall and briefly check the students' comprehension, often using techniques that did not require long or complicated verbal responses due to the fact that the students had just started formally using English. An example from Ms Cabot's (Ms C below) class on January 4, 2017 illustrates this general technique in her use of the Words Their Way curriculum (Bear *et al.*, 2011) and its systematic approach to teaching the fundamental phonetic elements of English (e.g. short or long vowels, diphthongs, etc.).

Note here that Ms Cabot makes no direct or indirect reference to the students' languaculture, but instead starts instruction with a reference to the prior material/background knowledge, both writes on the board and

Line no.	Speaker	Text
1	Ms C	Alright, today you have, we have gone through many words,
2		and many vowel sounds over the last several months.
3		Today we're gonna do the last of the five short vowels
4		that we've been learning, this is the short -i-,
5		the sound of the short -i- is 'eh' so everybody say with me 'eh'
6	Students	Eh
7	Ms C	learning the short i eh sound in the word,
8		ok,
9		ok, before I pass this out to you, I'm gonna show you,
10		((pauses and turns on overhead projector))
11		we have three families that we're gonna look at,
12		three word families we're gonna look at
13		Alright?
14		they are -ip, which is the sound 'ip' everyone say with me,
15		ip
16		ip
17	Students	ip
18	Ms C	((writes i p on the board))
19		i g, which is the sound –ig,
20	Students	ig
21	Ms C	ig
22	Students	ig
23	Ms C	and a new spelling, ill, or i double l –il,
24	Students	ill
25	Ms C	This is important, do we have two ps, no, two gs, no, two ls, yes?
26		some of the consonants in English when we put the sound at the end of the word we have to have two of the letter,
27		so it makes the same sound, one l le, two ls, le,
28		but for our spelling, we must have two, ok, so for example the word hill
29		ok?
30		or spill
31		or, here's a terrible one,
32		kill
33		all of those require this l l double l
34		so that will be the new one you have to remember, two ls
35		this time
36		alright?
37		alright, today you have, we have gone through many words
38		and many vowel sounds over the last several months
39		today we're gonna do the last of the five short vowels.

uses an overhead projector, prompts the students to repeat several words, offers moments of comprehension checking and provides a number of example words that should, at this point in the year, be part of the students' lexical repertoires.

This type of instruction is a large part of the corpus where teachers' instructional talk focuses on developing foundational language skills of reading, writing, listening and speaking through the four content areas of math, science, English and social studies. Following sections of talk similar to this, students were often given a handout or activity to complete, which will be discussed below in greater depth in addition to the related topic of computer-based learning.

However, the focus of this book is the degree to which the teachers made direct or indirect reference to the students' languacultural backgrounds. Thus, both during and after the transcribing of classroom events, I reviewed the transcript and coded moments where the home languaculture was engaged in some way. Similar to the monolingual–translanguaging continuum above, these moments can be organized on a continuum from curtailing to supporting the home languaculture. As I organized these moments, a corpus of moments emerged with 36 'curtailing' items and 88 'supporting' items. The goal of the remainder of this section is to categorize these and give illustrative examples.

However, before moving on to that task, one important point commensurate with the English-centric ideology of the space is that these are, again, relatively rare in the context of the broader corpus, representing only approximately three total hours out of the 145. On the other hand, it is important to underline that this number only includes moments where teacher talk focused on the home language, not on times when the students themselves were using their home language to make meaning. This latter number would in fact be the majority of the corpus, in that teachers generally limited their talk to initiating an activity in the first parts of the class and then released students to work on the task for the majority of the class while the teacher monitored or evaluated student progress. This was particularly prevalent in Mr Shahiya's and Mr Barre's classes where, on a number of occasions, students received no direct instruction but were simply given a handout to work on throughout class. Ms Cabot and Ms Popov both tended to dedicate the first 10–20% of their classes to direct instruction and on rare occasions engaged in direct instruction for the majority of the class time. The Reading Clinic groups, due to their small size, had more opportunities for teacher-directed talk and student responses but also generally reserved moments for students to work independently or as a group on various tasks.

Turning to the task of describing the 'curtailing' and 'supporting' moments, the curtailing moments are similar to those that have long been documented in research about linguistically minoritized groups, where students or families living in an area with a dominant societal language are either subtly or directly told across multiple contexts that their home language is not valued or valuable (Bourne, 2001; Gándara & Hopkins, 2010; K. Howard & Lipinoga, 2010). However, in the context of YES, the situation is perhaps nuanced in that the curtailing of home language use is relatively rare. Again, a significant amount of time in the corpus has students engaged in social or academic talk while the teacher either monitors the students' activities or provides some support. At only rare times, the roughly 35 moments mentioned here, does the teacher make any move to curtail or restrict home language use. Moreover, at no point throughout the corpus does the teacher attach any tangible punishment to home language use (e.g. threatening detention, lowing a grade or removing a student from the classroom). In other words, the home language is, at a minimum, tolerated throughout the majority of the classroom time. This general rule holds under certain circumstances, namely that the home language talk does not become too loud or disturbing. Thus, the first category of home language curtailing relates to volume maintenance, and this basic example from Mr Barre demonstrates the pattern.

Line no.	Speaker	Text
1	Mateo	((walks up to the front table and says loudly to the students there)) que paso?
2	Mr Barre	Shhhh
3	Mateo	((walks back to his desk and sits down, resumes quieter conversation))

Thus, home language use is tolerated as long as it is relatively quiet. However, the second type, code maintenance, shows how students are often encouraged to speak English although not forced to. This example from Ms Popov's class shows the pattern.

Line no.	Speaker	Text
1	Leonardo	((while sitting near Ms Popov and next to Mateo, speaks to Mateo in Spanish at moderate volume but indecipherable on recording))
2	Ms Popov	((hears Spanish)) guys, you remember to learn English, don't talk in your language.

The third type, register maintenance, is used only when students use home language that is considered offensive in some way. Again, students are rarely punished directly for this but rather encouraged to moderate their speech appropriately. Ms Popov's talk shows the pattern.

Line no.	Speaker	Text
1	Mateo	((answers Ms Popov's question then turns to insult Leonardo playfully)) puta miendo 'fucking whore'
2	Ms Popov	stop stop, you got it but don't say bad words. ((then smiles, holding back laughter at their banter))

The fourth type, code criticism, is slightly more nuanced and bridges to the supporting type. Ms Grey's Reading Clinic class frequently started with light talk intended to develop the students' general communicative ability. In this vein, Mondays often started with the prompt, 'What did you do over the weekend?', where students would describe and elaborate on their weekends, with their ability to do so gradually developing over time. One challenge that Ms Grey faced was that some students would offer an answer to this question such as 'sleep,' prompting Ms Grey to retort 'so you slept for 48 hours straight?' and push the students to give more extended responses. However, on occasion, Ms Grey's talk would border on a direct criticism of the home language which this example demonstrates.

Line no.	Speaker	Text
1	Ms Grey	((speaking to Francisco)) did you speak any English at home, at all?
2	Francisco	((shakes head 'no'))
3	Ms Grey	No ok.
4		do you know why you need to start?
5		why?
6	Francisco	((laughs lightly))
7	Ms Grey	I mean we've been talking about this like all year,
8		like all school year,
9		because right now, I'm asking you questions,
10		some you're like, um, I think I know what she's talking about,
11		and then the rest we have no clue what I'm talking about.
12		watch the news.
13		read at least 20 minutes.
14		English.
15		English.
16	Francisco	English.
17	Ms Grey	Listen to music in English
18	Francisco	((smiles))
19	Ms Grey	Yes.
20		Seriously.
21		even to your friends,

22		because that helps you improve your English,
23		your vocabulary,
24		helps you with your speaking.
25		ok?
26		so 20 minutes a night,
27		read a book,
28		in English.
29	Francisco	No have books.
30	Ms Grey	I have plenty of books.
31		I'll give you some,
32		and we'll start off easy.
33		we'll start off,
34		with colors.
35		the apple is red.
36		ok?
37		that is still helping with your English.
38	Francisco	English.
39	Ms Grey	what movie do you like?
40		you see, you remember how we did Nightjohn?
41		we watched a movie called Nightjohn?
42		that was in English, although there were things you didn't understand what they were talking about.
43		you could see it right, you knew what was going on?
44		same thing, you have a VCR or a CD player?
45	Francisco	No
46	Ms Grey	Do you have a DVD player?
47		I can get you one, and then you hook it up to your TV to watch it,
48		ok?
49		so I'll bring that in tomorrow,
50		ok?

In this section, although Ms Grey clearly intended to encourage independent English engagement and learning out of school, she moved into dangerous territory with her criticism of Francisco's inability to respond to her questions and her assumptions of what he does or does not know. Moreover, Francisco provided a reasonable explanation for his perceived lack of progress by describing the absence of relevant learning materials in his home. In other moments in class and also in discussions with me, Francisco emphasized that he is living with relatives and indicated that he has a number of household duties such as cooking and cleaning which, from his perspective, limit the time available for self-study. This issue is partly commensurate with Norton's insight that, just because a person is living in the midst of the target-language culture, this does not guarantee that the material or interpersonal conditions of an individual's life will be commensurate with target-language learning (Kanno & Norton, 2003; Norton, 2013; Norton & McKinney, 2011; Norton Peirce, 1995). In addition, Ms Grey's statements perhaps reveal an uncritical position on the (apparently unsatisfying) results of her own practice and what other methods or materials might be available to help a student like Francisco to develop conversational ability in English. This point will be taken up more below in the discussion of the handouts and other materials the teachers draw on to support student learning.

Thus, these four types of curtailing talk include:

- Volume maintenance: Being tolerant of home language talk provided that it is not perceived as being too loud; if the volume rises too much, curtailing ensues.
- Code maintenance: Being tolerant provided that the talk is not perceived as being off-task; if the talk is heard and perceived as such, curtailing ensues.
- Register maintenance: Being tolerant provided that the talk is not perceived as being offensive; if it is, curtailing ensues.
- Code criticism: Being tolerant provided that the teacher perceives student target-language progress; if not, curtailing ensues.

Moves supportive of the home languaculture were, to the program's credit, more plentiful with the nearly 90 items identified, but again generally rare. Moreover, these items range in terms of the length of talk and their connections to other meaning-making objects (e.g. handouts, Google Translate, etc.).

The most cursory moments are those that utilized the verbal modality only and provided or sought a one-to-one translation between English and the home language. These moments were partially moderated by the teacher's linguistic repertoire, such as with Ms Cabot's relatively limited range, evidenced by this section from February 13, 2017.

Line no.	Speaker	Text
1	**Ms Cabot**	soft green grass ((pulls up a picture of grass on the computer projector))
2		si?
3		oui?

Here, Ms Cabot uses the words '*si*' and '*oui*' to check the students' comprehension of the word 'grass.' Ms Cabot, who did not identify herself as having a very robust linguistic repertoire despite having some basic ability in Spanish, French, German and Latin, used this technique in multiple other instances. For example, she would tell students such as Francisco or some of the other Spanish male students who were perceived as difficult in the class to 'keep your hands, *manos*, to yourself' or 'don't be *loco*, crazy.' She would also give numbers in the languages she knew or say '*gracias*' or '*mañana*' or '*dice*' to some of the Spanish- or Portuguese-speaking students. This type of verbal one-to-one translation was also used by Ms Popov to, for example, help Spanish students understand 'birthday' as '*fecha de nacimiento*.'

The second type, also cursory in nature but perhaps more affirming of the students' languaculture, includes moments where the teacher is clearly attending to the students' talk and responding accordingly. Ms Popov's listening to the students' use of Spanish profiled above is a partial example, but there are other examples where she not only attends to student talk but also responds and connects with the students, such as in this example from March 2, 2017.

Line no.	Speaker	Text
1	Mateo	((sits next to Leonardo and says to him)) hace frío. 'it's cold'
2	Leonardo	((speaks towards Ms Popov)) necesito el baño. 'I need the bathroom'
3	Ms Popov	((to Mateo)) it's not so cold.
4	Mateo	si, esto frío. 'yes, it's cold'
5	Ms Popov	((to Leonardo)) you cannot wait? Ok, if it's emergency, write your name ((on the hall pass))
6	Mateo	frío. 'cold'
7	Ms Popov	if you are cold, zip your jacket, zip your jacket, and make it ((breathes in/out several times)) make the classroom warm, breath, breath, that's it.

In this example, Ms Popov is clearly noticing the students' home language talk even when it is not directed at her. Moreover, in contrast to the curtailing moments above, she responds to the students' talk in a humane manner, allowing Leonardo to go to the bathroom (contrary to the school policy of no bathroom visits during the first 10 minutes of class) and advising Mateo on how to deal with his issue of being cold in the room.

These two examples show how the teachers' linguistic repertoires are deployed in relatively short moments that are primarily verbal in nature. However, there were moments of longer home language talk, particularly from Ms Popov in Spanish or from Mr Barre and Mr Shahiya when the former would explain math or science issues in Somali and the latter in Somali or Arabic to students. These talks always occurred at the teacher–student level, that is, during one-on-one or small-group support, never as part of direct teacher–class instruction. This example from Mr Shahiya's class on November 15, 2016 demonstrates the pattern but requires some context to extract its full meaning. In Mr Shahiya's class, the first semester was primarily dedicated to learning about the conversion of units in the American or British (i.e. pound, foot, gallon) and metric systems. Omar, a Syrian refugee, had arrived in the first week of October and, due to having been out of school for nearly two years while in Jordan in addition to the challenge of a new city, school system and so on, was struggling in some classes, particularly in math with Mr Barre where he felt that he was not developing as quickly as he desired because it was difficult to understand the English on the handouts. Omar also often criticized, to me in private conversation, Mr Barre's lack of Arabic and, moreover, his pedagogical technique of offering brief direct instruction with a few examples followed by a handout that the students would complete in small groups or with his help. In turn, Mr Barre would tell me privately that Omar 'just wants to talk,' reflecting the fact that Omar was quite social, particularly with Salah, an issue that will be taken up more in the next chapter. In the class itself, Mr Barre's main expectation seemed to be that students at least make some effort, evidenced by his many statements of 'just try' to the students in the class. More specifically, Mr Barre's repeated phrase 'look look look,' although intended to encourage Omar to attend to the handout and attempt to answer the questions independently, often ran foul of Omar's expectations of good teaching because Omar felt this statement did not help explain the content to him. Indeed, on November 14, 2016, this event had happened, causing me to have a long conversation with Omar in which I tried to calm his frustrations, explain the material in Arabic and give him some personal and academic strategies to negotiate the transition into the school culture generally and with Mr Barre specifically.

The following example from November 15, 2016 picks up a moment when Mr Shahiya is explaining to Omar how to convert liters to milliliters, using an English-language handout generated from the website Super Teacher Worksheets (www.superteacherworksheets.com), which asked students to read a description of the process of either multiplying or dividing by 1000 and then to answer questions such as 'How many liters are in 5000 milliliters?' or 'How many milliliters are in 23 liters?'.

Line no.	Speaker	Text
1	Omar	tqsim² 'divide'? milliliter.
2	Mr S	ash althani? 'what's next'
3	Omar	liter, y3ni 'I mean', milliliter.
4	Mr S	u hadha 'and this one' milli shah 'right'?
5	Omar	shah. 'right'
6	Mr S	ok, 3in hna, ash baqi? 'look here, what's left'
7	Omar	xmsa bsir xmsa.' five becomes five'
8	Mr S	xhma ash? 'five what' xms alaf 'five thousand' ((corrects self)) xms miya shah? 'five hundred right'

9	Omar	xmsin 'fifty', xmsa 'five' ((turns attention to me)) ustadh shu al t3lim mu mithal ustadh riyadiat 'teacher, the teaching here is not like the teacher of math.'
10	Brian	((chuckles))
11	Omar	la baqulu lih shrh li lakin la yrd li. 'no, I tell him 'explain it to me' but he doesn't respond'
12	Mr S	ana 3rf al mudu3. ((or muqabala, audio not clear)) 'I know the issue/contrast'
13	Omar	bdi yshrh li, ytrjm ma bitirjm li, ma bdu al rd. 'I want him to explain, to translate, to translate for me, but he doesn't respond'
14	Mr S	ana bkllm 3rbi shah u huwa mish. 'I speak Arabic, right, but not him'
15	Omar	ay, ttklm 3rbi, sua fi ashasks yhtchi ajnabi u 3ni trjm li, ani jnbik hada, shaif, shu al t3lim, ma bi t3lim. 'yes, you speak Arabic, but there are those that speak a foreign language, and translate for me, who stay next to you, but you see the learning, it's not what it should be.'
15	Brian	so gul shukran. 'say thank you'
16	Omar	shukran. 'thank you'
17	Mr S	afuan, afuan. 'you're welcome, you're welcome (laughs a bit and walks away

In this section, Mr Shahiya is assisting Omar with the general concept as well as the question on the handout, specifically by translating many of the terms and walking him through the process using Arabic. After Omar works through the answer of 'five' in Lines 1–8 which required dividing 5000 by 1000, he turns in Lines 9–15 to a broader discussion or critique of Mr Barre's practice and comments positively about Mr Shahiya's work as a kind of 'real teaching.' Mr Shahiya, who is a friend of Mr Barre, is aware of and acknowledges the issues between Mr Barre and Omar but positions them as fundamentally about linguistic ability rather than pedagogical stance. Following this class moment, Mr Shahiya helps Omar with other questions and vocabulary such as the translation of 'oil' but also encourages Omar to try to use and speak English as much as he can. This push towards English continued between Mr Shahiya and Omar throughout much of the year, documented on occasions such as November 21, 2016 or March 13, 2017, and generally Mr Shahiya's talk towards Omar sought to bridge from more Arabic to more English talk.

This section illustrates the type of talk that goes beyond the one-to-one word or brief exchanges in the first part, but it must be emphasized that this talk is still fundamentally verbal in nature and not connected directly to any other pedagogical object that directly or indirectly engages the students' languaculture. This final type focuses on moments that can be considered more robust, where the teacher has explicitly connected other semiotic material (e.g. handouts) to the students' languaculture. Two examples demonstrate this, one from Ms Grey's class and one from Ms Popov's. Both require some contextualization.

Ms Grey, as an African-American woman, did not position herself as having a broad linguistic repertoire beyond English, nor did she explicitly claim African-American Vernacular English when I asked her about the languages she knew although she used this register frequently in her speech, with both peers and students. In her Reading Clinic class, she usually started with the conversational topics profiled above or engaged in vocabulary-building work around the Fry list that will be profiled below. However, a third key feature of her class was engagement with cultural-historical topics that, while intersecting with events such as Black History month (e.g. with the watching of the film *Nightjohn*), were directly applicable to her lived experience. For example, before, during and after Black History month, she emphasized the civil rights struggle, helped students build their vocabulary around this topic and connected it to their own backgrounds. Interestingly, Ms Grey grew up in the focal area and said that she had not experienced direct racism in the city but became more aware of the issue when she joined the Army Reserves after high school when, for the first time, she observed and experienced that some people did not like others because of the color of their skin. This is not to say that she was naïve about racism – her mother and grandmother had shared many stories about their experiences growing up with overt racism – but she was explicit about and thankful for the fact of growing up without many of these negative experiences. Thus, although her specific langua-cultural background may not be a clear overlap with the students, she recognized the importance of her work.

> **Ms Grey:** But I think, too, for me and my kids [her students], I talk about my experience. I talk about I'm here because a lot of kids think that I'm from some country in Africa. When I say, 'No, I've been born and raised here. All around here. Just went to school.' They hear that. 'You went to [name of a local high school]?' because they have friends there. We built that relationship, and they feel like, 'Oh, okay.' (Ms Grey, personal communication, April 10, 2017)

As this quote implies, part of Ms Grey's understanding of her role was recognizing and sometimes challenging the students' understanding of race and their broader lived experiences, both in the US and in their home countries.

> **Ms Grey:** Because I'm like, 'If I came to your country with the color of my skin, would there be an issue?' Some kids say, 'No.' Then there's some kids were like, 'Well.' Well, why? What does that mean? For them to be proud of their own heritage, where they're from, their culture, and to be proud and aware of it. Just understanding that everybody who is here in America, they're here for a reason. Better education, to find a job, to get away from war, to get away from famine. We're not going to

pick on a certain group just because they were in a refugee camp. We're not going to, even that, we look, depending on the group and where they're from, but we looked at the refugee camp that one of our Somali students were in. Then we also looked at the refugee camp the Nepali students was in. They were able to compare the differences of the structure of the houses, the food, the market [she gives examples of the comparison and transitions to questions about race]. We've talked about that too. 'What have you heard about black people before you came here? What have you heard about the Nepali community before you came here? What have you heard?' And we talk about all of those different things. 'What do you see that's the same, what do you see that's different?' And one of the kids tell me, 'I came over here. They said black people were bad. All I saw on TV were black people were bad. So when I ran into a black person, okay, because I used to, why when I go into a store and smile, they put their head down when I pass?' It's that kind of stuff. All of that is important in understanding. Especially when you're here, that everybody feels a certain way no matter where you come from.

These statements index Ms Grey's awareness of her own position in the program, what sorts of knowledge she feels she can authentically share with the students and how these have a goal of promoting understanding and reflective engagement with American society. These frame the activity structure and languacultural connections with her group on March 29, 2017 when I walked into the room and observed a lesson that was part of a several weeks-long exploration of the immigrant and refugee experience which started on March 22, 2017. During this time, the students had a packet of materials mainly compiled from the ReadWorks.org website. One of these readings was entitled 'Coming to the U.S.A' and featured the stories of Nimo and Fadumo, two Somali refugees; the other, 'I am Maria,' profiled a bilingual Spanish-English Mexican migrant from Juárez.

To make meaning of the readings on March 29, 2017, Ms Grey had the students read the text together and individually several times, and then worked through the text, focusing on key words such as 'civil war' and 'refugee,' spending time on the dictionary distinctions between refugee and 'immigrant.' Critically, she encouraged the students to collaborate and draw on their linguistic repertoire. The following exchange demonstrates part of this technique, with Ms Grey, Maria (a student from El Salvador) and the aforementioned Francisco from Guatemala.

Line no.	Speaker	Text
1	Ms Grey	what what is civil war?
2	Maria	it different people fighting.

3	Ms Grey	so is it where we both live in Somalia, it is me and you fighting, or is it someone from the outside coming in to fight us?
4	Maria	I think here.
5	Ms Grey	yes, it's inner fighting amongst the people who live there.
6		so it's just like Maria is opposed to Francisco because we're all in this group together,
7		they're fighting each other, there's a civil war, no no fighting you to.
8	Maria	es like guerre civil.
9	Francisco	huh?
10	Maria	la guerra civil.
11	Francisco	oh.

This section demonstrates the type of languacultural connections I wish to illustrate in the interaction between verbal utterances and more durable expressions in the form of written words or handouts. Indeed, when I walked into the room on March 29, 2017, Ms Grey had written 'civil war' on the board next to '*guerra civil*' and 'fighting' next to '*pelear*' and had asked the students to use Google Translate on their phones for other terms to add to the board. In addition, not forgetting the role of target-language rephrasing mentioned above, one of the students asked her for the definition of 'escape' and she said 'to run away.' She then explained to me that, following this vocabulary building exercise, the students would watch videos about their home countries on YouTube and would connect these to an autobiographical writing activity, subtly extending a previous activity that Ms Cabot had asked the students to do earlier in January.

This practice is generally positive in terms of supporting the students' languacultural backgrounds through engaging their individual, social and multimodal linguistic repertoires and was used to varying degrees throughout the program. However, this activity and practice is not without problematic elements, beginning with the one-to-one translation issues mentioned previously but extending to a more serious issue with Tara, a Bhutanese refugee with Nepali as a home language, who described his Nepali literacy skills as poor (for the history of this refugee population, see Evans, 2010; Kingston & Stam, 2015). Throughout this activity and others engaging the home language, Tara and students like him were limited in their ability to draw on their home language, particularly because Nepali is written in a script derived from Sanskrit. Moreover, the refugee camp education these students received in Eastern Nepal was formally English-medium except for a separate Nepali class. Although in practice these classes utilized the Nepali language heavily to help students make sense of the English materials, this decentering of the Nepali language in the students' formal education, in addition to the students' preparation for resettlement in the US, has led to uneven Nepali literacy abilities with this group, limiting in part their ability to connect their home language knowledge to their English learning.

Despite this complication, this second type of activity demonstrates a more coordinated integration of the languacultures of the students with the broader semiotic resources at their disposal. Critically, although Ms Grey's individual linguistic repertoire does not strongly overlap with that of the students, she draws in the social and multimodal aspects of the collective linguistic repertoire to make meaning and makes those meanings more visible by writing on the board and encouraging the students to write in their home language on their individual sheets.

The second example of this type displays what can be considered the most robust and coordinated efforts by a teacher involved in this research project to make connections between the home and target languages. Ms Popov, as has been implied and partially warranted, has a belief in the importance of the students' home languages and some strategies for engaging these in the classroom. This section will further describe her coordinated efforts to understand the students' home languages and connect these to target language learning.

YES's assessment protocols will be addressed more fully below, but the critical point is that the program neither assesses the home language systematically nor uses informal assessment results to make program decisions. This point will be emphasized below when discussing future orientations for the program and the barriers the English-centric ideology creates for multilingual pedagogy and practices.

However, Ms Popov's class is perhaps the exception that proves the rule. Ms Popov used a diagnostic test that had multiple sections – some on English grammar, reading and writing but also a 'Writing Sample' that asked students to write in their home language(s). Ms Popov administered this test with the first group that arrived and with any new student (despite the difficulty of high student mobility and the large sections that she had due to schedule changes). Figure 2.9 shows this assessment.

Although Ms Popov was not able to use this test for official purposes such as uploading it to the student's profile in the district's learning management systems, it provided her with a quick view into the students' previous educations and home language literacies. The range on these tests reflects the issues raised above. For example, Tara simply wrote 'cannot' in this section; another student, Salah (who will be profiled in detail below), could not (hand)write much in his home language beyond his name. On the other hand, others were already highly bi/multiliterate, such as Amal who wrote extended texts in Somali and Swahili (and was quickly transferred to a mainstream school) or Maria, who wrote/drew the charming story in Figure 2.10 with strong narrative links to 'Little Red Riding Hood.' Despite the administrative challenges of sharing this data, Ms Popov was able to use this information in the Teacher-Based Team meetings to advocate for or offer additional evidence about certain students.

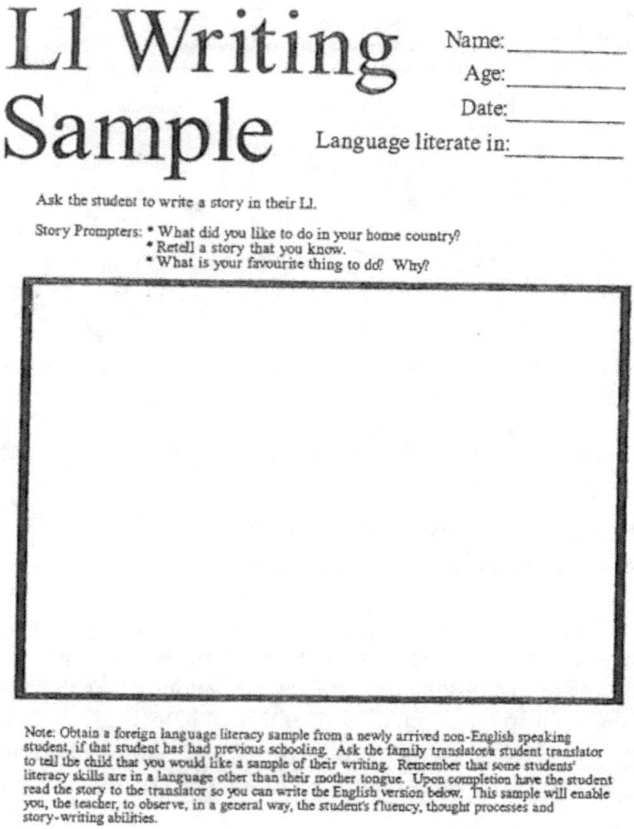

An English-centric Program with Multilingual Margins   79

L1 Writing Sample

Name:_____
Age:_____
Date:_____
Language literate in:_____

Ask the student to write a story in their L1.

Story Prompters: • What did you like to do in your home country?
• Retell a story that you know.
• What is your favourite thing to do? Why?

Note: Obtain a foreign language literacy sample from a newly arrived non-English speaking student, if that student has had previous schooling. Ask the family translator/student translator to tell the child that you would like a sample of their writing. Remember that some students' literacy skills are in a language other than their mother tongue. Upon completion have the student read the story to the translator so you can write the English version below. This sample will enable you, the teacher, to observe, in a general way, the student's fluency, thought processes and story-writing abilities.

Figure 2.9 Ms Popov's home language test

Figure 2.10 Maria's home language writing section

Vocabulary- Name_____ Class____ Date____			
WORD and VISUAL:	**WORD IN MY NATIVE LANGUAGE:**	**WHAT IT ACTUALLY MEANS:**	**CONNECTION:** (Text-text, text-world, text-self)
right			
freedom			
speech			
law			
vote			

Figure 2.11 Ms Popov's vocabulary building sheet

Thus, this initial test indexes Ms Popov's understanding of and commitment to the home languaculture. Next, Ms Popov was the only teacher to use or design a specific learning resource to help students make meaning of the target language with and through their home language. Figure 2.11 shows this resource, which has the target vocabulary on the left-hand side.

With this handout, Ms Popov asked students to first draw a picture of the target vocabulary, then write the word in their home language, then write a definition from the dictionary and then write a sentence of their own in the right-hand column or make some other connection to the target vocabulary. Crucially, Ms Popov used this tool from the beginning of the academic year and would dedicate extended class time to this task. For example, on March 9, 2017 Ms Popov oriented the students to a vocabulary sheet with the focal words 'conquistador, to sail, trade, route, to suffer' at approximately the 10th minute of the class. This was the second official item on the day's activities written on the board after 'Checking homework,' next to the regular activity 'Student on Duty' where a designated student would talk at the front of the class for three minutes. The third activity involved individual/small-group reading of a history text, but Ms Popov first held up the vocabulary sheet and said, 'So show me who finished at home. If you finished, you go to the next step.' As most students had not completed it yet, Ms Popov began an extended section of talk/student engagement lasting for approximately five minutes.

An English-centric Program with Multilingual Margins 81

Line no.	Speaker	Text
1	Ms Popov	I can show you some examples from my other groups, ok,
2		alright. ((goes to computer at front of room))
3		so, we have five words,
4		say together,
5		conquistador.
6	Students	conquistador.
7	Ms Popov	((continues with 'to sail, trade, route, to suffer' and students repeat))
8		definitions are here,
9		and on the backside,
10		on this side there are some definitions.
11		on this side, ok?
12		and let me show you examples,
13		a lot of students finished in my period 1 2 3,
14		I have different languages, let's see, please this,
15		Somali language.
16		do we have Somali speakers, yes, like four students, let me show Somali.
17		this is Spanish speaking,
18		nice picture, look at this picture,
19		((puts it on the overhead) funny pictures ((moves other papers out of the way)).
20		check, translation, oh you don't see very well? ((makes projection larger))
21		this is, Fatima, this is good, I think it is good Somali language.
22		check the translation in Somali, do you understand?
23		Mohammed, do you understand, is it correct?
24	Mohammed	(doesn't respond)
25	Ms Popov	yes no?
26	Mohammed	some are wrong.
27	Ms Popov	some are wrong.
28		this is Nepali language, check your,
29		guys and you can come and take the paper and look what other students do,
30		and check your translation.
31		French, no French.
32		that's, this student should be good in Somali,
33		she's always, she's usually very good,
34		check translation, Mohammed, is it good?
35	Mohammed	yeah, that's correct.

36	Ms Popov	this is good to sail, how do you say?	
37	Mohammed	fi3a.	
38	Ms Popov	to trade?	
39	Mohammed	garna.	
40	Fatima	gana3siga.	
41	Ms Popov	right?	
42	Mohammed	yeah, gana3siga.	
43	Ms Popov	route?	
44	Fatima	waddo.	
45	Ms Popov	waddo.	
46		to suffer?	
47	Fatima	((reads, audio-recording unclear))	
48	Ms Popov	good,	
49		so you are welcome to take what language if you need or you do by yourself.	
50	Fatima	I need Miss,	
51	Ms Popov	you need Somali?	
52	Dhan	I need Nepali.	
53	Ms Popov	ok, I'll give you, but try not to copy, just look, make up your own sentence.	
54		you, Nepali?	
55	Puspa	yeah.	
56	Ms Popov	((passes paper to Puspa))	
57		Nepali, she's ((indicating name of other student)) usually good	
58		and these are nice pictures. ((puts copy on the overhead))	
59		ha! look at the conquistador.	
60		he's, (with arms up like flexing)	
61	Maria	(laughs)	
62	Ms Popov	ok, Nepali language, examples,	
63		I find more, more Somali, do you want Somali language, yeah?	
64		you are good, Mohammed, you have it, do you need Somali?	
65	Mohammed	yeah, I need Somali.	
66	Ms Popov	pass to him. ((passes paper to Gabriela))	
67		she's ((the student's name from other class)) good, good pictures, I like the pictures,	
68		((laughs briefly)) I like this train, you see this is a modern train, like plane, people trade, do business by plane.	
69		trade routes.	
70		So, ((looks at some papers, laughs))	
71		oh my, look at this, these are interesting,	
72		to suffer.	

73	trade by car, you can do trading by car.
74	and the conquistador, ((laughs))
75	Ok,
76	ok, you understand right?
77	go ahead do it your way, you can copy a little bit,
78	but if you copy, understand what you're copying,
79	you learn it.
80	ok?
81	good.
82	I'm going to remove,
83	do it your way please.

The students then continued with their individual or group work as Ms Popov moved through the room, checking the students' work, collecting their papers and then directing them to the next activity working with the American history book. Overall, the students completed the activity and all of them, including those who had been struggling throughout the year, turned in the activity before the end of the period and moved on to the next task.

Thus, this activity shows Ms Popov's commitment to the home languaculture, but again it should be read critically. One of these is the aforementioned challenge for Nepali students. Ms Popov's activity, although she did not make this explicit, was interpreted by the Nepali speaking students as requiring them to write in Nepali script. This is partially reflected in the statement made by Dhan and Ms Popov's response/reminder of 'if you copy, understand what you're copying,' which subtly contradicts, for this population, the 'do it your way' statement. Thus, during these activities, many of the Nepali speaking students would bring up the translation in Google Translate and then rather painstakingly copy out the Nepali script rather than – as might have been easier and more useful for them – writing in transliteration. This relates to the brief discussion above about language loss and shifts, particularly for the Nepali speaking students, and indexes broader questions of what home language literacy means for adolescent students. On the one hand, the use of Nepali script is an important aspect of Nepali identity and literacy; on the other hand, the adolescents are developing their own ways of writing/reading Nepali which, I would argue, deserve to be recognized as legitimate and useful across various contexts from home to school.

A second issue is Ms Popov's repeated assertion, made to both Omar and Tara during the course of the class, that 'conquistador would be any language, conquistador, the same,' emphasizing that conquistador is itself a loan word from Spanish. However, of course, conquistador can be translated to English as 'conqueror' and then to other languages such as Arabic with '*fatih*' or other similar terms. As a result, it is possible that some misconceptions about the term or the task itself remained for the students; nevertheless, the overall structure of the activity and its discourse maintain a view of Ms Popov as one committed to supporting the home languacultures across a number of modalities.

In conclusion, this section reveals the range of teacher talk with respect to curtailing or supporting the home language. Although some aspects of this talk are positive and supportive of the home culture, it must be stressed again that these were relatively rare in the overall corpus of video data, with the majority being English-only teacher instruction or student group work. The student group work certainly is an element of languacultural support as the teachers were largely tolerant of the talk, provided it did not break the 'rules' above which, themselves, were not codified in any formal way by the teachers but were part of the invisible norms and systems of control that pervade all social situations. Within these norms, students were allowed to collaborate on group work and talk socially about a number of topics that, while not a direct focus of this book, partly index the kind of 'home' environment that Ms Johnston envisions. On the other hand, this analysis of teacher talk further warrants the argument that the program is English-centric in that no activities focused on developing the home language per se or asked the students to perform in their home language in a manner that would be more reflective of bi/multilingual programming. Indeed, these were the frontiers that Mr Braun had been exploring with his 'Bilingual Biomes' project (Seilstad *et al.*, 2019).

Instructional Materials

The teachers' use of various instructional materials, whether copied from books or taken from websites, has been discussed in part above, and this section will consider the issue more deeply and critically in terms of home languacultural support. This will show that, while the majority of the resources accessed are English-only, there is an interesting subset that have languages other than English available, raising the question as to why these are not used by the teachers. The answer I will provide connects directly to issues of national and named languages and Orellana's (2016: 91) 'things that were being held apart, or artificially constructed as separate and distinct.'

For this analysis, I reviewed all the handouts and websites that the teachers directly used in classroom instruction. This produced a list of 53 different websites or books. Some of these materials were used regularly in classroom learning, such as Raz-Kids (www.raz-kids.com) in the English class, Flowcabulary (www.flocabulary.com) in the social studies class, ST Math (www.stmath.com) in the math class and BrainPOP (www.brainpop.com) across all classes. The first three resources were used as the core activity nearly once a week in their respective classes, and BrainPOP was used occasionally to help students learn about particular topics. In general, Raz-Kids and ST Math were programs whose materials remained online, but Flowcabulary and BrainPOP had many handouts (e.g. song lyrics or quizzes) that could be printed out, if necessary, for classroom tasks.

Beyond these core websites, the teachers used a wide variety of websites to support their teaching. Some of these websites had broad P-12 materials such as Super Teacher Worksheets (www.superteacherworksheets.com), whereas others had more subject-specific content (e.g. www.sciencekids.co.nz). In addition, teachers often had core books that both guided and provided resources for classroom learning, such as the aforementioned Pearson's *Words Their Way* curriculum for Ms Cabot, AGS Publishing's *Basic Math Skills* for Mr Barre, Alston Publishing's *Science Smart* for Mr Shahiya or Great Source's *ACCESS American History* for Ms Popov, which they used either for making copies of activities or as a whole textbook (cf. examples from Ms Cabot's and Ms Popov's classes above).

In terms of grade-level content, these resources are primarily oriented towards early grade learning, particularly in terms of English language learning and corpus-based vocabulary lists such as the Fry (1980) or Dolch (1936) sight word lists, but not exclusively so. Teachers often drew on websites such as ReadWorks.org to provide more grade-level and complicated texts for students to work with, even if these might have been quite challenging for the students, as partially evidenced by Ms Grey's extended work about refugees and immigrants above.

However, the core issue is to what degree these materials engage with and support the students' home languaculture. Again, the short answer, reflecting the English-centric ideology of the space, is that these materials do not make many direct connections. The primary examples have already been shown above with Ms Grey's ReadWorks texts or Ms Popov's home language writing and vocabulary activities. Ms Cabot, however, did carry out a student autobiography activity mid-year which, while the final texts were written in English, allowed the students to write in their home languages as part of the brainstorming and early writing process.

The remaining examples of languacultural support are tangential. For example, some of Ms Popov's geography handouts might index aspects of the home languaculture (e.g. by linking volcanoes and Francisco's home country of Guatemala, which she did briefly during one of his 'Student on Duty' talk sections), but these connections are not central to the activity itself. Ms Cabot, in turn, conducted a written 'Reading Survey' taken from the Read-Write-Think website (www.readwritethink.org), asking the students questions such as 'What, besides books, do you like to read, outside of school, how often do you read, who are your favorite authors, and what kinds of books do you like to read?'. However, this survey was administered mid-year and mainly to help Ms Cabot do a case study of Puspa (attending to many of the aforementioned literacy issues) as part of a reading endorsement class she was taking through The Ohio State University. Thus, although it has some indirect languacultural elements and the class discussion around the survey raised interesting connections such as Omar's love of Nizar Qabbani, Puspa's reading of the Bible or students' literacy practices on social media, I did not include it above as an example of direct or consistent languacultural engagement.

Thus, these materials and usages warrant the English-centric argument, but there is an additional telling case about not only the teacher and school ideology but also the structural barriers within many of these websites to making languacultural connections. Out of the 53 resources, there were nine that had some connection to languages other than English. These were BrainPOP, Raz-Kids, ESL Fast (www.eslfast.com), Community Resources for Science (www.crscience.org), Common Core Sheets (http://www.commoncoresheets.com), Words Their Way, Hubbard's Cupboard (www.hubbardscupboard.org), Evan-Moor's *Beginning Geography* (www.evan-moor.com) and Teachers Pay Teachers (www.teacherspayteachers.com). While some of these have resources in, for example, Spanish, it can admittedly be difficult to find them, as is the case for Hubbard's Cupboard where the Spanish, French, German or Portuguese materials are several levels into the website as part of their 'Sight Word Booklets.' On the other hand, Community Resources for Science places prominent links to Spanish language resources such as Paso Partners (www.sedl.org/scimath/pasopartners), which consistently places grade-level lessons in Spanish and English on the same page next to each other, marking the connections between the content and languages. With such bilingual resources available, this raises the critical question of why such materials were not utilized during the course of instruction, which can almost immediately be answered by Mr Shahiya's expressed language and pedagogical ideology, quoted above. It is likely that this is an explanatory reason for many of the teachers at YES.

On the other hand, there is perhaps a telling counterexample with the BrainPOP website which relates to Orellana's point about languages being artificially (and unnecessarily) held apart. The BrainPOP website uses simple animations and texts to cover a broad range of academic topics. There is a core corpus of videos and texts as well as smaller BrainPOP Jr (K-3) and BrainPOP ELL sections. However, there are also BrainPOP Español and BrainPOP Français sections, which are essentially mirror translation sites of the primary BrainPOP videos, but as one navigates within any one of these video sections, unfortunately there is no direct link between these languages. This fact is perplexing in that any video is accompanied by a sidebar with a number of options to engage with the material, ranging from a quiz to conceptual map making, games and so on. Certainly, it would not be difficult for BrainPOP to add a link to the Spanish or French versions of the same video. Without this, interested teachers or students must find the corresponding video in the mirror sites – a task that is not necessarily difficult but is certainly unnecessarily time-consuming.

To explore this further, I emailed BrainPOP to ask why these features were not available and received a response on October 22, 2018 explaining that BrainPOP and BrainPOP Español or Français were separate products requiring subscriptions. They thanked me for my suggestion about linking the content. This response raises multiple challenges related to BrainPOP's notions of products, subscriptions and ease of use. A sustained critique of each of these would certainly be fruitful, but perhaps it suffices to point out that, as of Summer 2020, BrainPOP videos still do not have a direct link between the English, Spanish and French versions of their content.

These two examples reveal two sides of this English-centric environment in that, on the one hand, teachers and perhaps even some students prefer English-medium materials, commensurate with an English-only or immersion ideology. This might explain why teachers, with rare exceptions, did not utilize bilingual materials or learning strategies. One the other hand, some structural barriers exist within these websites in the way they keep material that is either quite similar or exactly the same segregated on the basis of language, thus reducing the visibility of those connections and the probability that connections would be made.

Assessment Practices

The final set of data warranting the program's English-centric nature with multilingual margins is the formal assessment practices of the program. As Mr Smith mentioned above in reference to the new Every Student Succeeds Act (ESSA), which replaced the No Child Left Behind (NCLB), all English language learners (ELLs) must be tested and tracked in schools, replacing a nexus of previous assessments that often delayed or removed these students from formal assessments. This skewed the overall student data and obscured the learning that was (or was not) happening with ELLs. Thus, although the decision to test these students is not uncontroversial, overall the added visibility of their results has been helpful.

These tests now include the state-level Ohio English Language Proficiency Assessment (OELPA), which is given once a year and is a summative assessment of the students' English proficiency, used most specifically as an exit requirement for a student to lose the LEP label. There are five levels of Beginning, Early Intermediate, Intermediate, Early Advanced and Advanced, and three broad bands – Emerging, Progressing and Proficient. The second test, NWEA's Measures of Academic Progress (MAP) is given three times a year and, while it is not strictly a formative assessment, its results are generally available within the week the test is administered. The numbers for this test are more continuous, allowing for more fine-grained analysis of the overall results. Both are now computer-based tests, and the district employs a testing coordinator whose job, among other duties, is to ensure that these tests are administrated on time and with adequate controls (e.g. proctors, space between students, etc.)

In addition to these computer-based tests, the Reading Clinic staff of bilingual instructional assistants administered the Dominie generally within the first week of a student's arrival and again, ideally, later in the year to measure the student's progress. Students were initially assigned to the Reading Clinic based on this test, with most students placed based on a 'pre-K' rating. However, as the main coordinator of this test, Ms Lee, pointed out, the Dominie and the 'pre-K' label may not be sufficiently differentiated for the program to conduct initial or ongoing assessment.

> Brian: So, what if you were just brainstorming, if you were going to design those pre-k levels, what would be the things that you would put in there, like say benchmarks, that you'd try to assess? ...
>
> Ms Lee: Well, if they know their letters and they know their words I would say its pre-k. But if they know some letters don't know words and they can't even form a sentence, I would say that was low and very, very low. Then in-betweens, they know some words but they just can't form a sentence. I don't know, I never thought about it. I just mentioned to Ms Sharp that maybe they should have some kind of a leveling system so we know because on the chart of the Dominie when I chart it. So yes, its pre-k, and the pre-test is pre-k but then the post-test's still pre-k. But then in-betweens they still make some progress but it won't show it. Teachers will say, 'okay they are pre-k and they are still pre-k and they have been through the Reading Clinic so they didn't improve.' But they have improved but they have no way of saying how they improved. You know what I'm saying?

(Personal communication, May 11, 2017)

This discussion and debate about the content and medium of the tests to which the students are subjected is part of a much broader discourse at the national and even international level about the degree to which student learning should be assessed and how those outcomes should relate to issues such as teacher or school evaluations. Ms Popov had personally complained to me about how her test scores in previous years had been negatively interpreted by district officials who, following state policy, evaluated her performance based largely on English-language gains on these standardized tests. She wrote letters to various leaders in the school system and government explaining how her high-quality teaching of YES students is unfairly judged because she worked with students at the beginning of the ELL process whose learning gains, while dramatic, simply did not register on the available standardized tests.

Internally, there was a debate about whether the time invested in conducting the Dominie on the part of the instructional assistants was useful or whether a test such as the MAP might yield similar insights. Additionally, the instructional assistants complained about being assigned to proctor the OELPA or other state tests such as the American Institute of Research (AIR) graduation test which had replaced the OGT, when they felt their time would be better spent helping students in the Reading Clinic or even administering the Dominie. This struggle over time and legitimacy dovetails with the aforementioned issues around the status of bilingual paraprofessionals, the overall hierarchy of the school and the micropolitical struggles that pervade educational spaces (Bales, 2007; Ball, 1987; Blase, 1993; Malen, 1994; Malen & Cochran, 2014). Indeed, although there have been shifts in school management style and discourse towards more distributed leadership in schools (Flessa, 2009; Piot & Kelchtermans, 2016) which manifest in the YES context with the Teacher-Based Teams, the Instructional Assistant meetings, the PBIS team and other groups, Malen and Cochran (2014) conclude that the overall picture of the politics of schools remains the same:

> Generally speaking, professionals have the relative power advantage vis-à-vis parents, particularly in formal decision-making arenas; principals hold the relative power advantage vis-à-vis teachers in both formal and informal arenas ... Insofar as teachers exert influence, they tend to do so within the boundaries set by the principal. (Malen & Cochran, 2014: 25–26)

The critical point is that all three tests – the OELPA, MAP and Dominie – only assess English language ability (in addition to content knowledge of math in the case of the MAP), reflecting the nation's practice of testing migrant students only in English, thereby ignoring the broad knowledge they bring in their home languages (Menken, 2005, 2008). Thus, it is possible that the insights gained from these tests are either redundant or a matter of fine-grained scale and that a more robust look at the students' home languages would yield more information. Indeed, the program did have a multilingual home language test that was very simple compared to the OELPA, MAP or Dominie, consisting of just eight sentences and 10 yes/no questions. Figure 2.12 shows the English and Arabic versions and the program had about 15 different languages available, including many of the focal students' or broader school population's home languages (they did not have Portuguese or Nepali available, but I arranged to have Nepali and Hindi versions made by a colleague). However, while this test was administered at the beginning of the year along with a written math assessment, it was not given continuously throughout the year as part of the regular intake process. This was partly an issue of policy in that the OELPA, MAP and Dominie already took many hours to complete, but it was also a matter of management in that the test, similar to Ms Popov's home language test, was not able to be included in the district data

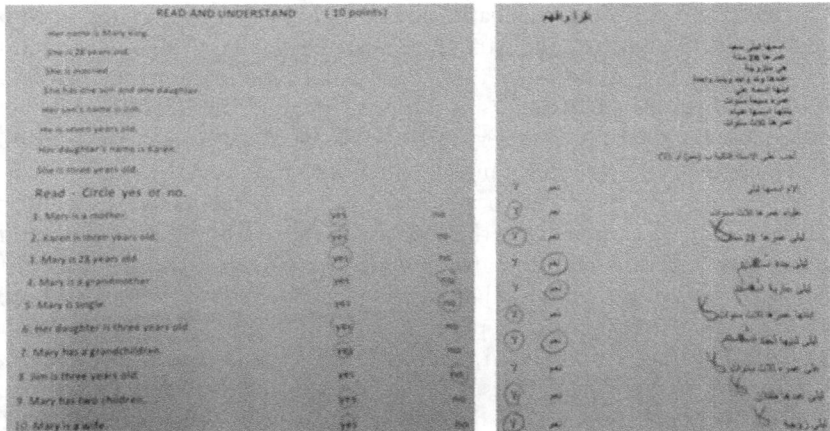

Figure 2.12 Home language test, original English version on the left, Arabic translation on the right: test on the left is Mohammed's, 9/10 correct; test on right is Salah's, 1/10 correct

management system and, therefore, was not part of any formal decision-making processes.

The peripheral but useful nature of this test is partly warranted by Ms Sharp's response to my question about the test's background.

> **Ms Sharp:** You are talking about that little survey, that little thing that we did, yes. (laughs) ... That was my idea because I think that with something we got. I don't know if it was from Seattle, Washington where we had a newcomers program or whatever. What I started to realize was that if this kid, just because a kid went to school or speaks his language doesn't mean that they were a good student or in their language. So I said we always do this little quick and dirty test. I had it translated into as many languages as they could by the instructional assistants ... It's very simple. But it tells you a lot. It tells you a lot. (Personal communication, April 27, 2017)

Ms Sharp's statement here and the overall discussion about the (lack of) home language assessment and the implications for individual students when English ability is the sole measure of a student's knowledge will be taken up further below where I will argue that the program is beginning to realize that some of their practices are not serving the students well and the oversight and neglect of the home language is at the core of these issues and embedded within the English-centric ideology and 'flexibility.'

Conclusion

This chapter has described the environment that the teachers and administrators created for the students in the 2016–2017 academic year. In general, this picture reveals the English-centric nature of the linguistic landscape, teacher instructional talk patterns, the use and availability of learning resources, and assessment practices. On the other hand, there are interesting bi/multilingual practices that exist in the margins which, if they could be more directly recognized, consolidated and expanded, would help YES further evolve to understand and support the students. Despite the somewhat dispiriting nature of this situation, some of these aspects such as the linguistic landscape might be seen as part of the frustrating trajectory of being moved from one school site to another and will almost certainly improve over time to become more languaculturally affirming. However, some aspects of the teacher talk, use of resources and assessment practices may reveal more longstanding instructional policies and practices undermining consistent engagement with the students' home languacultures which may take more focused effort to develop. This issue will be taken up in Chapter 4. In conclusion, this chapter admittedly foregrounds the teachers' and administrators' power and perspectives; however, Chapter 3 will consider more closely the students' responses to this environment through a deeper explanation of their backgrounds and analysis of their outcomes.

Notes

(1) Readers eager to learn more about the students can consult Chapter 3 and particularly Table 3.1.
(2) Transliteration conventions in Arabic vary. Most letters/sounds have clear counterparts in the Latin alphabet such as ا = A, but some of the sounds that are only in Arabic are transliterated here as ق = q, ع = 3, ذ = dh, ث = th, خ = x, drawing on the transcription conventions used in the Peace Corps Moroccan (2011) Arabic book I used as an Arabic learner.

3 Students and Outcomes

Chapter 2 provided a rich description of the context of the pseudonymous 'Youth English Services' (YES) program, from the state down to the day-to-day pedagogical activities. The goal in the chapter was to answer one central research question in this study: To what degree does the program support the students' languacultural backgrounds? The findings show a broadly English-centric environment but with some bi/multilingual perspectives, practices and possibilities for more robust languacultural engagement. This chapter focuses on the critical point of the students and their outcomes.

A key finding for this book is that home language literacy and prior education among adolescent immigrants is so consequential in shaping schooling experiences and outcomes that it should be the primary consideration in program design. Throughout this chapter and the remainder of the book, I will demonstrate that prioritizing English proficiency assessment over home language literacy creates blind spots leading to programmatic decisions that deeply impact students' abilities to benefit from instruction, imposes tiered challenges for students with differential levels of home language literacy, predicts elements of student resistance and program reactions to that resistance and isolates students who have normal adolescent interpersonal problems with the few home language peers in their immediate classroom context. Critically, while some of these issues can be overcome by certain learners, other students face deeply unsatisfactory and even potentially harmful outcomes such as weak learning gains, social isolation or dropping out.

Returning to the calligraphic metaphor, this chapter considers the all-important final image but also recalls that institutions, individuals and learning are a 'messy palimpsest' that has 'been written and rewritten and overwritten again, through which the original texts and even the original stuff on which the text is recorded is still dimly seen' (Song & Kellogg, 2011: 591). In the superdiverse YES context, so many aspects of the program change quickly and constantly that individual experiences can be overlooked or elided. Thus, this chapter seeks to shed light on students and situations that might have been unjustly ignored or forgotten.

The Focal Students and Superdiverse Context

Chapter 2's background to the program actors and development underlines the challenges that the program has faced in order to meet the superdiverse shifts that have been happening in Central Ohio over the past 20 years. In turn, these shifts are most directly represented in the student body with its dozens of languages and cultural groups. The focal student cohort for this book provides a clear example of this superdiverse context as well as the general complexity of migration today. Table 3.1 provides an overview of the students in the focal cohort. This table shows the students' country of origin, arrival/end date in class and the results of any movement in/out of the class. In addition, I indicate whether the student had developed home language literacy prior to arrival. Literacy is a specific and important skill, especially in schools, and the students who had not developed this prior to coming to the program faced the challenge of learning to read and write in a language with which they were not yet familiar.

Another important issue is whether the student is an *emergent bilingual*, that is, a person with primarily monolingual capacity and experiences prior to arrival in the program, or an *experienced bilingual*, someone who already has become bilingual at a relatively high level of proficiency, including biliteracy (García *et al.*, 2017: 32). This is important because, while the students are generally not at risk of language loss in the sense of forgetting their home languages (which is a more common concern with younger learners), their experiences with reading and writing in their home languages index multiple aspects of their prior schooling and may predict certain outcomes in the US context. Examples of emergent bilingual students include most of the students from Central and South America, who have parallel educations and are literate in Spanish or Portuguese but were just starting to learn English as a second language; examples of experienced bilinguals include many of the Somali or Congolese students who had lived in Kenya or Tanzania as refugees and learned Swahili and/or French at school in addition to their home language(s). Some of the Bhutanese-Nepali are marked as in between these categories in that their primary home language is Nepali but they had received a primarily English-medium education in the Nepali refugee camps. I mark these issues here to highlight that, just as there is a difference between monolingual and bilingualism, there is a difference, however subtle, between bilingualism and multilingualism (Higby *et al.*, 2013). Put succinctly and in the context of adolescent or adult language learning, monolingual learners will have a significant struggle to become bilinguals, whereas bilinguals will have less of a struggle to become multilingual. Among many factors moderating this phenomenon is the relative closeness between the target language and the home language (Nicoladis & Montanari, 2016).

Table 3.1 List of students, their national origin and start and end dates in class

Student name	HLit	ExpB/EmB	Start/end day in Lab section August 24, 2016 (first day of school)–June 1, 2017 (last day of school)
1. Gabriela (Brazil)	X	EmB	August 24, 2016–June 1, 2017
2. Antonio (Guatemala) (Moved to mainstream school in different district)	X	EmB	August 24, 2016–September 22, 2016
3. Lina (El Salvador)	X	EmB	August 24, 2016– June 1, 2017
4. Carla (El Salvador)	X	EmB	August 31, 2016– June 1, 2017
5. Maria (El Salvador)	X	EmB	August 24, 2016– June 1, 2017
6. Amal (Somalia/Kenya) (Moved to mainstream school in same district)	X	ExpB	August 24, 2016–September 6, 2016
7. Samuel (Haiti) (Moved up to CORE)	X	ExpB	September 1, 2016–September 22, 2016
8. Marcus (US-Mexico) (Moved up to CORE)	X	EmB	August 24, 2016– September 22, 2016
9. Shiva (B/N) (Moved to other LAB section)		Em-B-ExpB	August 24, 2016– September 13, 2016
10. Sudarshan (B/N) (Moved to other LAB section)		Em-B-ExpB	August 24, 2016– September 13, 2016
11. Puspa (B/N)		Em-B-ExpB	August 24, 2016– June 1, 2017
12. Tara (B/N)		Em-B-ExpB	August 24, 2016– June 1, 2017
13. Lakshmi (B/N) (Moved up to CORE around September 22, 2016)	X	ExpB	August 24, 2016– September 22, 2016
14. Dhan (B/N)	X	Em-B-ExpB	August 24, 2016– June 1, 2017
15. Fatima (Somalia/Kenya)	X	ExpB	August 24, 2016– June 1, 2017
16. Mohamed (Somalia/Kenya)	X	ExpB	August 24, 2016– June 1, 2017
17. Abdullah (Somalia/Kenya) (Went to charter school for several months)	X	ExpB	August 24, 2016–January 18, 2017 and April 26, 2017– June 1, 2017
18. Salah (Jordan)(Dropped out)		EmB	August 25, 2016–January 1, 2017
19. Beatriz (Brazil)	X	EmB	September 19, 2016– June 1, 2017
20. Manuel (El Salvador) (Transferred to mainstream school in same district)	X	EmB	October 4, 2016–October 11, 2016
21. Omar (Syria)	X	EmB	October 13, 2016– June 1, 2017
22. Iman (Somalia/Kenya) (Moved to 8th grade)		EmB	October 17, 2016–January 18, 2017
23. Hayat (Somalia/Kenya)	X	ExpB	October 25, 2016– June 1, 2017
24. Francisco (Guatemala)	X	EmB	October 27, 2016– June 1, 2017
25. Camila (El Salvador) (Mixed schedule – only math)	X	EmB	October 27, 2016– June 1, 2017

(Continued)

Table 3.1 (*Continued*)

Student name	HLit	ExpB/EmB	Start/end day in Lab section August 24, 2016 (first day of school)–June 1, 2017 (last day of school)
26. Abdelkarim (Somalia/Kenya) (Dropped out to work)	X	ExpB	November 1, 2016–November 28, 2016
27. Diego (El Salvador) (Maria's brother) (Mixed schedule, only English and math)	X	EmB	November 2, 2016– June 1, 2017
28. Mateo (Honduras)	X	EmB	November 3, 2016– June 1, 2017
29. Jhuma (B/N)(Moved out of state)	X	EmB-ExpB	November 3, 2016–February 28, 2017
30. Santiago (El Salvador)	X	EmB	November 12, 2016– June 1, 2017
31. Batuli (B/N) (Dropped out)		EmB-ExpB	November 12, 2016–January 24, 2017
32. Belvie (Congo/Tanzania)	X	ExpB	November 21, 2016– June 1, 2017
33. Yadu (B/N)	X	EmB-ExpB	November 28, 2016– June 1, 2017
34. Menuka (B/N) (Moved to 8th grade)		EmB	December 8, 2016–December 20, 2016
35. Leonardo (El Salvador)	X	EmB	January 4, 2017– June 1, 2017
36. Ahmed (Somalia) (Moved to 8th grade)		EmB	January 11, 2017–January 18, 2017
37. Juan (Honduras)	X	EmB	January 19, 2017– June 1, 2017
38. Valeria (El Salvador)	X	EmB	January 24, 2017– June 1, 2017
39. Zahra (Somalia)		EmB	January 25, 2017– June 1, 2017
40. Sabrina (Somalia) (Moved into section from another Lab section after attending YES for approximately three months)	X	ExpB	March 22, 2017– June 1, 2017
41. Ikram (Somalia) (Moved into section from another Lab section after attending YES for approximately three months)	X	ExpB	March 22, 2017– June 1, 2017
42. Gloire (Congo/Tanzania) (Moved into section from another Lab section after attending YES for approximately three months)	X	ExpB	March 22, 2017– June 1, 2017
43. Hajar (Somalia) (Moved into section from another Lab section after attending YES for approximately three months)		EmB	March 22, 2017– June 1, 2017
44. Aya (Somalia) (Moved into section from another Lab section after attending YES for approximately three months)	X	ExpB	March 22, 2017– June 1, 2017

(*Continued*)

Table 3.1 (*Continued*)

Student name	HLit	ExpB/EmB	Start/end day in Lab section August 24, 2016 (first day of school)–June 1, 2017 (last day of school)
45. Luciana (Honduras) (Moved into section from another Lab section after attending YES for approximately three months)	X	EmB	March 22, 2017– June 1, 2017
46. Sirad (Somali)		EmB	April 28, 2017– June 1, 2017

Notes: B/N = Bhutan/Nepal; HLit = student is literate in home language; ExpB = experienced bilingual; EmB = emergent bilingual.

In sum, these students had various levels of bi/multilingualism and home language literacy, which I was able to determine through: (1) analyzing the program's rudimentary home language and more advanced English language tests; (2) asking the students about their bi/multilingual abilities; (3) performing informal tests such as asking them to read in their home language; or (4) observing their literacy practices in contexts such as texting or online.

Thus, it is possible through this overview data to see how Blommaert's three categories of mobility, complexity and uncertainty fit this context quite well. First, mobility: throughout the year there were 46 students, of whom only 15 were present on the first day of school, and only eight of these remained in the section for the duration of the school year. By the end of the year 30 students were present, but manifold changes occurred for the other 16 students including:

- Institutional/administrative moves made by the school administration and teachers: (1) intra-program moves to transfer some students to Core, to 8th grade, to other Lab sections or from other Lab sections to the focal section; (2) inter-program moves by sending students to other district schools.
- Individual/family moves where the students or their families decided to: (1) move extra-program to other school districts in Ohio or out-of-state; (2) attend district charter schools; or (3) drop out to start work or seek other opportunities.
- Family/personal mobility in that the students often had erratic attendance due to the various doctor's visits, festivals and other events in addition to personal absences due to the challenge of adapting to the early morning school schedule while staying up late or missing the morning bus.
- Digital transnational mobility in that the students are recently arrived in the US and many of their strongest social connections remain in their home countries. For many students this might be family left behind, particularly in the case of the unaccompanied minors, or for

refugees it might be friends or family who are still in refugee camps in Kenya, Nepal or other areas. Thus, digital tools like Facebook or WhatsApp can diminish the felt distance between people.

Second, the complexity of the space manifests across the issues of home language literacy, prior education and even languacultural background. For example, several of the students above marked as 'Somali' were identified as Somali Bantu by the teachers, staff or students. This identifier distinguishes a class of Somalis who had been oppressed within broader Somali or East African society for generations. These students have a distinct language, Maay Maay, which is traditionally an oral, not written language (Birman & Tran, 2015; Roy & Roxas, 2011). However, in addition to languacultural background, there are other complexities, such as ability, sexuality, religion and immigration status. One of the students above, Hajar, had a clear learning or developmental ability issue that the school was working to address and there were other students where this was a possible issue of concern. In terms of sexuality, although most students expressed cis- and heteronormative attitudes, Gabriela expressed a bisexual preference and shared several websites related to homo- or bisexual adolescent literature. Also, although religion is closely aligned with many languacultural communities, these can be in flux, as in the case of Bhutanese refugees who are predominantly Hindu but with a growing population of Christian converts. This was reflected in the class group of six Bhutanese refugee students, where one identified more strongly as Hindu, one as Buddhist, two as converted Christians and two who demonstrated a certain hybridity through their appearance (one had a small tattoo saying 'Jesus') and expressed convictions. These aspects, in turn, created interesting class interactions and conversations. For example, the event below occurred mid-year in Ms Cabot's class towards the end of the school day. Ms Cabot had been doing a Reading Survey with the students designed to elicit the students' home literacy practices. Puspa, one of the Bhutanese refugee students who had converted to Christianity in Bhutan, listed the Bible as his favorite book, prompting me to engage in a conversation that then drew in the other Bhutanese refugee Jhuma and the Somali refugee Mohammed.

Line no.	Speaker	Text
1	Brian	What's your favorite story from the Bible?
2	Puspa	All.
3	Brian	All the stories? That's good.
4	Jhuma	He don't know, he don't know how to,
5	Brian	((to Jhuma)) Do you like to read religious books?
6	Jhuma	Yeah, I like.
7	Brian	Ok.

8	Jhuma	I love and trust in Jesus,
9	Brian	Uh huh.
10	Jhuma	But I can't trust with Christian people.
11	Brian	So are you Christian?
12	Jhuma	I love Jesus, I love Shiva.
13	Brian	Yeah, Shiva's cool, yeah.
14	Jhuma	Like, like Krishna.
15	Brian	Yeah.
16	Jhuma	In Hindu, there are different types of gods.
17	Brian	Yeah.
18	Jhuma	Ah, one, a god, I tell you, I show you the picture, I'll show you the picture of, I write you the story of an immortal Hindu god.
19	Mohammed	Mister, they make their god.
20	Jhuma	No no no
21	Mohammed	Yeah, how how how
22	Jhuma	You, you make a god.
23	Mohammed	No, I don't make my god, my god believe in Allah.
24	Jhuma	That's only what I said.
25	Brian	((addressing Mohammed)) you know, before before Mohammed came, you know in the Kaaba, in Mecca, there used to be lots of gods in there, but then Mohammed the prophet came and said, no, there's only one god, and that god's name is Allah, but there were lots of gods.
26	Jhuma	The medicine can prove the about the Hindu god.
27	Brian	Yeah.
28	Jhuma	You can search in the Googles and you can find a proof of god.

This brief anecdote reveals many aspects of the superdiverse context and how this impacts interactions. Puspa's conversion to Christianity is subtly criticized by Jhuma at Line 4 by critiquing his knowledge of the Bible, and then Jhuma's discussion of Christianity and Hinduism in particular is confronted by Mohammed from his Muslim point of view. The debate does not resolve directly or completely (nor could it be expected to), but ends with Jhuma asserting that a Google search can somehow prove the existence of god. At the end of the conversation, the bell rang and the students left the room, continuing their light banter briefly at the lockers before heading to the school exit.

Immigration status is perhaps one of the most challenging issues, and a number of the students were clear about their undocumented statuses. Moreover, although these did organize partly along languacultural lines with students from Central and South America more likely to be undocumented and students from Africa and Asia more likely to be refugees with authorized immigrant status, there were exceptions. For example, one student from Central America had been raised by grandparents, while the student's parents lived in the US for many years, eventually acquired citizenship and brought the student to the US, most likely (the student expressed ignorance about the details of the migration process) through the affidavit of relationship or 'chain' immigration process. Again, these aspects created interactions that revealed not only the challenges implied by individual statuses but also the challenge of being newcomers seeking to understand their new context and connections to these broader issues. As an illustration, again in Ms Cabot's class, an event took place directly before the Thanksgiving holiday. The students were engaged in an activity in which they colored a turkey and wrote a number of a 'What are you thankful for?' statements while they watched a YouTube video about the history of Thanksgiving. As this happened, I moved around the room to support the students and engage them in light but probing conversations. I approached Dhan and Abdullah, who frequently sat next to each other in class, due partly to Ms Cabot's seating chart but also due to their relative familiarity with each other as students who had been in the school from the start of the year, and started the following discussion.

Line no.	Speaker	Text
1	Brian	((to Abdullah)) So what are you thankful for?
2	Abdullah	Best friend.
3	Brian	Who? What's his name?'
4	Abdullah	Mahmud.
5	Brian	Where is your friend at?
6	Abdullah	My friend is in Africa.
7	Dhan	((to Abdullah)) You, Africa?
8	Abdullah	((nods head yes))
9	Dhan	Oh.
10	Brian	So, where does Mahmud live?
11	Abdullah	Africa.
12	Brian	I know, but which country? Kenya?
13	Abdullah	Kenya.
14	Brian	((to Dhan)) Do you know where Kenya is? It's in Africa.
15	Dhan	No.
16	Brian	((draws map of Africa on loose paper)) So if this is Africa, Kenya is like right here. ((indicates location of Kenya))
17	Dhan	Oh.
18	Brian	Kind of like it's next to Somalia, next to Somalia.
19	Dhan	So Donald Trump say, Africa go, not go, yeah?
20	Brian	I don't know, I think refugees will be ok.
21	Dhan	Ok.
22	Brian	But maybe people who came without papers,

23	Dhan	Oh, illegals are,
24	Brian	Yeah, they might have trouble but we don't know.
25	Dhan	I like Donald Trump.
26	Brian	Ok, why?
27	Dhan	Yes, because but because I don't like illegals because this time ((pointing at the ground)) I like because black people, black people country ((while making a gesture that seems to be like 'get out'))
28	Brian	Ok.
29	Dhan	Oh, people, my sister, my brothers, and me, we going going going beating,
30	Brian	Going where?
31	Dhan	I'm go, and black people, small small, two people, two biggers and two small, two boys, and Nepali total, eight and all Nepali running running running and black people back hit, beating beating beating,
32	Brian	You? ((points at Dhan))
33	Dhan	No no no, my neighbor.
34	Brian	Do you call police?
35	Dhan	I call the police and coming, police, and all black people go run run run.
36	Brian	The black people ran away? They were afraid, they were scared?
37	Dhan	Yeah yeah, I was scared, my brother, want, say, I don't like black people, all this time beating Nepali
38	Brian	Is this by your house?
39	Dhan	Yeah.
40	Brian	So, Abdullah's black, Abdullah is black.
41	Dhan	No, Abdullah, I like, no black, I mean black means Africa.
42	Brian	Abdullah's from Africa.
43	Dhan	Like this hair long and hair ((making gesture with hands in fists above head)), I don't like curly hair and long,
44	Brian	Ok.
45	Dhan	Strong ((while flexing arms)), look like, I look like, strong, I don't like this,
46	Brian	So Faisal's from Africa and he's black, but you like Faisal?
47	Dhan	Yeah, but Faisal is a refugee.

Abdullah's initial statement about his best friend in Kenya indicates aspects of his transnational experience in how immigrants maintain close ties across borders and physical distance. Dhan's questioning of Abdullah's origin opens a discussion that indexes, at a minimum, the complexity of race, immigration status and politics. Her statements about Donald Trump, 'illegals,' blackness, Africa and refugee status indicate an awareness of the shifting political landscape in the US, the threat to undocumented migrants from the Trump administration and a sort of relief that she, as a refugee, might not be targeted by these new policies. In addition, she describes how some African-Americans or other African migrants had been harassing some of her Bhutanese-Nepali friends and family members. From this, she says that she does not like black people, but when I reference Abdullah's blackness she describes a different type of Black person – somebody with long curly hair and strong muscles – that can be contrasted with Abdullah and his refugee status. Following this moment, I tried to understand more about the people bothering Dhan and offered some suggestions for staying safe on her walk home before moving on to help another student.

These two classroom moments demonstrate the complexity that emerges in superdiverse conditions. These aspects move beyond individual or group characteristics, combine in unique ways and produce discussions that are dynamic and layered even with the students' emerging English proficiency.

Finally, the space is highly unpredictable or, as Ms Sharp often said during bilingual assistant meetings, quoting Forest Gump, 'ESL is like a box of chocolates; you never know what you're gonna get.' For example, the arrival of around 10 Brazilian students in August 2016 was a surprise, and there were initially no Portuguese speakers among the school staff until, by coincidence, a Brazilian substitute teacher came in mid-November. This lacuna created manifold challenges to understanding these students' backgrounds and interests, including Gabriela and Beatriz above. As a researcher, I had very little idea about what sorts of students to expect other than that drawn from my knowledge of refugee or other migration patterns formed at the refugee support agency or the broader literature about migration locally, nationally and globally. On any given day, a new student might have arrived from a languacultural group that I had little knowledge about. In a sense, I was relatively lucky in that I have high proficiency in Arabic and French and there were a number of students who knew those languages in the class. Moreover, the class also had students speaking Spanish, Portuguese, Nepali, Somali and Swahili, relatively major world languages that I have some experience with. In addition, the students were developing their English ability, so many conversations were possible across our shared linguistic repertoires, as evidenced in part above.

These shifts may be well represented, in broad strokes, with images from the class demonstrating how the classroom started in August–September with relatively few students and then had two key expansions, one in November–December 2016 and one starting in April 2017. From August to October 2016, the class had about 17 students, then 25 from November 2016 to March 2017, and finally 30 from March 2017 to the end of the year. Figure 3.1 has images from Ms Cabot's class showing this growth across the academic year.

The first phase not only is commensurate with what most teachers desire in terms of small class sizes, but also is a particular feature of newcomer programs, as pointed out in the work of Short and Boyson (2012).

Figure 3.1 Images from Ms Cabot's class in August/September, November/December and April/May of the 2016–2017 academic year

Newcomer programs often consider small class size a very important feature. This is especially true for the programs that serve preliterate students or those with low literacy levels in their native language. Forty-five percent of the programs reported that their average class size was fewer than 15 students. Forty percent have an average of 15 to 24 students. Only 9% of the programs had an average class size of 25 students or more. The largest average class size was 34 students, and this was in the largest 4-year high school, which enrolls over 900 students. Only 3% of the students in this high school have interrupted formal schooling or low native language literacy, so the larger class size in this program may be less problematic. (Short & Boyson, 2012: 13–14)

However, the later stages of the class year show how this class size issue is strained as it jumps first to nearly 25 students and then to the union limit of 30 students by the end of the year.

In short, YES fits the definitions of superdiversity, which provides a framework for understanding some of the challenges and opportunities afforded in spaces designed to support adolescent newcomers. On the other hand, there are aspects of the students' lives that are not so easily categorized. Among the issues here are the fact that some students come from areas with open conflict, which weighs on their minds. For example, Omar reported having trouble going to sleep at night as he monitored events in Syria in the news and on social media. One day in math class specifically, he was having trouble following a relatively easy problem and told me that he was bothered by the images from the botched evacuation of Aleppo (Barnard et al., 2016). Similarly, Mateo discussed in an interview how he watched news sites for stories about violence in Honduras where his mother still lived, out of fear that something bad had happened to her.

In sum, this sketch of the students in the focal classroom demonstrates the superdiverse context that YES, in the nearly 20 years of development described in Chapter 2, is trying to address. As has been partially described, YES has certainly developed an array of tools and approaches to support these students. The remainder of this chapter will discuss the outcomes of YES's efforts through the prism of the focal students.

A Year in a Day: The Patterns and Changes in the Lab Year

This section draws more than the previous writing on the tradition of 'creative nonfiction' in ethnographic writing (Agar, 1990; Sayer, 2014; van Maanen, 2011) to frame a broader discussion about the students' experiences and outcomes in the program. My goal here is to provide a narrative description, drawing on the corpus of data, of the average school day from the perspective of the Lab students and how it evolved over the school year. This will set the stage for the qualitative case studies and critical discussion of the quantitative student results.

On the first day of school, August 24, 2016, the students and staff arrived relatively early. I met Ms Cabot in her classroom at 7am, and we walked down to the cafeteria to meet the students and other teachers. Inside the room, Ms Lincoln and I fell into conversation about her upcoming OSU classes, and she said that she'd got to school at 6:30am to get ready for the day. Then, Mr Smith contacted her on the walkie-talkie, and she walked up next to him as another teacher with a loud voice started the school year off with a booming 'Good Morning!' which he repeated a few times until the students were quieter and, presumably, listening. Mr Smith stood up with each teacher, welcomed the students to the school and then started a process whereby each teacher read the names of the students in their homeroom section. Ms Cabot, the homeroom teacher for the focal Lab section, took her turn with her names and the respective students came to the front of the room with her, and we all walked out to her classroom. On the way, I started to talk to a few students, beginning the research project in earnest. In the room, Ms Cabot began to get to know the students, identifying them by language and recognizing those like Mohammed who were already relatively conversant in English and could help others, and then dove into the students' overall schedule. She explained the flow of the day with frequent repetition and rephrasing, drawing on her various language abilities where possible (e.g. by asking me for 'eight' in Spanish and recognizing that 'it's the same "*ocho*"' as the Italian she is more familiar with), and then discussed some of the class materials they needed and rules such as no gum or cell phones in class. Towards the end of class, Mr Smith came over the PA system to announce that the next period would start in five minutes and commented, 'Great job this morning, teachers.' The bell rang a few minutes later, and the students walked out to their 2nd period class with Mr Barre. Thus it began. Student enrollment was approximately 200 and the focal Lab section had about a dozen students.

Beyond this first day, students continued to arrive at the school sometimes before 7:30am. Some students were bussed to school, sometimes waking up to catch the bus as early as 5 or 5:30am, others walked to school because district policy does not provide bussing for students who live less than two miles from school, and some were driven by their caregivers or a friend or even drove themselves. When they arrived, they went to the cafeteria or to the auditorium when the school population increased up to nearly 700 students by the end of the year. In the cafeteria they could eat free breakfast. Although it was not a hard and fast rule, most students sat with other students from their shared languaculture and talked. Administrators and other teachers were in the cafeteria to monitor student behavior and to interact. When the first bell rang at 7:30am, the students got up to go to the first class, which was a combined homeroom and content area class. The focus group had Ms Cabot's English class first, but normally the first 10 minutes or so were occupied with Ms Cabot giving out various administrative announcements (such as requests for immunization records), listening to school announcements and doing the Pledge of Allegiance (a school board policy), before regular instruction began.

As the students entered the first period room, they interacted briefly and eventually took their seats. Ms Cabot often organized the students in different ways throughout the year, sometimes by English ability, sometimes by language group and sometimes to deal with disciplinary issues (generally by separating students considered troublesome or unproductive together or locating those students closer to the teacher).

When instruction started, a good portion of the English class was devoted to foundational skills with the Words Their Way curriculum. Students frequently engaged in 'sort activities' with various phonemes organized into 'families' where words that end in -ot or -at are discussed and then put together – for example, variations like hot, pot, got – with pictures of the words given as definitions. Ms Cabot would often engage in repetition with the students and move around the room to help students with organizing their words and pictures together. Other kinds of activities the students regularly did were 'stations' where Ms Cabot would describe various assignments that the students would do throughout the class, computer-based learning with programs such as Raz-Kids, writing activities such as autobiographies, or quasi-competitions where students might listen to a word the teacher said, write it on a white board and then hold it up. Rarely were students asked to give any formal presentations in front of the class. As mentioned above, Ms Cabot might draw on her linguistic repertoire for one-to-one verbal translations of words – often numbers or other basic lexical items such as 'tomorrow' or 'hands.'

The 2nd period was math with Mr Barre, or Reading Clinic for students identified as 'pre-K' by the Dominie assessment. The students left Ms Cabot's class, walked down the hall to math class, sat down, and then Mr Barre would briefly take attendance before releasing the students to the Reading Clinic, which served 5–15 students throughout the year, leaving a similar number to begin the math assignment with Mr Barre.

Math class would generally proceed with a quick introduction to the topic by Mr Barre with some examples on the board, and then the students would receive a handout with a number of practice problems. This would often have 30 or so simple math items of the same type, or it might be a certain number of basic arithmetic problems with more complicated word problems or other types which, if not more mathematically difficult, were certainly more linguistically complex. The students worked on this handout for most of both periods. When the Reading Clinic students returned, they either received direct instruction from Mr Barre or simply received the activity and relied on the teacher's one-to-one support or clarification from students who had remained in math class. About once a week the students would study using ST Math. Mr Barre was a Somali male teacher who frequently used Somali to describe the math activities to other Somali students in their one-on-one sessions, and because he also was highly proficient in Italian he would sometimes use associations with Italian, for example with numbers, to connect with the Spanish or Portuguese speakers in the class. If the students completed the activity, Mr Barre usually had another handout they could do, or the students might simply engage in social talk for the remainder of the period.

The Reading Clinic students walked down the hall and went to one of their several groups. These groups, with no more than five students in each group, sat around a small semicircular table with the instructional assistant in the middle. During this time, the students generally started with light conversation and then turned to reading a text, completing a packet of Fry list words, coloring or some other kind of activity designed to link vocabulary and concepts. On occasion the students would watch a movie, such as before vacations or during special events such as Black History month. Generally, these small groups offered many opportunities for engagement with the teacher, casual discussion, repetition of vocabulary items and focused writing. Moreover, these groups allowed the instructional assistants to become close to the students in the small-group atmosphere and encourage them to practice English as much as possible without (it was hoped) denigrating the students' home languages. Occasionally the students would use Raz-Kids or Rosetta Stone. Although many of the instructional assistants were bilingual, the students in the Reading Clinic were not assigned to the instructional assistant by language background. Therefore, the students might be in a group with a fellow bilingual, but that bilingual person might or might not share the same linguistic repertoire with them. Thus, the instructional assistant might use the home language with students if the linguistic repertoire was shared; if not, the instructional assistant might use Google Translate or other media to help the students make meaning.

After math class the students had 'Encore' classes where they would split up into music, gym, art or computer classes. These classes were with students from other Lab sections and focused on the assigned topic but also English language development. For example, in computer class the teacher might ask the students to develop a PowerPoint about a certain topic, in music class to sing various songs in English, in art class to make and describe a medieval crest or in gym class to discuss various health-related aspects.

Following Encore classes was social studies. After sitting down and taking attendance, Ms Popov would start class with the 'on-duty' student, who was asked to stand up and talk in English for three minutes about some topic. At the beginning of the year this was as simple as discussing the student's home country, language spoken and general experiences with school, but it evolved over time to discussing topics such as their morning routine, favorite movie or the like. The 'on-duty' student rotated daily, usually by alphabetical order unless a new student arrived who would be asked to present immediately or over the next few days. Following the three-minute drill, Ms Popov would engage in the social studies curriculum by teaching key vocabulary, often drawing directly on the students' home languages with the vocabulary learning sheet described above. Throughout the year, the teacher would use a form of computer-based learning approximately once per week with websites such as such as Flowcabulary or BrainPOP. Although Ms Popov's Russian home language was not directly useful to the students, her background as a Spanish teacher allowed her frequently to engage passively or actively with the students' home languages, particularly those who spoke Spanish or Portuguese.

After Ms Popov's class it was time for lunch; students went to the cafeteria to eat. Some students took their free lunch and ate it, whereas others did not and sat at the back of the room to talk, play on their phones or even play cards. Many of the Arabic-speaking boys sat at the back, and I had multiple opportunities to talk with them casually during this time throughout the school year. After about 20 minutes, students could walk down the hall and go outside if the weather was nice or go to the gym when it was not. During this time, some played basketball or other sports and some sat at the side to talk. On occasion, students would become romantic with each other and kiss, leading one of the school security staff to yell later in the year, 'This is not the [Youth Kissing Services], it's the [Youth English Services].'

After lunch it was time for science class with Mr Shahiya, who had a similar pedagogical method to Mr Barre with relatively brief instruction followed by a student handout. However, Mr Shahiya did not use computer-based learning as frequently as the other teachers, relying more on the various handouts. On a few occasions Mr Shahiya had the students take part in activities that bridged art and science, with his 'Gallon Bot' or 'X–Y coordinates art,' and the results of these were put up in the hallway for other students to see. Mr Shahiya conducted his classes in English but frequently used Somali or Arabic to describe and explain the content to the students at their individual seats.

After science, the students were supposed to return to Ms Cabot's class to complete their double period of English. However, due to the increasing numbers in the school (approximately 500 by the end of December), Ms Cabot's last period combined two Lab sections, leaving her with more than 30 students. Thus, she first devised an A–B schedule with one of the instructional assistants whereby each section of students would alternate one day with her and the other with the assistant, who would take students to the library to do computer-based learning with Rosetta Stone, Raz-Kids or Starfall. When this became untenable due to further rising numbers, Ms Cabot devised a schedule with another teacher so that three sections of Lab students would be combined and divided by a perception of their level, with the more advanced group staying with Ms Cabot, the intermediate group with the instructional assistant and the novice group with the other teacher. This arrangement continued until mid-January when the third quarter started and the school was able to hire six substitute teachers to address the rising enrollment. Thus, from January Ms Cabot worked with the original focal Lab section until she went on maternity leave in late March and Ms Tucek took over until the end of the year.

During 8th period, Ms Cabot or Ms Tucek generally tried to connect and extend the work the students had started during 1st period, but this was difficult in many ways. Ms Cabot frequently commented on the difficulty in transitioning across these periods, lamenting the break in momentum and additional time lost as students came in and sat down. Moreover, the administrative task of taking attendance again made it difficult for her to engage in the more whole-language tasks (e.g. extended readings, discussions, etc.) that she liked to do after the more fundamental work with the Words Their Way curriculum. Therefore, during 8th period students often spent a portion of the time completing the assignment started in 1st period and then moving, if possible, to other tasks. This difficulty was exacerbated by the fact that Ms Cabot and all the other teachers did not have instructional assistants in their classrooms, because Mr Smith had made the decision at the beginning of the year to allocate all the instructional assistants to the Reading Clinic due to his perspective drawn from observations over several years that many instructional assistants were being used by the teachers just to do simple tasks such as make copies, take attendance or grade papers rather than engaging in more productive educational tasks commensurate with their backgrounds and abilities (particularly bilingualism). Overall, Ms Cabot felt that the loss of both her double period of English and her long-time instructional assistant, Mr Dahal, made the academic year more difficult.

This day-to-day schedule for the focal Lab students was punctuated from time to time with events such as regular fire, tornado or lockdown drills, fieldtrips in the Fall to the Ohio Statehouse and in the Spring to a museum in Dayton, Ohio, and school assemblies or special events that are, in general, activities that occur regularly in American schools today.

By the end of the year, when the school had nearly 700 students, the focal Lab section had also evolved and expanded considerably, with nearly 50 students having some experience in the class. A small core of about 15 students started and finished the whole year, whereas others came in for a month or less before being transferred or transferring themselves to other sections or schools or simply dropping out.

Analysis of the Student Experience

The notions of continua and trajectories are key to this book and have been invoked at various points in the previous pages. This section uses case study theory and practice (L. Bartlett & Vavrus, 2016; Mitchell, 1984), integrates this with a language socialization perspective (Duff, 2008; Duff & Anderson, 2015; Garrett, 2008) and includes triangulating information from the broader ethnographic inquiry (Wolcott, 2001) to focus on students, their movement through the program and some indications of their future directions. These insights bridge to the next chapter, which considers the possibilities of and challenges to the future of the program.

In this chapter I will draw on these frameworks to look across the cases in the Lab class and argue that there are three groups. Although all the students in the Lab class were labeled as 'pre-functional' by the

Dominie assessment in terms of their English language ability, the first group are those with home language literacy and generally positive or parallel prior school experiences. The second are those where either of these two issues is unstable. The third is where both are lacking or highly unstable. In the context of the program, the first group was often labeled informally as 'High' performing by the school actors because they were more likely to understand the school structure, patterns and academic content. These students, when they also had reasonable English proficiency, were the most likely to be moved from Lab to Core or even transitioned to a mainstream school in the district. The last group was often labeled 'Low' because the students frequently demonstrated manifold confusions about the schooling process and would receive significant remedial support from the program actors. The 'Mid' group was generally considered somewhat normal for the school provided that they did not display significant gaps or behavioral issues. However, through these cases I will argue that the trajectories are far from assured and that three things must happen in the school context for the trajectories to be bent in a positive direction. First, the students must have their academic needs addressed early and systematically. Second, any frustrations that manifest must be met with compassion and understanding. Third, the broader learning environment must be built on collaboration and any conflicts understood and addressed as early as possible. This harkens back in part to Krashen's (1985) theory of comprehensible input and the affective filter. Krashen states that 'people acquire second languages only if they obtain comprehensible input and if their affective filters are low enough to allow the input "in"' (Krashen, 1985: 4). It has been shown above that a wide variety of comprehensible input strategies are deployed in the school, particularly in the use of early childhood English development techniques, allowing significant time for students to make meaning together with and through their home languages and occasional teacher use of the home language itself for meaning-making. However, the affective filter indexes the broader issues around the highly contested areas of 'motivation' and 'investment' (Norton, 2013; Waninge *et al.*, 2014).

> I argue that a learner may be a highly motivated language learner, but may nevertheless have little investment in the language practices of a given classroom or community. The classroom, for example, may be racist, sexist, elitist or homophobic. Alternatively, the language practices of the classroom may not be consistent with learner expectations of good teaching, with equally dire results for language learning. In sum, a learner can be highly motivated to learn a language, but not necessarily invested in a given set of language practices. (Norton, 2013: 3)

I take it as a given that many if not all YES students are motivated to learn English and subject area content. However, we have already seen hints of the challenges YES students face to remain invested in the classroom, especially when their home languages are not incorporated into the learning process – the example given above of Omar's criticism of Mr Barre is illustrative. The remainder of this chapter seeks to explain more of the variables and processes at YES that contribute to student investment in learning and lead to certain outcomes.

Case Studies

As implied with the above description, students may be justified in viewing their school experience with some confusion or frustration due to the linguistic landscape, changing schedule, student arrivals and departures, assessment practices and different teachers' pedagogies and personalities, in addition to the generally English-centric environment or lack of target-language peers. On the other hand, the changes and variety of events can be seen as fun and motivating. Thus, students generally conformed to the structure of the school and classes by arriving on time, attending classes, sitting where assigned and working (or appearing to work) on assignments (cf. Bloome *et al.*, 1989).

This section turns to a description and analysis of the focal students organized into the aforementioned three groups. However, as this analysis will show, these groupings and trajectories are not static or deterministic, and the shifts in these trajectories reveal much about the overall functioning of the program and factors that should be addressed as the program evolves. Table 3.2 provides a general profile of these students: however, it must be emphasized that these distinctions are porous in that students who might have an initial academic profile in a certain category may not necessarily remain there nor the potential needs, frustrations or roles manifest.

Table 3.2 General profiles of 'High, Mid and Low' students

	'High'	'Mid'	'Low'
General initial academic profile	Home language literacy and parallel education	Instability in either home language literacy or parallel education	Instability in both home language literacy and prior education
Potential academic needs	Access to target-language peers	General academic support	Home language literacy or specialized support (content or learning difference)
Potentially expressed frustrations	Boredom	Occasional off-task behavior	Disengagement or disturbance (including possibility of violent anti-social behaviors)
Potential roles in sociocultural learning environment	Supporting other students	Providing or receiving support	Receiving support

'High' students: Those with home language literacy and parallel schooling

Students of this type include Gabriela and Beatriz from Brazil, Maria from El Salvador, Jhuma from Nepal, Gloire from Congo and Tanzania or Mohammed from Somalia and Kenya. This group clearly demonstrated to me their home language literacy and parallel educations, often positioning themselves as excellent students in their home countries. The following statements from individual interviews with Maria, Jhuma and Gloire are standout examples:

> Brian: Yeah, I think, before you came, here in the school, I think you are an excellent student, you're very like serious, hard-working student?
>
> Maria: I think all the time, I am a good student from Salvador, yo gané primeros lugares, como papel de reconocimiento, todo el tiempo. 'I got prizes, like recognition certificates, all the time.'

(Personal communication, March 30, 2017)

> Brian: How were your grades in Nepal?
>
> Jhuma: I can easy to read science and maths. I'm easy. I am. Here in Nepal, out of 100, I can get 95 in Math. It's too hard here. In Nepal, in total 100, we can pass in 32, right? We can pass. I get 95. But many, in Nepal, we can take 28 maybe about 98 or 93. It's too hard. It's hard.

(Personal communication, February 28, 2017)

> Brian: Quelles étaient tes notes? 'what were your grades' I think you are about 100?
> Gloire: Moi? 'me?'
> Brian: Les notes du camp de Tanzanie, ils sont sur 100, oui? 'Grades in the refugee camp in Tanzania are out of 100, right?'
> Gloire: Oui, c'est de 100. 'yes, they are out of 100'
> Brian: Ok, tu étais quoi, plus ou mois? 'you were what, more or less?'
> Gloire: 60.
> Brian: Ok, yeah, ok, c'est bien, parce-que tu dois avoir juste 50. 'that's good because you just have to have 50'
> Gloire: 50.
> Brian: 50 c'est passable. 'that's passing'
> Gloire: Passable commence a 50, mais mois je passe a 60. 'passing starts at 50, but I passed with 60'
> Brian: Vous aviez un mention, un mention très bien, pour les notes? 'did you have any distinction, distinction "very good" for the grades?'
> Gloire: J'etais très bien. 'I was "very good".'

(Personal communication, April 27, 2017)

Although Gabriela and Beatriz did not identify themselves as having the same outstanding academic identities, they both had grade-level and parallel educations, moderated only by the fact that they entered the US in the Summer as unauthorized migrants, spending a month or so in juvenile detention centers before being reunited with either their parents or members of their extended family. However, both were highly literate in Portuguese, with Beatriz often bringing various books to 'quench the fire' of engagement with her home language (Personal communication, March 23, 2017). In turn, Gabriela would read extensively on WattPad (www.wattpad.com), particularly enjoying gay literature, commensurate with her expressed (to me, not necessarily with other peers) bisexual identity. Both used social media extensively with sites such as Facebook or Snapchat to connect with their national or transnational friends.

Thus, this group was generally ready to engage with YES and its academic demands. However, their sole complaint about the space was that it was not demanding enough and that there were no 'normal' Americans there to help speed their English-language acquisition. Maria points out her perspective on the academic demands.

Brian:	so in your opinion what are some things that are not good about the school? Things that could be better?
Maria:	I think, I don't know.
Brian:	Like say, if you were the director.
Maria:	I think more work.
Brian:	More work?
Maria:	Yeah, porque es very easy 'it's very easy'
Brian:	Oh.
Maria:	The first class I think is very easy.
Brian:	Yeah yeah, what do you want? What kind of more work?
Maria:	Um,
Brian:	Like more speaking, more writing, more homework?
Maria:	I think speaking, writing, homework, um.
Brian:	Do you have homework most of the time, tu tienes homework? 'do you have homework?'
Maria:	Algunos tiempos. 'some times'
Brian:	Yeah, but not all the time.
Maria:	Um, pero some muy faciles le creo, 'but I think some are very easy'
Brian:	What is the hardest subject for you?
Maria:	My favorite subject?
Brian:	No, the difficult, the mas, le sujeto le mas difficile? 'the most difficult subject'
Maria:	No have.
Brian:	They're all easy?
Maria:	Yes.

(Maria, personal communication, March 30, 2017)

In turn, Gabriela and Mohammed separately elaborate on the desire to have a demanding academic environment with target-language peers:

Brian: If you were like the director, quel sorte de escuela? 'what kind of school would you want?' una escuela comme ici con multas personas? 'a school like here with many people'
Gabriela: Oh, si, eo carito una escuela americana por aprendre englais. 'oh, yeah, I would like an American school to learn English'
Brian: Ok, un escuela americana, normale. 'ok, an American school, a normal one'
Gabriela: Si, pero necessito aprendite mas un poquito. 'yes because I need to learn a little more.'
(Gabriela, personal communication, November 21, 2016)

Brian: And now you're here, and then maybe next year in different school, we'll see. I want to ask you. If you were the director of this school, and you wanted to make it better for students like you, what would you do?
Mohammed: I want to do, whoever English is perfect and get almost all As for the whole school, I want to make them go to different schools from this school.
(Personal communication, March 2, 2017)

As a result, these students rarely engaged in behavior that was seen by the teachers or other students as disruptive or anti-social but were usually the first students to begin an assignment, seek confirmation or clarification about their answers and turn it in well before the end of class. On many occasions, students from the 'Mid' or 'Low' groups would come to these students for help or even to copy answers – an issue that teachers vacillated between tolerating and curtailing depending on their perception of whether the copying was educational or not. As Ms Popov said to Ms Tucek, a novice teacher seeking to understand the nature of this copying activity which, to others, is a form of cheating, 'What other option is there if they don't understand?' (Personal communication, March 23, 2017). Thus, these students would often be seen as critical classroom support for the teacher and gained access to various privileges and responsibilities. Mohammed, for example, almost always took Ms Cabot's attendance sheet to the office. In addition, these students could nearly always be counted on to respond to the teacher's whole-class questions, forcing the teacher to silence them from time to time in order to elicit answers from other students. Additionally, they might be indirectly or directly asked to help new students acclimate to the classroom environment. However, it is an open question to what degree these students were open to and accepting of these roles. From my observations, Maria would often become exasperated with the 'copying' type of student and either ignore their petitions for help or just write the answers for them. Ms Cabot and I reflected on this dynamic and challenge in the context of creating a space conducive to sociocultural learning.

Brian: The other challenge, the flip side of that is, it's good to have kids in a class that are kind of leveled because you talked about the previous year, you guys had done this kind of tracking thing that didn't work. You put all the really low kids and they stuck in the whole year, then they all got progressed up to Core and there was just a mess because they had the same levels. You talked about how it is good to have in a classroom with some kids of mixed abilities who can help each other but it's finding that balance so that you can allocate the right resources.

Ms Cabot: Yes, it's also not the more advanced kids' job to teach the kids who are behind. Their job is to accelerate, to get better and so anyways ...

Brian: I wonder, I never asked Maria directly because so many kids in the class are coming to her for help.

Ms Cabot: I know, she was like the mother hen (laughs)

Brian: And I never, she didn't really seem to mind exactly but what I noticed in her behavior was for certain people she would actually kind of teach. For other people, she'd just be like, fill out their thing and get out of there.

Ms Cabot: 'Get out of my face, I'm tired of this.'

(Personal communication, June 29, 2017)

Thus, these 'High' students clearly came to the program ready to learn and fill an important role, but it is unclear whether they felt the program was appropriate for them. Indeed, if these students did display any behavior that the teacher did not approve of, it would usually manifest in some notion of 'boredom' or being seen as disengaged in the learning task. For example, on September 21, 2016 Ms Cabot asked Gabriela, who was slouched in her chair and unresponsive to Ms Cabot's questions, 'Are you bored or are you tired? Do you know it all?' In turn, I would often find Mohammed playing a game or watching a video on his phone during Mr Barre's math class, causing Mr Barre to eventually demand he return to the activity.

I end this section with a focus on Beatriz and particularly her interactions with Gabriela because it underlines the importance of sociocultural learning. Again, both Beatriz and Gabriela entered the school under similar circumstances, backgrounds and legal statuses. As the 'luck' of classroom placement had it, they were the only two Brazilian students put into the focal Lab section and initially displayed a budding friendship as they sat near each other, talked socially, gave each other high fives and collaborated on projects. This continued from the start of school up to the first week of October when a dramatic shift happened. Beatriz is a 14-year-old woman, with a fair complexion that marks her as 'White' in Brazil's racial categories (cf. Degler, 1986), and conventionally attractive, becoming an object of desire for many of the male students in the class and school throughout the year. Gabriela is 18, darker skinned and considered 'Black,' and also attractive, becoming an object of desire for several students, most notably Omar. The issue arose when Beatriz started to develop a friendship and romantic relationship with Gabriela's younger brother, which Gabriela didn't like for reasons that remained unclear to me despite much questioning on this topic. As related to me by both Gabriela and Beatriz, Gabriela informed her mother about this situation and then forcefully told Beatriz to break off her relationship. Beatriz complied, describing the situation in this way (conversation conducted in English-Portuguese with interpretation assistance from a Portuguese-speaking colleague):

Beatriz: She (Gabriela) said, she just kind of got angry at me and never said anything else about that situation.
Brian: Did she ever threaten you?
Beatriz: No.
Brian: Because it was like night and day in the class, and the beginning of class you were at the table talking to each other and collaborating and then like, I think maybe in the middle of October or in the September, like,
Beatriz: To be honest, I didn't try to reach out to Gabriela and try to figure out, I just said 'I'd rather just leave it be' then try to, try to mend things because I was under the impression that it was going to make things worse if I tried to reach out.
Brian: I think in general, Gabriela is a bit older than you, and you're not the same people, she's interested in different things, you're interested in different things.
Beatriz: Yeah, of course she is 18 and I'm 14, but it's my impression that Gabriela maybe was being a little less mature about it, but obviously it's just a lack of understanding.
Brian: Ok.
Beatriz: Don't tell Gabriela what I said.
(Personal communication, March 23, 2017)

This rift put Beatriz in a difficult situation. In the class, Gabriela had developed strong personal connections with Maria and other Spanish-speaking students who would often work with Gabriela, even allowing her to copy answers. However, despite an expressed weakness in mathematics that had existed even in Brazil, I never observed Beatriz collaborating with the Spanish-speaking students; she preferred to sit near Mohammed and other Somali students and spent as much time as possible on her phone, chatting or texting online with other Brazilian students in the school or elsewhere. As an additional unfortunate twist, the Reading Clinic staff placed both Beatriz and Gabriela into the same group with Omar, assuming that their shared langua-culture would support each other. However, this did not manifest, leading Ms Son, the Cambodian bilingual assistant to be confused by their (lack of) interaction in the class until I explained the situation. Despite my clarification, both Gabriela and Beatriz remained in the Reading Clinic group and only partially started to collaborate late in the Spring semester as, presumably, the ice had thawed a bit. Nevertheless, Beatriz generally worked silently and independently in the Reading Clinic, which was interpreted by Ms Som and Omar as a lack of intelligence. Indeed, on November 7, 2016, Omar told me in Arabic that Beatriz 'doesn't know much,' and another interaction from March 6, 2017 further illustrates the situation:

Ms Som:	See this is for all the vocabulary that we did, like 1 2 3, so this is Gabriela, current review, so she did all this,
Brian:	That's good, good Gabriela.
Omar:	Gabriela is very good.
Ms Som:	You too.
Omar:	((looking at Beatriz)) And Beatriz.
Ms Som:	Beatriz too, you know what, you too, because you need to speak more, everybody,
Omar:	Beatriz is, ((sort of shakes his head pejoratively and waves hand dismissively))
Gabriela:	((looks at Beatriz))
Omar:	((leans towards Gabriela, smiles, and looks at Beatriz))

This example shows how Ms Som positions Gabriela as a good student and Beatriz' reluctance to speak as a personal choice rather than something imposed by the situation. Moreover, Omar praises Gabriela and directly, through the use of head and hand gestures, identifies as Beatriz as a poor student. Of course, the irony is that Omar was in a very similar situation to Beatriz in terms of educational background and overall proficiency in English at the time. The sole difference is that he has (at least) me and Mr Shahiya to speak to among the adults he interacts regularly with in the program. Beatriz has only a substitute teacher in another Lab section who speaks Portuguese, and because Gabriela and Beatriz are not speaking, this has isolated her considerably, putting her in a frustrating situation. Indeed, on January 26, 2017 Beatriz was visibly upset in Mr Barre's class, crying silently and then putting her head down on the desk for the majority of the class. When I asked her if she was ok she shrugged off my requests, and when I asked other students, particularly Mohammed and the other Somali women, if they knew what was wrong, they all explained that her boyfriend had broken up with her, which might have been true but was not the explanation the Beatriz gave when I interviewed her, again with the help of a more proficient Portuguese-English interpreter.

Brian:	I want to ask you a personal question, do you have a boyfriend now?
Beatriz:	No, only my mom.
Brian:	Did you have a boyfriend or multiple boyfriends throughout this time?
Beatriz:	I had started to date (another Brazilian student), but then that's stopped.
Brian:	Is that, because maybe a month ago in class you were crying, you seemed really sad, was that about the breakup, or something else?
Beatriz:	No, I was crying because I wanted to be back in Brazil.

Brian:	Okay, but did it have some relationship breaking up with your boyfriend?
Beatriz:	I was also a little bit stressed out with some of the Somalis, that there was one boy in particular that would sometimes be critical of me and say that I don't know English, and so I was crying out of anger/frustration.
Brian:	Yeah. It was a boy in our class, who was it? Mohammed, Abdullah, or who? I'm not going to tell them.
Beatriz:	He goes to the clinic.
Brian:	Omar?
Beatriz:	Yes.
Brian:	But Omar is from Syria.
Beatriz:	he's not Somali? That's why he's even more annoying. I thought that he was Somali because he was talking to another kid there that maybe was Somali.
Brian:	But he has white skin, I mean more or less white skin, you know Omar with the hair and the gel.
Beatriz:	Yes.
Brian:	I speak with him in Arabic a lot.
Beatriz:	Oh, I never really knew about how Somalis were darker skinned and that there were lighter skinned people.
Brian:	So, sorry, so you were sad because Omar was saying,
Beatriz:	I have a difficult time with English, and I try to do my best, but he will perpetually find ways to criticize me and there are times where the teacher will tell him to stop and he will kind of continue needling me, and you know sometimes it's just too much.
Brian:	Yeah, Omar, I got to know him well because I speak Arabic. He's very sarcastic, but he's not trying to be mean.
Beatriz:	That's fine as long as he doesn't keep giving me a hard time.
Brian:	Even like, for example in the Reading Clinic, Omar sits here and Gabriela sits here, and he is always like touching Gabriela, and I'm trying to tell him, like 'man, respect other people' but,
Beatriz:	Yeah, I'd rather kind of do my own thing and focus on my work.
Brian:	Yeah, what's interesting, like say if I would ask somebody to watch the video from the class they would say 'Oh this girl Beatriz is always sitting by herself' and I'm concerned about it, but do you feel like isolated in the class or do you feel connected to people, how do you feel in the class?
Beatriz:	No. there's a student, is his name Abdulkabir?
Brian:	Mohammed?
Beatriz:	Yeah, Mohammed. With Mohammed and some of the girls that he's friends with, I feel comfortable sitting with them in the class, and the only class I don't have with him is the music class which is kind of the other activities class. So, yeah it's easier that way.
Brian:	Yeah.
Beatriz:	The day I was crying I was just really stressed out.

(Personal communication, March 23, 2017)

This perspective supported some of my underlying suspicions about what was happening for Beatriz in the class. On the one hand, although I knew that she was exploring some romantic relationships and that some of the other male students saw her as desirable, I was skeptical of the other students' explanation that her crying in class was solely based on a breakup. This interview reveals that the silence she employed in the Reading Clinic was a move to avoid conflict with Gabriela but was interpreted as ignorance by Omar and Ms Som (and other actors in the program). Moreover, Omar's criticism and teasing was not interpreted by her as the light sarcasm that he likely intended, a strategy that he used with many other students, and this situation compounded over the course of the year. Perhaps more tragically, when this frustration manifested in tears of longing to return to Brazil or the stress of an unproductive learning environment, this was interpreted as a typical romantic breakup situation by the very friends that Beatriz purported to have in the class, indexing, in addition to the fact that Beatriz did not even know their names well, the overall shallowness of their friendship. This recalls McDermott *et al.*'s (2006) query, 'At any given moment in a cultural arrangement, just what interpretations are available and called into use?'. In this situation, Beatriz' silence was interpreted as ignorance and her tears as some kind of girlish naiveté.

This final point is essential in the broader sociocultural learning environment of a superdiverse, translanguaging context. Although it is likely that students who share a similar linguistic repertoire will collaborate, this anecdote underlines that this is only a potentiality that the rest of the learning environment must work to create. The fact that the simmering conflict between Beatriz and Gabriela goes unnoticed and unresolved throughout the vast majority of the year is disappointing, resulting in highly differentiated results for the two students: Gabriela has strong gains on the Dominie and MAP (going from 149 to 180 in Reading from Fall to Spring) and gets As and Bs in all her classes; on the other hand, Beatriz' MAP Reading scores actually decline, going from 183 to 169, and she receives Ds and Cs in most classes.[1] This is a disappointing result for a student whose initial profile is so strong.

Thus, students in this 'High' group are characterized by strong academic backgrounds, including home language literacy, and are almost immediately recognized as crucial academic supports for the teacher and other students despite the fact that this role is not one that they have been actively engaged in creating or negotiating. Nevertheless, this group can be a powerful source for student support in the classroom as long as interpersonal conflicts do not impede collaboration and communication. However, it must be underlined that this group does not see the program as being challenging enough for them or adequately supportive of their English-learning process, which they pin directly on the lack of access to English-speaking peers, the 'normal' Americans mentioned by Gabriela above. This point will be taken up again in a discussion of the future trajectory of the program.

'Mid' students: Those with either home language literacy or prior educational issues

In a sense, the 'Mid' student group is the group that the program is most attuned to and most supportive of their academic journeys. These students arrive with some challenging elements in their backgrounds in that they might have been out of school for several years or have not fully developed literacy in their home languages. On the other hand, the school is aware of these issues and has a broad array of structures in place to support the students. Academically, just as students in the 'High' group may find the academic material and activities too easy, this group likely find them challenging but not overwhelming. In terms of home language, they may not be at the same literacy level as their peers in their home countries, but they may have reached a theoretical 'tipping point' where their home language skills can effectively transfer to the target learning context. This issue of transfer has been theorized by a number of second language researchers (Cummins, 1979, 2005; Ortega, 2008: Ch. 3) and recent research from multilingual environments in India has suggested 'an empirical tipping point of approximately 60% Lit 1 decoding ability for a significantly higher likelihood of "transfer" of knowledge to Lit 2 decoding, and thus effective biliteracy outcomes' (Nakamura, 2014: 31). Thus, students in this category might include: the aforementioned Omar, who was out of school for a few years in Jordan but read and wrote Arabic very well; most of the Bhutanese-Nepali refugees with their generally parallel educations yet uneven literacy skills; many of the Central American Spanish-speaking students, particularly the males; Belvie, another Congolese refugee from Tanzania; and many of the Somali students, particularly Abdullah, who expressed an inability to read/write Somali but was very strong in Islamic studies and Arabic, having memorized much of the Koran.

As such, these students have a general set of academic needs that are largely met by the program through its manifold meaning-making processes and pedagogies. These students were often those who might struggle with a handout but would be able to draw on their own knowledge or collaborate with the 'High' students or seek support from the teacher in order to complete the task. The example given from Omar's talk with Mr Shahiya above is a good example; although Omar was highly frustrated with Mr Barre's approach in math, he complained and persevered in getting academic support from Mr Shahiya.

Thus, in class, these students are often moving towards other students, collaborating or engaging in various social talk which, while generally tolerated by the teacher, might at times violate the informal rules explained above and receive some correction from the teacher. It is within this group's talk that examples of translanguaging occur that illustrate the meaning-making processes for this group that often remain invisible to the teachers but are highly meaningful for student cohesion and identity.

For example, one 'rich point' (Agar, 1994: 231–232) that emerged was how the word 'chick' evolved across speech events. The focal events began on January 24, 2017 during a Words Their Way lesson with Ms Cabot on the difference between the phonemes 'c,' 'h' and 'ch,' including 'comb,' 'heart' and 'chick.' When 'chick' was introduced, Dhan, a Bhutanese refugee girl, quietly identified 'chick' as a 'Nepali bad word,' and I asked her what it meant. Although she was initially reluctant to explain, it was eventually revealed by Jhuma to mean 'f*ck,' which he did not say aloud but rather wrote in his notebook for me to read. Later, on February 13, 2017 in Mr Barre's class, Dhan explained that another Spanish-speaking boy, Santiago, had learned the Nepali phrase *'chicki-chicki'* 'I want to f*ck you' and was saying it to her. As she didn't like that, she asked me to intervene, and I moved to Santiago's table and asked him if he knew that the phrase was offensive. He explained that he didn't but had just learned it from Puspa who had encouraged him to say it to Dhan. I suggested that he should be more mindful of his words. However, on March 7, 2017 back in Ms Cabot's class, Dhan and Santiago were sitting at the same table, and Dhan complained again about his use of *chicki-chicki*, but later in the class resisted by making fun of Santiago's laugh and used Google Translate on her mobile phone to say to him in Spanish 'your voice sounds like a goat' *'cabra.'* The use of *chicki-chicki* continued in the class in this relatively congenial way but gained additional meaning on May 1, 2017 when three other students – Omar, a Somali girl named Hayat, and Belvie – asserted to me that *chicki-chicki* was Spanish and came from the Daddy Yankee song 'Shaky Shaky.' A group of Spanish-speaking girls sitting nearby clarified that this was their understanding as well; in contrast, I explained how *chicki-chicki* had another resonance going back to 'chick' in both English and Nepali, which they found amusing, and Hayat commented, 'All the boys are saying this (*chicki-chicki*),' revealing how the phrase had become a kind of class lingua franca.

Thus, 'chick' has a specific, salacious and insulting meaning in Nepali, but by being taken up by a Spanish speaker in a translanguaging context, the students collectively draw on their own languacultural repertoires to make meaning, in this case bringing in the popular song 'Shaky Shaky' by Daddy Yankee – itself a song that is mainly in Spanish but also with some English lyrics. The sexuality of the song with lines such as *'Que mueva to' lo que tiene. Vamo' a ver cómo lo sostiene'* 'she moves everything she has, let's see how she holds it' has a semiotic relationship with 'chick' and '*chicki-chicki.*' Through this example, the 'named languages' of English, Spanish and Nepali deteriorate and are replaced by the coherence and conviviality of adolescent social belonging. In the end, these adolescent students seem to have little interest in the exact linguistic background of this phrase but are mainly focused on it as a tool for creating laughter, mild provocations and explorations of sexuality outside the gaze and control of the adult teachers in the room, which is emblematic of adolescence itself.

Thus, this 'Mid' group can be considered the most amenable to the program's design and structure. They do not express the same degree of desire for target-language peers or rapid transfer to a new program nor show boredom or frustration with the academic activities or expectations. In a sense, they are where they are supposed to be – in a space designed for them where they can develop their language and content knowledge before eventually moving on to another environment.

'Low' students: Those with both home language literacy and prior educational issues

The 'High' and 'Mid' groups have a partially distinct yet overlapping set of academic needs. Both are working to develop their English-language ability but may struggle to do so because of, in the 'Mid' group's case specifically, some challenges in their prior educations or home language literacy. The key difference between the two centers on (1) the desire for target-language peers and (2) the perception of difficulty in the academic tasks presented to them. Specifically, the 'High' group are more likely to complain of boredom whereas the 'Mid' group engage more in the languacultural semiotic environment. In short, the 'High' group seem to resent being at the program whereas the 'Mid' group may genuinely enjoy it.

The 'Low' group, on the other hand, come with the most significant challenges. These students have significant gaps in their educational backgrounds (i.e. no formal education or three or more years out of school) and may not have reached the theoretical threshold of home language literacy necessary to create a pathway for transfer. Moreover, the issues presented by these students may mask other difficulties such as undiagnosed learning differences that could impede learning at a cognitive level. Students in this category include Salah, an 18-year-old Jordanian male, Mateo, a 16-year-old male from Honduras and Hajar, an 18-year-old Somali woman.

Salah is a Jordanian male, 18 years old, who came to the US in 2013 primarily to have surgery on his hips due to some physical handicap that had existed from birth but was not severe enough that he could not walk. However, this condition was debilitating, so his father, who had been in the US for many years and co-owned and managed a number of businesses, most notably a convenience store in the southern part of the city, brought him to the US for orthopedic surgery in late 2013. Although his medical history was never clarified completely, it seems that Salah had several surgeries in 2014 requiring extended hospital stays, which led the school counselors to question why he had not received schooling at the hospital and his family to respond that their primary concern at the time had been Salah's health and therefore they had never registered him for school nor were they aware that in-hospital or home schooling were available. However, Salah did recuperate enough to visit Jordan at least once after the surgeries and returned to the US to enroll in school, arriving at the program on the second day of school, August 25, 2016, walking with a slight limp but eager to learn.

Due to our shared linguistic repertoire with Arabic, Salah and I became relatively close from the start of the school year. I would frequently sit by him in class, talk to him about his life and attempt to help him with the classroom activities. However, it became more and more clear to me and the other teachers that Salah had manifold educational challenges in terms of home language literacy (see below his 1/10 on the home language test), general English ability, school organizational habits and issues such as working memory. For example, Ms Cabot would frequently give him exercises to practice the English alphabet, which he could complete in the moment but would struggle with the next day. For instance, on October 11, 2016 I sat with Salah and worked on the English letters extensively, using Arabic and English to explain their sounds and their correspondence to Arabic, and to engage in various forms of repetition, writing and object manipulation to help make connections. Although he was able to master A–F well and then L–Z, G–K remained consistently difficult to recognize. In addition, when his answers were not being closely monitored, he would quickly read or mumble through a list of, for example, sight vocabulary in a sort of hope that the teacher or I would overlook the lack of detail; however, when told to slow down and read more carefully, he would often struggle, saying about many activities '*hadha s3ab*' 'this is hard.'

On the other hand, Salah had many positive moments of academic and personal development. For example, on October 25, 2016, Mr Shahiya helped him in Arabic to understand the conversion activity they were doing and, when he had demonstrated competence several times and received Mr Shahiya's compliments, he looked up and said '*Ana shatr*' 'I'm smart' and smiled. He was often surprised to learn that words like 'gallon' or 'kilogram' were the same in English and his Jordanian Arabic and, moreover, despite being initially the only Arabic speaker in the class, he made many social connections with other students such as Abdullah or Dhan and frequently sat with the Bhutanese-Nepali student group to work on activities. In short, similar to students in the 'Mid' category, he was able to address the relative instability in his language and content knowledge by working with others.

However, one of the key challenges in the situation was his home life. Salah's father had left for Jordan on an extended vacation and would not return until the middle of December. This left him living at home with his brother, who worked long hours at the convenience store, and his brother-in-law who also worked. Thus, simply getting up on time and meeting the bus early in the morning was a challenge, leading to many late days and unexcused absences, in addition to a number of excused absences for various medical appointments he still had. Nevertheless, in order to understand the situation further, the teachers and I contacted his brother and brother-in-law and they came to the school for a conference with the Lab teachers, school counselors and me on September 29, 2016. During this time, we worked to understand more about Salah's academic background, the nature of his physical impairment and any prior diagnoses of learning disabilities.

What emerged from this conversation was: (1) that Salah's prior education was sub-par, with his brother describing him as a 'not good' student; (2) that Salah's home language literacy was emergent, with his brother-in-law telling me several times that Salah had only recently started writing in Arabic on Facebook and WhatsApp; and (3) that Salah's academic home practices were uneven, with neither much time spent doing homework nor support from the brother or brother-in-law provided. On the other hand, we learned that Salah liked to go to the gym to swim and was competent working in the store, and that his father imagined a career for him in tourism in Jordan, particularly with his emergent English skills. However, his brother-in-law acknowledged that 'we never asked' Salah about his own interests. At the end of the meeting, the counselors requested a medical history for Salah, counseled them to seek transcripts from his school in Jordan as it was possible that some academic credit could be applied, and offered to see if it would be possible for Salah to join the swim team at his home school (due to the school's 'program' status, there were no sports offered but, theoretically, students could join their home school's teams).

This generally positive meeting provided useful context for the teachers and, it was hoped, signaled to Salah and his family that the school was committed to his success. However, this was severely impeded on October 7, 2016, when I came into school and learned that Salah had been suspended for five days for fighting during the lunch hour with a Pakistani student. Seeing this as extreme and unproductive, I questioned Mr Smith about it in the office, but he said that he wanted to 'nip it in the bud' even though he didn't 'like to make an example of a student,' and made an oblique reference to how things 'used to be' and that he 'didn't want to go down that road' of being permissive about violence or fighting in school. During and after this time, I learned from talk with multiple students and staff involved that the Pakistani student had gotten another French-speaking student to say something to Salah which he interpreted as an insult about his mother. However, what also emerged is that the Pakistani student might have been developing a relationship with the sister of a Syrian student that Salah might also have liked. In any case, these events led him to fight, resulting in both Salah and the Pakistani student receiving a five-day suspension. When Salah returned to school, I tried to understand the situation more deeply and also counseled him to solve any conflicts with words and not violence.

The issue of violence and culture emerged with a key figure in the school, Ms Abadi, the bilingual Arabic-English teacher and translator. She had been called in to interpret for Salah during this situation and explained to me that she saw 'a lot of anger in him,' which she seemed to understand as an individual or even cultural issue whereas I interpreted the anger as coming from the social context of the new school, English instruction, no Arabic support, etc.

Following this time, Salah was fully on the teachers' radar and his name frequently came up in the Teacher-Based Team meetings as a student who needed special support. At one meeting, the group resolved to pair him with Ms Lincoln as a faculty mentor, to arrange for him to be in Ms Abadi's Reading Clinic group, to start the process of diagnosing a learning disability and for me to continue supporting him in and out of class. However, the first three items never fully manifested, most consequentially the pairing with Ms Abadi, likely because her 2nd period was for planning, not Reading Clinic. Critically, Salah never received a formal assessment for special services.

Nevertheless, Salah continued to attend school after the suspension and showed some progress across his classes, despite other frustrations such as a repeated unrequited request to change from art to gym class to be with a Syrian boy he liked and admired or not being allowed to wear a hat one day in November when he felt that his hair was too long and didn't want to be seen by Beatriz, whom he joked or wished was his girlfriend.

A significant lift occurred in mid-October when Omar arrived, giving Salah a same-language peer in the class, particularly one who (theoretically) could help him academically. However, in a manner similar to Gabriela and Beatriz, this eventually deteriorated in that Omar began to resent helping Salah because he perceived Salah to either be unable or unwilling to complete the work; Omar frequently accused him of 'copying' and quasi-joked by saying '*skt unta*' 'shut up' to Salah repeatedly. This escalated to the point that, on December 5, 2016, Omar said to me 'keep Salah away from me teacher,' and they eventually got into a verbal fight in which Omar drew on cultural beliefs regarding mothers' food cravings while pregnant (*twahm*) to subtly suggest that Salah's physical handicap was the result of his mother not satisfying these cravings (Kruk, 1987). This happened while they were both standing near Gabriela, and Salah had asked in Arabic 'does she have a boyfriend?' to which Omar replied, 'you're the last one in the world someone would think of, I swear to God.' This escalated in class, which I was able to observe, and after class into a significant verbal confrontation, which I did not see but which Omar described on February 2, 2017, resulting in their cutting off their friendship for some time and sitting apart in all classes. Although they eventually started to talk again, their friendship, according to Omar, was not 'the same as it was' and they would just talk about general things but not support each other in any active way.

Thus, leading up to the Winter holiday, Salah had directly stated or implied that he was thinking of dropping out. Although his father returned from Jordan at the beginning of December 2016 and his attendance improved significantly, the frustrations remained, leading to perhaps the proverbial straw on December 13, 2016 when, while walking to the Reading Clinic, Ms Lincoln stopped Salah and a few other Reading Clinic students and asked them rather forcefully where they were going. When I rounded the corner and explained that they were going to the Reading Clinic, she released them, but as Salah and I walked down the hall he said to me in Arabic, 'Did you see? The animals, they're better than them,' and when I asked him for clarification, he said in Arabic, 'Wherever I go, they say "stop!", but what have I done wrong?' Later that day, apparently Salah engaged in what Ms Cabot called 'multiple little defiances' that resulted in Ms Lincoln receiving several teacher complaints, leading her to give him a two-day suspension. However, Salah came to school on December 14, 2016 anyway (likely to avoid explaining the situation to his father), and Ms Lincoln worked with Ms Cabot to allow Salah to stay in her class throughout the day until his father could come in to talk. When his father came in on December 15, 2016, he met with the school administration and Ms Abadi to come to an understanding of the issue, and the two-day suspension began. Salah returned to school on December 19, but then the Winter holiday started, certainly a welcome break for many but also just another interruption in Salah's academic trajectory. When the school year resumed on January 4, 2017, Salah also returned, demonstrated knowledge of the most vocabulary in Ms Cabot's class, and we talked about the vacation. However, another week passed, and he stopped coming to school on January 11, 2017. I reached out to him a number of times by phone and text but received no answer. Eventually, I visited his father's shop on February 23, 2017 and saw him confidently working the cash register. His father was there and explained that Salah had said that he was just going to school but 'not understanding anything' so decided to quit and either work at the shop or at another place. The school also eventually inquired about Salah, but he told them that he was moving back to Jordan, a falsehood as he continued working at the shop where, as of my last direct interaction later in Summer 2017, he remained.

A fuller explanation of Salah's case will be explored below, but the key elements are that Salah was capable of learning and had many things to draw upon from his experiences in Jordan, his languacultural background and his work at the shop. However, the confusion of the English-centric environment led to frustration, and when his response was violence he was given a suspension rather than engaging in a process of deeper reflection or support. Ms Lincoln and I discussed his case in the broader context of how well YES supports struggling students.

Ms Lincoln: I feel that we do because the reason why I feel that way is because during the Teacher-Based Team meeting, we have the counselors coming here. Then, we try to identify those kids that have problems and we try to get them help. Whether it's on the inside or outside of social services, counseling, [a specialized local program particularly for students with criminal/prison involvement], mentors. I feel like that we have a support system here in place and we're trying to do everything we can to help. We even contacted the parents and let the parents know, 'Hey, you need to do this. Get the kids so we can get them on the track.' I feel like we're doing all that we can to help them. Some of it has helped. It seemed like some of the kids that got some of the help, it seemed like we've turned them around. They're not on our radar now as far as we know, coming to the office with problems. It seemed like some of them are getting under control.

Brian: Do you see the kids that are suspended actually tend to improve their behavior or get worse or stay the same?

Ms Lincoln: Sometimes that's a, when they get suspended for something major, for the most part, I think they're getting better because I'm not suspending the same kids that I was suspending at the beginning of the year. I think that message has gone across that it if you don't do what you're supposed to do then, you're going to get in trouble. Most of the kids that we've suspended here, it has been mainly for fighting, for the most part. I feel like that they're getting better. It's sending the message when you take school away from them and this is where they want to be. Then, they come back and do what they're supposed to do.

Brian: One of the kids that's kind of, well, a focal student for me in the class I've been following is that kid we talked about a lot, Salah. Salah, the kid from Jordan. At the beginning of the year, he was here and had that miscommunication with the other kid. I think you suspended him for three days for one of those instances. I think you told me at the moment like, 'I'm just going to nip this in the bud.'

Ms Lincoln: Was that the kid with the limp?

Brian: Yes. 'I'm going to nip this in the bud. Suspend him for three days. Send a message not just to him but to whole school. We're not going to put up with this.' But over the year, unfortunately, Salah dropped out. He stopped going to school here in December.

Ms Lincoln: I've been wondering where he was.

Brian: Yes. I've been worried that, my basically feeling that him being suspended twice really decreased his motivation to be in school even though I think he wanted to be here in the beginning. I found it to be a little bit, the policy of suspending is still problematic to me. What do you think? In his case, I don't think it was productive but

Ms Lincoln: There are some kids where it's not productive. Even though it might not be productive, we try everything we can because, I'm going to be honest with you, at other places that I've been at, we suspend them more days at other places. Here, they don't get suspended as many days here. Most places that I've been, they get suspended anywhere from five to ten or more. Five or more days. You can go up to ten. Once you get the parent involved, sometimes, that's why we call the parents up here, we're trying to get them involved. We try to keep them in school as much as possible. There are times where, hey. You can take him home. Then, come back tomorrow. You might have a set day on your mind, but as you talk to the parent and you see that their level of involvement in it, you see their concern and it is not as much. So for most of the kids, suspension is productive because once you do it that one time, they might not have to do it anymore. Some kids it

	doesn't matter what school that they were at, it can be unproductive where they go right back out and they can come back in and do the same thing. So it works with some kids and you really, really not want to suspend them, now some schools have what you call is school suspension.
Brian:	Yes, like restorative justice kind of thing.
Ms Lincoln:	Yes, so that tend to work. Instead of putting them out, you've got somewhere to put them rather than letting them go home. And then sometimes you suspend them and they're out there on the streets. I'm concerned about that but sometimes you just, it's just part of the job. You have to, you've got to send the message to them and then, not only that but the staff that you're working with, you don't want to seem weak, like you're not doing your job, you're not doing what you are supposed to after they've done all they could do and after I've done all I can do. Suspension to me is a last resort you know. I don't want to suspend anybody but I will if I have to.

(Personal communication, April 26, 2017)

This anecdote demonstrates some of the gaps related to suspensions and working through core issues with student frustrations at their academic environments. The next two cases, Mateo and Hajar, will be explained more cursorily, due to overlap and contrast with Salah's situation in addition to the fact that my data on these two students are not as robust as Salah's.

Mateo was 16 years old, came from Honduras and had been out of school for five years, or since the fifth grade, due to the presence of multiple gangs, most notably the infamous MS-13 which had essentially infiltrated his community and school. Thus, during this time, he said that he primarily stayed at home, helped his mom with the house, played video games or soccer and received some kind of tutoring from his older sister. He entered the US in late Summer 2016 through a coyote and then spent time in a detention center in a manner similar to Gabriela and Beatriz as well as several other Central and South American students. After being released into the custody of his sister, he arrived at the school on November 3, 2016 and began the process of acclimating to the class.

In the beginning, Mateo was relatively quiet, sitting in the class and, according to my reading of events, not connecting directly with the Spanish-speaking students, Lina, Carlos or Maria, who had been in the school from the first day. However, he soon started to make contact with Francisco from Guatemala, who had arrived on October 27, 2016. Francisco eventually got the nickname '*chapi*' and as other Spanish-speaking students arrived in mid-November to early January, especially the males Santiago and Leonardo from El Salvador and Juan from Honduras, they formed a relatively coherent group who frequently spoke and moved together in the class. These students fit much better in the 'Mid' or even 'High' category in that they had generally parallel educations and strong home language literacy but also similar experiences with gangs and the migration experience. However, critically, this group started to break many of the informal rules in the class about volume and codes, leading to multiple censures by the teachers across contexts. By the end of the year, both a novice teacher such as Ms Tucek and the experienced Mr Barre felt quite exasperated with the group.

The issue of gangs is illuminating in Mateo's case. Although he was a victim of gang violence in Honduras, in class much of his identity reflected a gang persona. He wore clothes that might be read as such and even made statements such as 'I'm gangster' on February 22, 2017 to Jhuma and Dhan, punctuating his statement with a hand symbol with index and pinky spread out with the middle and ring fingers down, reminiscent of the '*Vatos Locos* "crazy cows"' gang sign. He also wore a bandana from time to time, put his hood up and carried around his backpack to classes, all direct violations of the stated policies of the school. Moreover, during computer-based learning or moments when he could look at videos on his phone, he would often look at videos such as clips from the 2009 movie *Sin Nombre* or the 1993 film *Blood In Blood Out* which both feature heavily gang-oriented themes. Thus, Mr Barre might be forgiven for asking Mateo about his bandana on April 3, 2017: 'What's this? Gang? Take it off.'

However, in conversations in the class and an interview facilitated by a Spanish-speaking colleague, Mateo offered a more nuanced view of these displays. Of the various gang gestures, he said that these were just imitating gang signs within the *Grand Theft Auto V* game, which he played frequently outside of school. Of the bandana and specifically how Santiago would sometimes put it on and do a flying kick in the air, he explained that this was referencing the *Karate Kid* movies. Perhaps most significantly, he explained that many of the videos that appeared to be gang related were actually news items from Honduras or Central America, and he watched them to keep track of his mother and other sister, both still living in Honduras and subject to this threat of violence daily. Thus, Mateo's explanation is more consistent with an adolescent boy's identity and common interests and concern for his family's welfare. Mateo stated several times that he was not involved with any gangs in Central Ohio and, as I did not follow Mateo after school, I can make no independent claims about this other than to point out that he never had any physical signs of violence on his body such as cuts, black eyes or bruises.

Nevertheless, Mateo's various displays and performances were part of an identity that was read differently by the teachers, administration and even other students. Mateo received frequent criticism from teachers for not doing the assignments in a timely manner, was often placed in a specific seat to separate him from other students and, when he had a fight on the bus on February 15, 2017, was suspended for five days, causing Ms Popov to comment the following day, 'I thought so, he's been building. He needed somebody to talk to him.' Critically, in contrast to the behaviors of the 'Mid' group, he seemed unable or unwilling to seek help from other students such as Maria, who interpreted this as Mateo not wanting to study.

Brian: So, you know, in our class, in the class, and I've been there all year, Santiago, Mateo. You know, like say Mateo, Santiago, ok, so they're having, I don't know problemas 'problems,' Leonardo,
Maria: Si, yo creo que el más enfoca es Leonardo, pero yo creo que Mateo, Leonardo, como que, no gusta estudiar. 'yes, I think the most focused is Leonardo, but I think that Mateo, Leonardo, like how, he doesn't like to study'
Brian: Ok, no gusta estudiar 'he doesn't like to study,' so like, like como, por los professors 'how, for the teacher, teachers' here, would be your advice for students like Mateo, Santiago, Leonardo, how can the school help students like that?
Maria: I think more work, and, más como más, presionarlos mas. 'and more like more, press on them more'
Brian: On Mateo?
Maria: Yeah, I think.
Brian: But maybe if Mateo doesn't like, if he doesn't like studies, how can more pressure?
Maria: No, I think no.
Brian: Do you think that like maybe Mateo, because Mateo didn't go to school for like five years?
Maria: Yes,
Brian: He was out of school because of the pandillas 'gangs,' that kind of thing,
Maria: Mateo quiere convertir a otra escuela. 'Mateo wants to transfer to another school'
Brian: Oh, which one?
Maria: Um, no se como se llama, pero, habla mucho sobre eso, como se llama? 'I don't know the name, but he talks a lot about it, what's its name?'
Brian: Escuela publica? 'public school?'
Maria: Publica. 'public'
Brian: Publica 'public,' like (I give names of several schools, including a vocational school)
Maria: I think, (confirms name of the vocational school I just said)
Brian: Oh, that's a school like special for trabajo. 'work'
Maria: Yes.
(Maria, personal communication, March 30, 2017)

Maria's perspective, on the one hand, potentially reveals a deficit perspective towards Mateo in that she thinks that he does not want to study. On the other hand, it is clear that she has been listening to his talk in class and perceives that the main issue is that the school is not giving him the education he desires. This is a valid criticism, and the vocational education programs are certainly one possible solution but also demand a relatively high level of English, so it is difficult to assess how aware Mateo is about these programs and what they offer.

Critically, it seems that Mateo himself may have adopted a sort of deficit perspective about his own behavior and performance in the class, which may impede his ability to consider other alternatives to the programming he is experiencing during an interview I have with him facilitated by a Spanish-English speaking staff member.

Brian: So, in your opinion, if you were like the director of the school or somebody, you know, with power, to change schooling to help students like you, what would you like it to be like? like a teacher or director?

Mateo: First I would change the behavior of the students. And a lot of students are missing English. And all the teachers they speak English, and then I speak with my friends, and I could speak more English with my friends. To explain the homework.

Brian: Okay, so you, I don't get, you mean that you think you should, you should speak more English for yourself.

Mateo: Yes.

Brian: So you're saying that part of this is changing yourself.

Mateo: Sure.

Brian: Yeah, so, this will make sure I understand, you're giving yourself a self-criticism, you're saying that you think you should be more serious.

Mateo: Yes.

Brian: Ok, that's good, I want to try to get this at the level of the system, the actual way that the teacher asked the class and the kind of classes, because right now you have English, science, math, and social studies, all in English, imagine that you can build a new school with any kind of classes, any kind of teachers, what would be the best kind of thing to encourage a student like you.

Mateo: First of all, I would ask teachers to learn Spanish because when they say words, I don't know all the words, and if they say something I don't know, I just don't know it, so if they're able to say in Spanish than I could understand it.

Brian: Ok, second thing.

Mateo: It's really just that for the Spanish speakers, cause Spanish speakers are missing a lot of English.

(Personal communication, April 9, 2017)

Mateo's comment indexes the fact that, in a way similar to Beatriz above, the 'luck' of the program organization put him in a schedule where only one of his teachers – Ms Popov – knew Spanish in a robust way and used it occasionally to help students.

Brian: Ms Popov, for example, speaks Spanish. Do you speak Spanish with her sometimes? She was a Spanish teacher in Russia.

Mateo: A little, very little,

Brian: Okay, what does she say, what do you talk about when you talk to her?

Mateo: Whenever I don't understand something I ask and she'll explain it.

Brian: Ok, is it helpful?
Mateo: Yes.
(Personal communication, April 9, 2017)

Again, just as with Salah, Mateo received the maximum intervention from the school by being assigned to the Reading Clinic, but his teacher was Mr Dahal, a Bhutanese refugee whose multilingualism in English, Nepali and Dzongkha is impressive but not well aligned with Mateo's needs. Also, as mentioned above, Mr Barre could have theoretically drawn on his Italian linguistic repertoire to communicate more robustly with Mateo and other Spanish or Portuguese speakers, but he rarely did so, possibly indexing his personal monolingual ideology or the constraints of the English-centric space. Regardless, it is clear from Mateo's perspective that these interventions and connections to his linguistic repertoire were not robust enough for him, leading to generally frustrated behavior inside and outside class. As a result, his test scores show beginning proficiency and his final grades are two Fs for math and science, a D in social studies, and Cs in English and Reading Clinic.

The coda for Mateo's experience is that he was picked up for trespassing in May 2017 and put back in immigration detention for two months in the Summer. However, during this time he received a hearing, was granted temporary asylum status and was released back to his sister. When I contacted him last in the Fall of 2018, he was working at a shop in the city to pay back the loan he had accrued for the legal fees in the asylum process and was thinking about coming back to the school or other educational experiences.

The final illustrative case is Hajar, an 18-year-old Somali woman with a clear physical or mental development issue. By 'clear' I mean visible and audible, and her situation is noteworthy as a contrast to Salah's. In Hajar's case, when she arrived in the class in the third group of students on March 22, 2017, the teachers and school counselors had already started the process of identifying her for special services. This included a number of actions including providing both regular Lab and differentiated activities for her to work on and documenting her ability to do these. This is important to determine with some precision because the history of the intersection of learning disabilities, ESL services and racism is replete with examples of misdiagnoses leading to students with only a physical ailment or students who simply do not speak English being placed in special education programs separated from the mainstream, severely limiting their academic potential. In Hajar's case, she had never gone to school and had epilepsy, requiring medications that made her frequently tired, even to the point that she would sometimes fall asleep in class. On the other hand, in the classroom environment she was able to follow a number of tasks; she could communicate socially with the other Somali students in Somali and was developing some English ability. Her case, in some senses, is positive and an argument for the inclusion of all students in the process of language and content learning.

However, her case contrasts with Salah's in that, although Salah may have had some sort of cognitive issue, he never received a full assessment from the school psychologist or any other special education professionals. This was certainly due to his spotty attendance and the perception of a negative attitude or violent tendencies, but the suspensions were a significant barrier as well, which seems to have not been appreciated by Ms Lincoln above and may have even been a barrier to his getting the assessments for special services that could have supported him.

Brian: Do you regret at all that we didn't get Salah promoted to get a special ed assessment?

Ms Cabot: Well, we were trying. We were in process for that. I was in process, I had filled up all the paper work and I had taken it to, he was in process with, what were we on? We were on the interventions. I was trying to get my colleagues on board with doing interventions and we were in that phase. That was phase one or whatever in that process and so he was on the track, he was in the process, but then he kind of disappeared and,

Interviewer: Yes, and got kicked out.

Ms Cabot: Oh, did he? Okay, I forgot that.

(Personal communication, June 29, 2017)

Ms Cabot's forgetting of this detail in the Summer interview should not be construed as inattention or callousness – Salah left school in January, her class size by the end of the year was at 30 and she had just recently given birth. However, these statements underline the challenges inherent in the intersection between language learning and special services. On the one hand, it is positive that special services are no longer an immediate reaction to any student who presents some difference in the classroom; on the other hand, Ms Cabot's statement reveals that getting students assessments they might need is a complicated process that relies, in part, on the student's behavior and attendance so that interventions can be documented. Seen in this light, Salah's suspensions are all the more tragic in that they not only disrupted his personal learning process but may also have contributed to him being passively denied the very services that might have helped him be successful.

Hajar's case adds another layer to the sociocultural nature of the classroom context in that some students in this context might not be prepared to share space with a student with a physical or mental impairment. Omar, for example, initially complained to me about Hajar's presence bothering him for some reason, and I had to tell him with some firmness that she had as much right to an education as he did and that he should work to be understanding and compassionate with others. In addition, Belvie and her female Somali friend Hayat frequently made lighthearted, from their perspective, jokes about two people being boyfriend and girlfriend, particularly towards Omar or Mateo in reference to women such as Hajar or

Zahra, an 18-year-old Somali woman who also had never gone to school and who was perceived somehow as being a funny or undesirable match for these young men. In these interactions, either of the students would protest these insinuations strongly, only further provoking Belvie and Hayat. On the other hand, these jokes never seemed to become too barbed or insidious and, in general, Hajar appeared to be well supported by her peers, particularly the other Somali females in the class.

This section has focused on three distinct types of students within the 'pre-functional' Lab classes, given here as 'High,' 'Mid' and 'Low.' These student groups are theorized and organized based on the students' home language literacy and prior educational experience. The analysis of these types has led to three broad arguments. First, Lab students with strong home language literacy and parallel educations may feel bored or demotivated in the program due to the lack of access to target-language peers and generally lower academic standards. Second, students with some instability in either of these areas may feel comfortable in the program and even thrive in the superdiverse translanguaging milieu despite some interpersonal challenges. Third, students with instability in both of these areas have a serious risk of feeling frustrated with the lack of home language support, the demands of an English-centric environment and a school support apparatus that may be too slow to address students' academic needs or may even directly undermine learning through suspensions. These issues illustrate that a 'one-size-fits-all' approach to program design, in-class work, disciplinary policies, etc., is not sufficient, particularly when considering the 'Low' group. From these general and specific issues, there are therefore at least three possible solutions that could address student concerns most robustly:

- developing a system of home language assessment and support;
- understanding the distinct types of potential student frustrations and being prepared to respond accordingly;
- monitoring student interpersonal conflicts and intervening when necessary to ensure that all students have access to supportive peers, especially those that share a similar linguistic repertoire.

The first point underlines that any school and especially those serving English language learners (ELLs) must have a strong understanding of the students' home language(s) ability and particularly their prior literacy experiences. These sorts of questions are often included in district or state required home language surveys, and Ohio is no exception (Ohio Department of Education, 2018). However, these forms, even the updated Ohio version, can focus more on speaking ability while not including a specific home language literacy test which could provide more fine-grained analysis of the students' literacy ability, a key factor for transfer to English literacy. This is especially true considering the wide variety of languages in any state, district or school, but even YES's rudimentary home language reading or writing tests documented above would be an improvement. Thus, assessing the home language would be a key first step; however, the next would be designing specific systems to support students, especially those who have not developed prior literacy. The most direct way to address this issue would be some form of home language classes, either for all students or focused on those without home language literacy.

In addition, the systems must take account of the fact that many students will likely display some frustration throughout the year, but that these frustrations will be specific depending on the group and require distinct interventions. 'High' students might show boredom or low-level defiance or 'Mid' students may seem off-task at times; however, both of these are relatively easy for a teacher or system to address. On the other hand, the 'Low' group's frustrations might boil over into violence, and if the administration or counselors have no recourse other than suspending students, this leads to inadequate and inequitable outcomes. This was certainly the case at YES for many students, and announcements, usually delivered by Ms Johnston, included on several occasions the statement, 'Students, if you wanna fight, you wanna go home.' This approach is, at a minimum, unproductive for many students and can lead to significant frustration or even dropping out, as was the case with Salah.

The final point underlines the subtle difficulty that students often work well together but frequently have conflicts that can impede their learning. The cases of Beatriz and Salah show that this can be most frustrating when they are in a class with only one same-language peer and if that relationship breaks down over time. This is challenging in that the verbal exchanges in their home language have all the subtlety and potential for inadvertent offence present in any interpersonal communication, but as these languages are often not part of the teachers' or other staff's linguistic repertoire, in addition to the fact that the students themselves may intentionally mask these disagreements, it is highly possible that their interpersonal conflicts can go unnoticed or unaddressed for some time. Indeed, throughout the year, many of the staff expressed confusion about Beatriz' and Salah's lack of collaboration with Gabriela or Omar or simply assumed that they were friends and continued to pair them for group work. The result here was that Beatriz and Salah both spent significant time in class without a collaborative peer, same language or otherwise, a significant constraint to their learning and investment.

These conclusions and recommendations are focused on the students' languacultural and educational backgrounds as the primary source of friction with the English-centric environment. However, this should not obscure other potential sources of frustration such as the fact that many of the students are living in the US with the significant stressor of undocumented status (Allard, 2015; Allard & Mortimer, 2008; Gonzales, 2011; Murray & Marx, 2013; Suárez-Orozco *et al.*, 2011) in parallel with tenuous home situations or work demands. Nevertheless, I focus on these factors because they are the ones most firmly within the program's ability to address.

On the other hand, I worry that my presence as a researcher may have impeded the students in some ways, for Salah in particular. It is clear that the teachers and staff considered my engagement with him as a kind of intervention. Although I welcomed this level of connection with Salah and the program, I wonder if there would have been more dramatic moves on the part of Ms Lincoln to mentor him or place him in a class with Ms Abadi if I had not been present at all. These more systematic moves might have helped him more. On the other hand, it is possible that without my support Salah would have become frustrated and dropped out more quickly. Clearly it is impossible to know the answer to this situation, but I believe that these larger structural issues in the school, namely the lack of attention to his home language literacy, SLIFE status, possible learning issues, unfair and inconsistent discipline practices and difficulty in forming collaborative relationships in class, in addition to his unsteady home life without his father, were the most significant contributors to his dropping out.

English-centric Assessments and Results: Invisible, Dramatic and Debatable Growth

> At the staff meeting on March 6, 2017, Ms Johnston, filling in briefly for the Mr Smith, announces that 'the MAP scores have been good,' that there were increases in every level, and that overall they were 'fabulous.' When Mr Smith arrives at the end of the meeting, he takes the floor and reinforces that these MAP scores had gone up 'across the board.' (Fieldnotes, March 6, 2017)

The previous sections have focused on the English-centric nature of the program and how that is a partial contrast to the 'flexibility' offered by state policies and a strong contrast to the academic consensus of what types of programs would likely best support newcomers. This English-centric nature has been evidenced across a number of data, including the program history, the current actors' perspectives on bilingual approaches, the linguistic landscape, in-class teacher talk, learning resources and assessment practices. The case studies show how this environment is interpreted and responded to differently by three theoretical types of students. The final part of this chapter takes up the critical question of YES's quantifiable learning results and interpretations that emerge from the various actors.

The brief anecdote at the start of this section frames a broader discussion about interpreting the results of the program, with a focus on the Lab students. The overall argument will be that these 'fabulous' and 'across the board' gains raise important questions about the nature of student growth, testing, targets and the interpretation of data. Table 3.3 includes the students' assessment data, with those focused on the home language in the columns on the left and those on English language and academic content performance on the right.

There are several key take-aways from this data. First is the inconsistency in the home language assessment. Only nine of the students were administered the quasi-formal home language test. In addition, Ms Popov, despite her best intentions, was not able to continue delivering her home language diagnostic after the initial period of the year, and Ms Cabot's home language activity occurred mid-year. Thus, institutional knowledge of the students' home language literacy levels is quite limited. Second is the variation in the more official English language data. For example, for students with longitudinal MAP Reading scores, there are eight students with fairly large gains of roughly 10–30 points, 10 with modest increases of 0–9 points, and three – Mohamed, Beatriz and Yadu – with decreases. The Dominie shows similar gains and variation to the MAP scores. On the whole, this speaks to the program's educational potential.

In the remainder of this chapter I will focus on the interpretation of the OELPA and MAP data. In this section I will argue that there are at least three interpretations of this data – invisible, dramatic or debatable – that have implications for the overall assessment of the program's efficacy. My argument, centered on the Lab students' experience, is that these results support a 'good but not good enough' interpretation, particularly when considering language development as evidenced in the MAP Reading scores.

Looking over the OELPA results reveals a classic 'good news and bad news' situation. Table 3.3 reveals the negative side in that all 27 students who took the OELPA in the Spring of 2017 were evaluated as a '1' 'Beginner' overall proficiency status. However, the skills results are perhaps more encouraging in that five students had a '2' 'Early Intermediate' for speaking, three had a '2' for listening and one had a '2' for writing. Regardless, it is perhaps less than ideal that all the students were still in the lowest possible band, even the 13 students who had been in the program for the entire year.

On the other hand, the OELPA does not allow for particularly fine-grained analyses of student learning. The MAP data do and reveal a more positive story, particularly for the students who were in the program for the entire year. This group had an average Reading level of 163.8 in the Fall and a 172.2 in the Spring. Keeping in mind that the stated goal for the Lab year is to cover, more or less, the first half of elementary language content, the negative aspect here is that this final level is still in the lowest 10% of 3rd grade compared to the population average (which includes target language speaking peers). On the other hand, the program has succeeded in moving the students as a whole up, on average, nearly two grade levels in an academic year. This dovetails, more or less, with the Dominie results which had been the source of some controversy throughout the year. For the focal students who had been initially assessed as 'pre-K' readers, placed in the

Students and Outcomes 137

Table 3.3 Student assessment data

Student name	HL test (/10)	Ms Popov's Diagnostic (Yes = some HL writing; No = no HL writing)	Ms Cabot's partially HL autobiographies (Yes = some HL writing; No = no HL writing; Eng = wrote in English only)	OELPA (Instability in both home language literacy or parallel education)	MAP (Reading: Fall, Winter, Spring)	MAP (Math: Fall, Winter, Spring)	Dominie (Initial, Mid, Final [if available] by reading grade level)	GPA (Good = A/B; Ok = B/C; Poor = D/F)
Gabriela	N/A	Yes	Eng	All 1	149, 158, 180	190, 195, N/A	PK, Mid1, Beg2	Good
Antonio	N/A	Yes	N/A	N/A	N/A	N/A	PK	N/A
Lina	7	Yes	Eng	All 1	153, 172, 167	179, 188, 184	PK, Mid1, Beg2	Good
Carla	10	Yes	N/A	All 1	157, 175, 172	177, 181, 188	PK, N/A, Beg1	Good
Maria	9	Yes	Eng	1,1,N/A,2,1	163, 167, N/A	191, 191, N/A	PK, Mid1, End1	Good
Amal	N/A	Yes	N/A	N/A	N/A	N/A	N/A	N/A
Samuel	10	Yes	N/A	2,3,3,4,3	N/A	N/A	End5	N/A
Marcus	10	Yes	N/A	2,3,3,2,2	N/A	N/A	BegK, Beg3	N/A
Shiva	N/A	No	N/A	All 1	N/A	N/A	BegK, EndK	N/A
Sudarshan	N/A	N/A	N/A	All 1	N/A	N/A	EndK, Beg1	N/A
Puspa	N/A	No	Eng	All 1	146, 159, 161	166, 167, 178	MidK	Good/Ok
Tara	N/A	No	Eng	All 1	158, 162, 154	180, 185, 202	PK, N/A, Beg1	Good/Ok
Lakshmi	N/A	Yes	N/A	2, N/A, N/A,3,2	N/A	N/A	Beg3	N/A
Dhan	N/A	No	Eng	1,2,1,1,1	170, 175, 179	189, 198, 200	EndK	Good
Fatima	10	Yes	Eng	All 1	179, 184, 183	190, 192, 192	Mid1	Good/Ok
Mohamed	9	Yes	Eng	1,2,1,2,2	192, 185, 184	191, 201, 195	MidK	Good
Abdullah	5	No	N/A	N/A	161, 162, 181	160, 162, 178	EndK	Poor
Salah	1	No	N/A	N/A	N/A, N/A, N/A	148, N/A, N/A	PK	Poor
Beatriz	N/A	N/A	N/A	All 1	183, 161, 169	175, 178, 190	PK, N/A, Beg1	Poor/Ok
Manuel	N/A	N/A	N/A	N/A	N/A	N/A	N/A	N/A
Omar	N/A	N/A	Eng	All 1	158, 152, 160	141, 177, 204	PK, EndK	Ok

138   Educating Adolescent Newcomers in the Superdiverse Midwest

Name								
Iman	N/A	N/A	N/A	N/A	N/A	N/A	N/A	N/A
Hayat	N/A	N/A	N/A	All 1	157, 156, 165	N/A, 171, 170	BegK, MidK	Good
Francisco	N/A	N/A	N/A	All 1	N/A, 161, 164	N/A, 172, 179	PK, MidK	Ok
Camila	N/A	N/A	N/A	All 1	166, 166, 183	179, 194, 206	PK, MidK	Ok
Abdelkarim	N/A	N/A	N/A	N/A	N/A	N/A	N/A	N/A
Diego	N/A	N/A	Yes	N/A	N/A	N/A	BegK, Mid1	Ok
Mateo	N/A	N/A	N/A	All 1	N/A, 158, N/A	N/A, 160, N/A	PK, BegK	Poor
Jhuma	N/A	N/A	Eng	N/A	N/A	N/A, 207, N/A	Mid2	N/A
Santiago	N/A	N/A	Yes	All 1	N/A, 157, N/A	N/A, 159, 157	PK, BegK	Poor/Ok
Batuli	N/A	N/A	N/A	N/A	N/A	N/A	N/A	N/A
Belvie	N/A	N/A	Eng	1,2,1,2,1	N/A, 168, 175	N/A, 180, 195	Beg1	Good
Yadu	N/A	N/A	Eng	All 1	N/A, 184, 171	N/A, 194, 200	Beg1	Good
Menuka	N/A	N/A	N/A	N/A	N/A	N/A	N/A	N/A
Leonardo	N/A	N/A	N/A	All 1	N/A, 143, 156	N/A, N/A, 165	PK, PK	Poor/Ok
Ahmed	N/A	N/A	N/A	N/A	N/A	N/A	N/A	N/A
Juan	N/A	N/A	N/A	All 1	N/A, 161, 169	N/A, 201, 193	Beg1	Good/Ok
Valeria	N/A	N/A	N/A	All 1	N/A, 144, 159	N/A, 187, N/A	PK, PK	Poor
Zahra	N/A	N/A	N/A	All 1	N/A, N/A, 151	N/A, N/A, 166	PK, PK	Good/Ok
Sabrina	N/A	N/A	N/A	N/A	N/A	N/A	PK	Poor
Ikram	N/A	N/A	N/A	All 1	N/A, N/A, 168	N/A, N/A, 174	Beg1	Poor
Gloire	N/A	N/A	N/A	1,1,1,2,1	N/A, N/A, 196	N/A, N/A, 207	Beg1	Poor/Ok
Hajar	N/A	N/A	N/A	1,1, N/A, N/A,1	N/A, N/A, 138	N/A, N/A, N/A	PK	Poor
Aya	N/A	N/A	N/A	1,1,1, N/A,1	N/A, N/A, 174	N/A, N/A, 182	BegK	Poor
Luciana	N/A	N/A	N/A	All 1	N/A, N/A 170	N/A, N/A, 186	PK, Beg1	Poor
Sirad	N/A	N/A	N/A	N/A	N/A, N/A, N/A	N/A, N/A, 154	N/A	Poor

Note: N/A indicates that the test or test section results are unavailable due to factors such as the student's arrival date, attendance on testing day or lack of valid data.

Reading Clinic and assessed at the middle or end (or both) points of the year, the average gain was nearly one grade level and, for those present for the entire academic year, nearly a grade and a half. Thus, Mr Smith's and Ms Johnston's assertions of 'fabulous' growth are partially warranted.

Complicating this picture is a discussion of effect size with the MAP data. Effect size is a useful measure of growth that has started to be used to avoid 'the slippery slope of significance' in social science research due to the fact that large populations can more easily generate low p values, and then lead to dichotomous declarations that a certain result is 'statistically significant' rather than a more continuous understanding of 'the amount of something that might be of interest' (Cumming, 2011: 51). Effect size is traditionally measured by Cohen's d, calculated by taking the difference in the means of two groups divided by their pooled standard deviation (Cohen, 1988).

Therefore, considering only the group that was in the program for the entire year, the effect size given through Cohen's d was 0.693. Interpreting effect size can be tricky, and Cohen initially gave levels of small at 0.2, medium at 0.5 and large at 0.8. Seen in this light, the result for this group is relatively strong, commensurate with Mr Smith's and Ms Johnston's interpretation. However, Plonsky and Oswald's (2014) meta-analysis of effect sizes in the SLA field argues for interpreting values of 0.6 as small, 1.00 as medium and 1.40 as large when considering within-group comparisons (Plonsky & Oswald, 2014: 889). Seen in this light, the Lab program's results should be considered much more modestly. However, stepping back further, one must question whether the program goals of students achieving a 3rd grade reading level in one year is realistic. The norms set for the MAP by NWEA in 2015 for RIT score for the Spring 3rd grade reading level is 198.6. For the students in the focal group, who had an initial RIT slightly above 160, to achieve at or near this result would require an effect size of over 2, well beyond Plonsky and Oswald's review of what can be expected. This is perhaps confirmed by the Dominie results where the highest growth for a focal student, Maria, with an initial 'pre-K' was 'beginning 2nd' and, beyond the focal group, only two 9th grade students who started at 'pre-K' reached into the 3rd grade reading levels.

Thus, these test results do show that student learning as measured by English reading development is happening; however, the gains fall short of the stated program targets, and perhaps more troubling are those cases where students documented no or even declining growth across the year. These results prompt two big questions: (1) Are the stated goals realistic for this population? (2) Would other program features accelerate growth?

Conclusion

The implications of the program design and student outcomes recall the complexity of this program's work but also some of the broader issues involved in working with adolescent newcomers. These are highlighted by the fact that many actors are aware of program gaps and their consequences, as evidenced from this statement from Ms Cabot.

> Brian: The class sizes is, I don't know how students can really move along, except within the context of just kind of what goes for schooling in some ways, like just progress, coming to class, move along, and so on.
> Ms Cabot: Limp along, which is what it ends up being.
> (Ms Cabot, personal communication, June 29, 2017)

However, Ms Cabot points out that, without some broader shift in the program, these issues are likely to remain.

> Ms Cabot: To me, I think it's a structure thing and I think that's something that we at [the program] can fix. The problem is getting everybody on board with the same idea and it's like too many cooks in the kitchen. (Personal communication, June 29, 2017)

This quote dovetails with statements made by Mr Smith during my final interview in June 2017. Despite the fact that his expertise is not in SLA and it is highly unlikely that he has read the Plonsky and Oswald article and considered its implications for management of the program, he has a clear awareness that the program 'isn't there yet' in its quest to discover how to ensure the best possible outcomes for this student population. However, Ms Cabot's comment that the various 'cooks in the kitchen' may feel they are working at cross-purposes must be seen in the context of Ohio's 'flexibility' which allows, even promotes, a range of program activities and allocation of resources that may not be well suited to the adolescent newcomer population.

In conclusion, the fundamental argument of this chapter is a belief that all students, even those who have never set foot in a formal learning environment, who have physical or mental differences or who have manifold external or legal pressures on them, can learn well in environments that are designed for them, staffed by qualified individuals and adaptive to their needs. The next chapter will take up the issue of the program's future trajectory and consider the ways of, and possible barriers to, supporting all learners equitably and effectively.

Note

(1) See Table 3.3 for a summary of the student assessments.

4 Aspirations for Better Program Futures

> Every minute is precious.
> Ms Popov to focal students, February 15, 2017

> If you cannot measure it, you cannot manage it. ... If all you have is a hammer, everything looks like a nail.
> Wagner, 2017: 239–240

Overview

There are no sure things in life; there are only probabilities. This is one of the challenges in education and even sociological or journalistic thinking, as Nate Silver (2017) discussed in the context of the election of Donald Trump. Just as Trump's 2016 election seemed (or was presented by writers as) improbable, this outcome was within the available polling at the time even if it was among the more unlikely outcomes.

This actual result led to, among Democrats especially, a number of explanations discussing everything from sexism in US society, the role of Russian interference on the broader electorate, the Clinton campaign's decision to essentially ignore Wisconsin and James Comey's last-minute statements about Hillary Clinton's email investigation, to the aforementioned immigration trends causing the White racial resentment and backlash embedded in many of Trump's statements connecting to the overt xenophobia and racism of the alt-right, Richard Spencer or the Charlottesville attacks. If there is a key takeaway at this point, it is a growing awareness that seemingly small factors impact outcomes, and when some or all of these are pushed with intensity, the improbable can become reality.

This insight connects well to the pseudonymous 'Youth English Services' (YES) program. Just as Beatriz' fall from the 'High' group to the 'Low' group is improbable based on most theories available in sociocultural learning theory, SLA or immigration patterns, it happened, and the factors that contributed to this are recognizable in retrospect – a lack of a supportive peer environment and active or passive oppression from a same-language peer leading to a decrease in investment. In turn, Zahra's situation, briefly mentioned above, is equally improbable. Zahra was an 18-year-old Somali woman without home language literacy or formal education. She had spent many years in Ethiopia as a refugee but either had not enrolled in or had been denied access to formal education. She did not have home language literacy and did not report being bi/multilingual in Amharic or other Ethiopian languages. However, when she entered school in the Spring semester she became conversant in English relatively quickly, demanded and received extra help and support from the teachers and, at the end of the year, was on a path towards academic success with decent grades in all courses, even As in English and Reading Clinic. On the other hand, many of the trajectories above are consistent with predictions. Maria and the other students with home language literacy and prior educations were progressing in their language and content knowledge, whereas Salah, Mateo, Abdullah and a few others without these factors were struggling or had even given up.

However, despite the unpredictable nature of the world, social scientists, educators, politicians and others remain stubborn in their hope and belief that, if only the right systems and incentives can be found for general or specific populations, good things can happen. For progressives today, this might mean a more just distribution of income and wealth, efficient and high-quality human services and rising standards of living. Conservatives might share in these goals broadly but foreground other priorities or prefer indirect (i.e. non-governmental) methods to achieving them. This chapter focuses on this reflective and forward-looking spirit and will first discuss the current structure of the program and the various imagined futures the program actors – from the students to the director – envision or hope for to make the program more responsive to the students' needs. Then, I will critically assess these and offer my own opinion and evidence. Finally, I will discuss some of the personal, ideological and structural challenges to achieving this vision.

Returning to the calligraphic metaphor, this chapter reminds us that art (and education) is a constant process in which certain elements may seem beautiful or compelling to some but not to others. Moreover, the metaphor reminds us of the role of power in creating change – no-one, absent a revolutionary situation, can climb on a ladder and repair, remove or modify the calligraphy on Topkapi Palace without the permission of some higher authority. However, shifts do happen as tastes evolve and, critically, new actors bring forth visions of beauty that represent and enrich the human experience.

Visions of Changes to Current and Future Programming

The previous chapters outlined some of the program changes over time, and Ms Cabot's reflection on how Lab students used to be sorted into three groups by English reading level is a useful starting point for this section. The challenge here was that, as the students matriculated to the next level of the program, the academic distances between the students were only exacerbated. The realization that this tracking apparatus was contrary to the overall goals of the program led to the current change where Lab students would be broadly defined as newcomers with below 3rd grade English reading levels. If any student was initially placed in Lab but shown to have a stronger reading level, they could be moved to Core or even out of YES altogether. This happened to several students, particularly in the first three months of the program, and is indicative of the new program goal to transition students to the mainstream environment as quickly as possible. However, once these initial issues were settled, the Lab sections focused on the language and content necessary to transition to the Core level.

This section explores the various recommendations for program improvement made by actors across the program's contexts. These comments have been implied previously but will be more fully examined here. The evidence draws on interview data, whether semi-formal, audio-recorded interviews or shorter talks in class, in meetings or in other contexts. Specifically, throughout the research I asked actors two questions: (1) what changes to the program would they like to see based on current resources; and (2) if there were a modest increase in resources, how would they use them. I will report the responses in a manner similar to the above by first describing recommended changes to the overall program and then focusing on the issue of languaculture and prior educations.

General program changes

The proposed changes to the program include three key themes: (1) improving the overall environment; (2) focusing resources where they are most needed; and (3) developing new trajectories for student development. The first theme involved a broad range of recommendations. One of these, improving the linguistic landscape by repainting the building, refurbishing the inner courtyard and putting up more distinct markers of the program's identity, has already been implied through Ms Johnston's statement about the maps above and even realized in the subsequent years. Again, as the program has recently moved to the new building, this type of work is sorely needed to create an environment that students would immediately recognize as supportive of their backgrounds and languages.

The next area includes extracurricular support systems such as school counselors, after-school activities, school clubs, sports and summer programs. The issue of overworked school counselors, nurses and psychologists is a broad complaint and challenge across the US where many of these social service providers have hundreds of students in their caseloads. In terms of extracurricular activities, these were regular features of the previous school but were removed as part of the downgrade to program status. Thus, issues with bussing or funding for after-school staffing make this a larger logistical task demanding more human resources. A similar issue extends to sports, in that the program status of the school connects the students administratively to their home schools from which they are, in practice, separated. Thus, as in the case of Salah above, although it might have been theoretically possible for him to join the swim team at his home school, in practice this was very difficult due to transportation issues in addition to the social challenge of playing sports at a school that the student does not actually attend. On the other hand, there are some internal opportunities for the school to develop engaging programming such as student clubs that might work during lunch hours or the students' free periods. For example, the program already had a 'Service Above Self' program that generally worked with Core students; the only challenge from the perspective of the Lab students is that participation in this club was informally restricted to students with more advanced English ability. Beyond the school, there are manifold opportunities for nonprofit or community-based organizations to provide extracurricular activities during after-school or summer periods. Indeed, one local organization ran an after-school program primarily for the Bhutanese refugee population and hired Mr Dahal as its site coordinator. The primary challenge with these programs is ensuring that the students who most need the support are enrolled in addition to those who are already doing well and seeking further enrichment.

The third area would impact the students' trajectories in the program. Mr Smith, as the director of ESL, is fundamentally concerned with improving the students' English ability so they can access the opportunities offered by the broader district. Throughout our conversations, he expressed some frustrations and reservations with the current model whereby the students move from YES to sheltered sites in mainstream urban schools. These schools, in his perspective, are areas where ESL students struggle with 'General Education' teachers who do not understand ESL issues, direct or indirect racism or xenophobia from the students, and a bewildering social culture in schools with more than 2000 students. Thus, Mr Smith and the district are working on improving two trajectories for YES students.

The first is a smoother transition or connection to the district's vocational programs. Mr Smith feels that many of YES's students would appreciate a pathway to a program that would not only confer high school graduation but also prepare them directly for a career in an upwardly mobile field such as education, construction or health care. However, the challenge for Mr Smith and the district is, similar to mainstream programs, ensuring that these vocational programs are also aware of the issues YES's students might bring in terms of English language acquisition and bilingual learning strategies. Supporting migrant families is also a challenge in addition to other logistical issues such as transportation to and from YES, assigning academic credits across programs and sharing staff. Although vocational programs should not be seen as a panacea for this population (Salerno & Kibler, 2015), as Maria implied above about Mateo, this type of pathway might be appreciated by some students.

The second pathway is creating a direct connection to the district's magnet high school which is focused on international languages and global issues. Currently, the students in the three bilingual elementary programs for Spanish, French and Chinese matriculate directly to this school. Other district students can attend the school via the school choice lottery, and the goal is to add YES students as a third population that would both contribute to and benefit from the schools' bilingual and global focus. The district's master plan during 2016–2017 was to build a new complex that would co-locate YES and the international high school on the same site, allowing for intentional sharing of space and time so that the focal students have access to target-language peers and the international school could also benefit from YES students' emergent or experienced bilingualism. At the time of writing, this vision has partially been achieved with the co-location of YES and the international high school at the same site; however, the possibility of razing and rebuilding remains a future goal. This arrangement should be an improvement over the current 'mainstream' focus and would address the 'High' group students' concern about lack of access to a 'normal' school with target-language peers.

The second broad theme is focused on the distribution of classroom resources at YES. The first issue here is simply class size. Virtually all actors, particularly Ms Popov due to her having several combined classes of nearly 30 students throughout the year, cited the challenge of teaching language and content in a large classroom. Ms Lincoln felt that this was such a significant issue that she was planning on writing her doctoral dissertation on the relationship between class sizes, ESL students and educational attainment (e.g. grades, MAP, OELPA, AIR, etc., scores). More generally, Ms Cabot and others simply wished for class sizes to remain in the 20–25 students range, particularly if the teachers would not have the support of instructional assistants, which was the second issue.

As mentioned above, Mr Smith had made the rather surprising decision early in the year to allocate all the bilingual instructional assistants to the Reading Clinic. He made this decision based on his perspective that the assistants were often not used well by the teachers, being asked, for example, to make copies or input attendance rather than actively engaging in instruction. Although few teachers disputed this rationale directly to me, the decision did create some confusion and friction in the program. Ms Cabot, for example, often complained that she was not prepared for this situation and struggled to adapt. She specifically missed the instructional assistants' ability to work with a small group of students or to help new students make their Word Study notebooks, homework folder or other basic classroom elements that both take time and cause confusion for new students. Thus, most actors wished for either a general increase in the number of instructional assistants or, failing that, for some proportion to return to the classroom. However, the basis for the reallocation of these was sometimes unclear. For example, Ms Lincoln or Ms Grey simply mentioned adding more assistants; on the other hand, Ms Cabot stated that some instructional assistants should remain focused on the Reading Clinic and some should be allocated to the Lab sections.

> Ms Cabot: So, if we could pull back some, not all, but some of the assistants, back to Lab, at least in English, that would be really helpful, because we also this year, we also lost 30 minutes of English everyday. And yes, we have Reading Clinic, but it's not the same quality as, I guarantee, these two periods right in a row. Or at least, or maybe one before lunch and one after lunch, that's fine, but I'm guaranteed these two periods, solid with these kids, and that extra 30 minutes goes a long way if you don't have an assistant. So getting a few of the assistants back, and then really focusing on the lowest level kids for Reading Clinic, because I think that will help accelerate them, especially kids who are pre-literate, who are learning the alphabet for the first time ever in any language, those kids, it just takes them much, much longer to get anywhere with the language and with the reading. Usually, they get the oral language pretty quick, but their reading skills, their literacy skills, it just takes such a long time. (Personal communication, October 28, 2016)

Implicit here is that the Core students, with their improved English ability, have less of a need for the assistants than the 'pre-functional' Lab students. This is a perspective that I generally agree with, which will be elaborated more below.

Languaculturally specific changes

The issue of languaculturally specific changes essentially addresses two concerns: (1) helping students to have access to target-language peers; and (2) the SLIFE or home language literacy issue. The first issue has already been addressed above in large part through the various possibilities for clubs, after-school programs and especially the co-location of the international high school and YES. However, the issue of how to support SLIFEs or students struggling with home language literacy remains challenging.

As discussed above, students in the 'Mid' or 'Low' groups often have some challenges in the program related to their level of prior education or home language literacy. Unfortunately, due to the program's English-centric nature, particularly in terms of initial intake and English-only language assessments, these issues are basically ignored. As Ms Lee indicated above, even a face-to-face test such as the Dominie can struggle to give any indication of the students' capabilities. Thus, students who do not perform well on this test acquire a host of labels, from the more institutional 'pre-functional' to Ms Lee's informal 'very very low' (p. 88). Despite this institutional blind spot, the program has both adopted and imagined various ways to support SLIFEs. The adopted methods include all the programming and the suggested changes mentioned above in addition to more specific initiatives such as cultural orientation classes that cover 'basic' issues such as how to walk safely home on the sidewalks or various aspects of personal hygiene.

However, Ms Cabot had perhaps the most focused idea about how to support SLIFEs, who 'we've never been very good at figuring out' (Personal communication, June 29, 2017), with a 'self-contained' class that had existed in the program before and that she would like to resurrect. The idea is to create a 'newcomer center within a newcomer center' which would have the students spend all day in one classroom as they develop the basic knowledge – letters, phonemic awareness, etc. – to join the Lab class.

Ms Cabot: We need to really deal with the problems that we have with kids with the interrupted educations who need more very, very foundational skills. Those kids if they don't get it quickly and right away, I think they struggle for a very, very long time. We know from research that the newcomers struggle no matter what. They all as a group, they struggle and they struggle for a long time but I think we could do a much better job of giving them foundational skills, if we were able to identify them, and then, okay, (names two teachers, including herself), why is what you do with those brand new kids and what we usually call self-contained, why is it that? Is it because they're with the same teacher all day, they're not worrying about transitions, and they are really focusing on foundational skills all together, and they're not getting just 10 or 20 minutes of the teacher's time every week, they're getting concentrated attention? ... That's why it was called self-contained because it was like an elementary classroom. I think maybe they switched, maybe they did, like one teacher did the English and History stuff because on this schedule, you have to make it still official individual classes, but then, maybe they had a teacher who did science and math, so they flipped some. The more they did with one teacher, so it's like an elementary class in structure and so in a way, even if the class is really big, the teacher has fewer students so they can really focus in because maybe they only have two different groups. (Personal communication, June 29, 2017)

This idea may have some merit and clearly Ms Cabot felt that it addressed aspects of SLIFEs' needs. However, stepping back from these discussions, what the program actors are essentially describing is a move away from a current Lab (and broader program) structure that treats the 'High-Mid-Low' students in the same way to a tripartite program

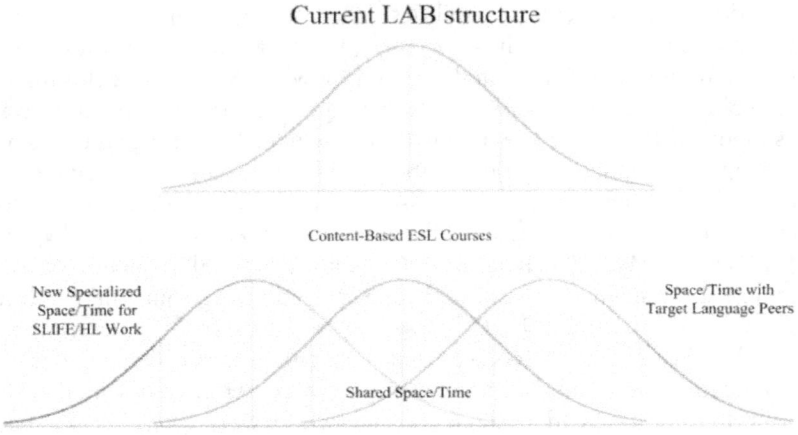

Figure 4.1 Current and envisioned future Lab structure

structure where the core content-based ESL courses remain but the 'Low-SLIFE' students have some specialized programming and the 'High' students some access to target-language peers. Figure 4.1 imagines these theoretically overlapping program structures.

A key point that this figure shows is the program's realization that long-term segregation of the students in space and time is undesirable and that intentionally designing opportunities for general collaboration in addition to specialized programs or experiences is key. Thus, although Ms Cabot's recommendation of the self-contained classroom may be desirable in some ways, it may not meet the approval of Mr Smith or other program actors concerned about students being placed into a class or program without clear learning goals, exit criteria or access to more knowledgeable peers. In other words, the self-contained idea might easily be countered or defeated by issues of tracking and segregation, which have been shown across multiple contexts to be deleterious to student progress. Thus, this recommendation and others must be interrogated critically based on this book's focus – the degree to which the students' languacultures are integrated into YES across multiple contexts.

Critical Reflections and Recommendations

This book has made a number of claims that are now necessary to explain directly and evaluate critically. These extend across contexts and consider change across time:

- The 'flexible' approach to LEP programs in Ohio is inadequate and not aligned with current research on bilingual programming and support of languaculturally minoritized groups.

- The district's ESL program's interpretation of Ohio's 'flexibility' by implementing an English-centric set of programs is based on and reinforces an English-centric ideology that dominates across program structures and practices. This, in turn, is inadequate and unreflective of current research and trends.
- This English-centric approach may be navigable for some students but is wholly inadequate and even harmful for others, especially SLIFEs or students who have not developed home language literacy.
- The results of the English-centric approach may appear robust under some measures, but when understood in the proper context are poor or lukewarm at best.
- The English-centric approach blinds the program to a key factor, home language literacy, which could reorganize program structures in a more efficient and equitable manner.
- The English-centric approach also blinds the program to the range of bi/multilingual practices occurring on the margins that, if recognized and consolidated, might support students more robustly.

In this section, I will turn a critical eye onto the program in light of the statements above and argue that one critical factor – greater attention to the home language and literacy specifically – would have impacts across the program and might even make certain aspects of the work easier.

> In all districts, it is important to identify newcomer students early in the school enrollment process. In approximately half of the programs that participated in our survey, this takes place at the district intake or registration center. Some parents and children find out about a local newcomer program through the media or by word of mouth through friends, former newcomer students, and family members. In many cases, enrollment of refugee newcomers is often facilitated by staff from the refugee resettlement agency. During registration, students and parents complete a home language survey. If they indicate that they speak a language other than English in the home, their English language ability is assessed. If it is determined that students have had no education or interrupted formal schooling, an evaluation of their academic skills in the native language is conducted *when possible*. (Short & Boyson, 2012: 11, italics added)

> They (SLIFEs) must first develop basic literacy, in their home language *if possible*, and definitely in English ... *wherever possible*, based on district resources and public policy, heritage language classes and/or bilingual classes are invaluable. (Custodio & O'Loughlin, 2017: 10, 100, italics added)

These quotations, the first taken from the national research on newcomer programs and the second from a recent book on supporting SLIFEs, are certainly useful for general program management; however, my criticism is with the combined phrasing 'when, if, or wherever possible' and the English-centric ideology that it encodes. Both of these perspectives treat knowledge of the students' home language literacy ability and provision of home language classes as something optional rather than something essential to effective and equitable program management. Moreover, as has been argued above, this approach ignores critical facets of the students' background, is dismissive of important language acquisition theories such as transfer and downplays critical differences between the students in the program.

Indeed, combining English and home language assessment, particularly home language literacy, is essential to the equitable and efficient support of students. Even YES's rudimentary home language test offered would have helped distinguish students in need of interventions such as the Reading Clinic or home language classes from those who would benefit from, for example, greater exposure to advanced classes or target-language peers, therefore helping to improve the efficiency of program interventions. For instance, there were only three students among the first group of focal students to arrive from August to October – Salah, Iman and Tara – who scored 'pre-K' on the Dominie as well as demonstrating poor home language literacy. However, by only focusing on the Dominie's 'pre-K,' 11 students – Gabriela, Lina, Carla, Maria, Tara, Salah, Beatriz, Omar, Iman, Hayat and Francisco – were placed in the Reading Clinic. Alternatively, more borderline students with home language literacy and low Dominie scores such as Puspa, Dhan or Abdullah could have been included in the Reading Clinic. This focus would have not only directed support to students more in the 'Mid' or 'Low' categories but also led to a dramatic gain in human resources with the instructional assistants, allowing them to assist Lab classes, improve the intake process or design bilingual materials. This is not to argue that the 'High' group students who did receive the Reading Clinic are not worthy or would not benefit from small-group interventions; however, in a program where human resources are often stretched, developing the ability to focus interventions where they are most needed is critical. In this case, considering both English and home language ability for intervention selection would have achieved this.

Home language literacy assessment would certainly improve the program's understanding of the students and help tailor interventions. However, this book also argues that, for many if not all students, home language classes would be critical. This point can be warranted based on a host of factors including transfer theory, efficient identification of possible learning challenges and general support of languaculturally diverse students. Most importantly, study of the home language need not be separated from learning English but can certainly be in parallel, reminiscent of one-way or transitional bilingual education. For example, the school could organize the schedule so that students, particularly those with a demonstrated lack of home language literacy, have a home language class as their first period homeroom. This could not only address issues of literacy but also improve the efficiency of explaining administrative information, announcements, rules and so on. Moreover, home language classes would have the best chance to more quickly identify learning challenges with students. For example, although I had some indications of Salah's (or Abdullah's or even Hajar's) learning issues, a bilingual teacher or assistant such as Ms Abadi, in partnership with qualified staff such as a counselor, psychologist or therapist, could certainly have made more grounded and documented assessments about his language ability or cognitive development, thus speeding up the provision of any necessary special services. Indeed, it is difficult to understand how these assessments could be made outside of the home language.

Although home language assessment and targeted interventions for those with demonstrated home language literacy gaps would be a critical change, home language courses for all students would likely be beneficial, and students with more developed home language literacy could be a support to those who are still developing in this area, so it might be preferable to organize the schedule in that manner. This is particularly the case with YES in that, in contrast to less well-developed programs, the human resources exist in terms of teachers or bilingual instructional assistants who are skilled in the home languages of the majority of the students. If necessary, the school could reach out to community groups or even qualified parents to help facilitate these courses. This is not to say that home language courses would be a panacea or easy to implement; certainly manifold challenges would arise in terms of finding or developing educational resources, deciding what literacy practices to develop with primarily oral home languages, understanding and supporting multiple varieties of a given named/national language and documenting student progress across time. However, I argue that this would ultimately lead to greater understanding of the students' backgrounds and create new opportunities to assess and build on their prior knowledge.

It is in this light that I am skeptical of Ms Cabot's idea for the self-contained classes. It is hard for me to understand or support the expenditure of key human resources – highly qualified bilingual teachers – to work with a heterogeneous group of SLIFEs using English-centric pedagogies. Even if these teachers used the students' home languages considerably to help them make meaning, it begs the question as to why the resources would not simply be organized for home language coursework at the same time as the SLIFEs are integrated into the broader Lab coursework structure.

I am sensitive to the challenges of providing home language courses in the superdiverse context – as Ms Lincoln says, 'First of all, we just have too many languages' (Personal communication, March 29, 2017). However, looking across the focal group and considering issues of efficiency and human resources to support a translanguaging pedagogy, it may not be necessary for each national or named language – Spanish, Portuguese,

Somali, Arabic, Nepali, French or Swahili – to be isolated and given one specific class, but rather for students to be grouped by language family or broader linguistic or geographic affiliations. For example, the Spanish and Portuguese emergent bilinguals could be combined to draw on their shared linguistic repertoires. A similar situation might exist for any Hindi, Nepali or Urdu emergent bilinguals in the school. Alternatively, there are some students who are already experienced bilinguals learning English who could make some choices. For instance, Gloire and Belvie speak Swahili and Kibembe at home and know French as an academic language. Depending on the number of these multilingual students' languages, their personal preferences about which language(s) to develop further and the availability of teachers, these students could fit into a number of home language classes. Of course, there might be some challenging situations such as Somali-ethnic students who speak Maay Maay, or Central or South American students who speak Indigenous languages, but these could be further differentiated with available teachers/assistants, new staff hired or community connections made to support these students.

Moreover, these changes would likely have ripple effects across the program and encourage broader conversations about how to support the students' home languages more effectively. This labor would spur the identification and use of bilingual materials, including those embedded in the websites and other materials the teachers already use. It would create synergies with the other bilingual programs in the district and perhaps attract new students and professional staff. In broad terms, it is impossible to predict what this shift would bring, and of course not all changes would necessarily be positive. Some students might feel an additional academic burden of developing their home language in parallel to English. Families that have invested heavily in coming to the US might question the validity of learning or developing the home language when English is so clearly necessary for social success. Moreover, it is possible that this shift might, if made more public, incur various backlashes or that the results might be lukewarm, prompting some doubt about the return on investment.

However, my perspective is that this program change is the 'low hanging fruit' with the most theoretical weight to make a significant impact on the program's efficiency and equity. On the other hand, implementing this change will require confronting the significant issue of ideology because, without a more coherent approach, much conflict and confusion may occur.

Challenges to Change

There is no doubt that a shift to a more languaculturally oriented space is necessary. However, even if the ideological issues can be overcome, which seems possible in that no actors expressed hostile opposition to home language support, just some hesitation about how to implement the approach given the program constraints, perhaps the most significant issue is micropolitical or, put more simply, the challenge of collaboration. Here there are three broad and intertwining issues: interpersonal communication, staffing and leadership.

> Based on what we have, I would love to see my teachers collaborate more to make sure that the content that they're teaching in their rooms interconnects a little better because they don't have another teacher. We don't have it, we don't have that resource. We've given them as many resources we can technology wise, given them as many resources we can, materials whatever they needed, we've tried to give them as far as physical resources. However, I would love to give them more time or even get their buy in to meet together to do interconnected methods and not to continue teaching in silos. Because then, I think, it would be so much more rich in learning English. (Ms Johnston, personal communication, March 29, 2017)

> Ms Popov and I walk together down the hall, and she says (about a wide ranging discussion in the Teacher-Based Team meeting about testing, allocation of instructional assistants, district/state advocacy, and about bilingual options), 'There's always lots of talk like this every year, but things don't happen because of practicalities' and adds, 'There's always lots of ideas, but there's little change,' stating that this kind of pattern has been going on for about 15 years. (Fieldnotes, December 8, 2016)

Any institution struggles with interpersonal conflict and micropolitical challenges. At YES, however, these issues are perhaps compounded by the diversity of the staff, the hierarchical arrangements from administration to students, pay inequalities and the stress of an environment that is perceived to be constantly changing and under-resourced. For example, Ms Lincoln said in the December 8, 2016 meeting that she felt there were 'the children, step children, and outcasts' in the district's schools, with YES being one of the outcasts. These issues can lead to a feeling of disjointedness or even conflict as the program shifts. For example, schedule changes made in the online learning management system by the school counselors at the beginning of the 2nd semester caused such problems with the grading interface that Mr Barre became angry during the weekly Teacher-Based Team meeting, blamed Ms Fey, one of the school counselors, and left the meeting early. As I followed up after the incident, both Mr Barre and Mr Shahiya explained that these issues between themselves and Ms Fey were longstanding, stemming from a perceived lack of professionalism in addition to communication ability rather than issues of gender, race or ethnic background.

Thus, with a well-established program it is likely that certain patterns would emerge, just as Ms Popov mentions above. For her, many things could be done that would be 'just common sense' (she used this phrase at least three times in meetings, on January 12, 19 and 26), such as some kind of home language classes, having instructors in the program who reflect the languacultural or ethnic backgrounds of the students, not giving Fs to students who come at the end of a grading period, or having reasonable class sizes. However, programs must and do evolve, and Mr Smith, responding to his perception that more bilingual approaches and staff are desirable, expressed in both formal and informal interviews that hiring bilingual staff, whether new teachers or instructional assistants, was a goal, but not one without some barriers. One of these is the program's English-monolingual teachers who, while they have certainly developed a certain expertise in teaching English and working with languaculturally diverse students, lack the broader linguistic repertoire to support students and might be better suited to working with more English proficient students in 'mainstream' schools or other contexts. However, many actors such as Mr Smith and Ms Lincoln made clear that these teachers were unlikely to accept such a move because the 'mainstream' schools were seen to be more difficult environments to work in due to school violence, drugs, poverty, etc. Mr Smith makes this situation clear:

Mr Smith: Of course, it (improving the program) would require the addition of course, first people that could speak the language, teachers that could speak that language.

Brian: Which you have you got, you got the bilingual, some of the bilingual assistants could be like Ms Abadi, they're certified.

Mr Smith: They're certified. We have some of those things in place that we'd have to make, like some of those bilingual assistants teachers and things like these so as matter of things that we would have in place but see, what I would be afraid of, that would be just thinking right off the bat, that would be an all out war, within our own union and the teachers that we have here because they of course, what would the teachers think immediately, 'I'm not bilingual, you're trying to get rid of me out of my job.' That's an overall and see I immediately have to go to those things that you have to think about. It would be a good thing because we have those resources in place now maybe, we probably have pretty much of course, we have, we could cover the languages almost with what we have here. It's just that my problem with that would be the perfect scenario to just hire the ones we have, make them teachers and maybe we can work the schedule where we funnel, let's say Ms Abadi is an English teacher and (another monolingual English teacher) is an English teacher, that course can be set so that the kid has half and half and it can be blocked back to back. It's things that we could do in every area, we got we got Somali covered, we got Arabic covered, we got even that situation like for example, (names another bilingual assistant who speaks Haitian Creole, French, and Spanish) in French. We got a lot of things that covered. We got a lot of people that could get certified in the area which would be of course, better for them, be better for the school but then they've would open the door to a whole another situation, I mean just being honest.

Brian: I think you're right and I wonder though if it would be worked out because some of the teachers here I know that they're in ESL by default. They started off as English language arts, they started off as real science teachers and I wonder if they can move on like, 'Okay, I don't have to be an ESL teacher, I could go teach English language arts,' you don't think?

Mr Smith: That won't happen I'm just telling you Mr Seilstad. Right now you could probably offer most of these teachers here another 2,500 bucks a year and they wouldn't leave here because first of all, a lot of them know or in their mind they know it's better here and I know they wouldn't leave. I mean, let's take a virtue of just the tool in my process year after year now I've been back here. I was in, been in ESL really off and on from 2001 to 2009, so 12 out of my 16 years in the ESL. I'm going to be honest, and I've checked for sure, in the last four years it's only been one person of staff reduced themselves to leave here because they didn't like it. I can't remember ever from 2001, and I'm sure that maybe in some other places, but nobody from (the program's) staff reduced themselves. Nobody. Never happened. (Personal communication, November 17, 2016)

Thus, Mr Smith's non-confrontational and long-term approach is to gradually hire bilingual teachers or promote a bilingual assistant when a monolingual teacher retires or leaves. This approach may bear fruit, but it is unclear to what degree this will result in more direct support of the home language, particularly for Lab students. During the final interview with Mr Smith, he expressed satisfaction that the program was going to pilot Spanish and possibly Arabic home language classes but was unclear about who would be in the classes, how they would be selected and what the curricular goals would be. Overall, he felt that the Lab students need some focused attention.

Mr Smith: I have to be honest, I'm really, that's something that we probably, with my team, that we're probably going to have to address a little bit more because right now our main focus is always the second year students and leaving out. Realistically, when you look at it, we don't have it in place like we should. What's our goal, what's our focus on these LEP kids that we're getting in? Because we're going to have to do something because they're all pre-functional. If you don't get them now they're going to drop out, so, what are we going to do to make sure that these kids other than the focus here of two years is got to be tied around, of course, the two years of what we do here. I don't think we've addressed, that's something that they're going to have, probably going to have to sit down and address more because I don't think we have a true focus on what it should be or

> what we should be looking to get or getting what we need or where we need to get these kids in the two years that we have them. (Personal communication, June 26, 2017)

I concur with Mr Smith and am hopeful that these conversations will take place; however, as mentioned above, I am concerned that the overall framework of Ohio's deficit and English-centric approach, indexed in Mr Smith's use of 'LEP' and 'pre-functional,' will be a barrier, in addition to Mr Smith's and the other administrators' relative lack of knowledge about SLA and bilingualism, from both a personal perspective with none of them being bilingual, or a theoretical perspective with none of them having studied these issues in depth. Ms Sharp expresses this relationship between leadership, personal experience and academic training well:

> I think sometimes if you don't have a strong instructional background, if that's not your focus, then you can be a good administrator because you can follow all the things. I can organize a school, lunch, and the times and whatever. But you also have to be an instructional leader who understands the process of learning and especially schools like this, how do students acquire English? … it depends on again how well the administrators understand acquiring the second language and some of the implications from the research that's been done how to support them. (Personal communication, April 27, 2017)

This might be rather pessimistic about the school administration but, returning to the Goffman quote in Chapter 2 about assigning 'less praise and blame' to individual actors in a system, one must recall the general goals of the district's ESL program, of which Mr Smith had only recently taken control. Thus, one can hope that his curiosity and stated desire to adopt a more bilingual program model might lead him to explore other newcomer programs or states with similar demographic shifts. One example might be Minneapolis Public Schools which, rather than having an ESL department, has a 'Multilingual Department' (www.multilingual.mpls.k12.mn.us) articulating the following vision, mission and core values:

Vision: Every English Learner bilingual and biliterate, college and career ready

Mission: The Multilingual Department empowers educators and leaders to develop language-rich learning environments that raise the achievement of English Learners through:
- Consistent, high quality programming
- Research-based instructional strategies
- Shared accountability for student learning
- Affirmation and development of student, family, and community assets

Core Values: Our work is guided by the following values:
- Bilingualism is an asset
- All teachers are teachers of English Learners
- All staff are responsible for the success of English Learners
- Every parent is a partner

Conclusion

This connection to Minnesota and Minneapolis is relevant because this state too has been experiencing superdiverse shifts in the past 20 years but its vision for multilingual learners contrasts strongly with Ohio's. Each context and state is different, but it can be hoped that experience and exposure to the broader fields of adolescent newcomer programs, bilingual schools and even TESOL, which has consistently challenged monolingual bias and supported bilingual approaches (e.g. Auerbach, 1993; Cummins, 2007, 2009), may help to form new connections and understandings for Ohio and YES's actors which can impact overall program design, classroom pedagogy and learning outcomes.

Conclusion

Nelson Flores, through his blog, *The Educational Linguist*, recently raised the question, 'Do we need a revolution in educational linguistics?' in which he underlined that 'language education is a tool of social transformation' and that the policies and practices can be described on a continuum with the following five theories of change: assimilation, accommodation, evolution, transformation and revolution (Flores, 2019). Flores argues that a 'revolution' perspective holds that 'the foundation of mainstream schooling has historically and continues to be oppressive to language-minoritized students. Therefore, the only way to truly empower language-minoritized students is to completely restructure the institution.' I fully agree with Flores in this regard, in terms of both policy and practice, and believe that this restructuring should embrace multilingualism and reject linguistic hierarchies so that all people's languages and cultures can be reflected and developed throughout society and particularly in the (public) educational sphere.

Summary of Central Findings and Recommendations

This study had three key research questions about YES. First, how do YES's policies and practices support its students' home languacultures? Second, what are the students' outcomes in this context? Third, how do YES program actors envision program improvement? Following Flores' point above, this book argues that, despite the superdiversity of many regions and the potential of translanguaging pedagogy to serve adolescent newcomers well, the English-centricity of the US, Central Ohio and YES is minoritizing to its students and a significant barrier to the social and educational transformations necessary to support all students equitably and effectively. In terms of restructuring, the revolution that YES could engage in is a radical focus on understanding students' home language literacy as the key consideration in program design. Other factors such as English-language proficiency, prior education and the need for special services would then be considered appropriately as co-factors. Students' instructional time and space can then be organized to ensure appropriate, equitable and efficient development of the home language, English language and content knowledge. Moreover, this focus on home language literacy and instruction can help the program anticipate and respond thoughtfully and humanely to the various frustrations that may arise in and between adolescents, especially without resorting to suspensions or other punishments that reduce the potential for constructive dialogue and restorative justice. Finally, this shift can develop multilingual materials and learning ecologies that increase the possibility for students to benefit from instruction and, therefore, to progress academically towards the lives of dignity that they imagine for themselves.

Building on Figure 4.1 above and considering the specific flows and organizations of time and space and the allocation of resources, this revolution might include the following practical points related to program management and pedagogy:

- Assessing home language literacy at intake in parallel with English language proficiency. Many appropriate professional home language tests exist, but even YES's 'quick and dirty' test would provide some insight.
- Ensuring that, minimally, students without home language literacy receive direct instruction in it as part of their schedule. Ideally, all students have home language courses.
- Ensuring that all students have some instructional and recreational time with home and target-language professionals and peers, thereby promoting translanguaging spaces and pedagogies to support meaning-making.
- Anticipating normal adolescent frictions and frustration ranging from withdrawing socially to violent outbursts and responding proactively with dialogue and restorative justice rather than neglect or suspensions.

YES, in my analysis, is working in this direction, although some policies, practices and actors may not be perceived as revolutionary at the current moment. However, I do believe that the program and its actors understand and embrace the demographic changes brought by superdiversity and the pedagogical recommendations of translanguaging in a shared goal of creating equitable systems for all students. On the other hand, it remains clear that, although some promising practices exist, the English-centricity of the space is a barrier to equity and is not sufficiently challenged to move towards a true revolution. However, it is also important to remember that the program itself is not an island but is rather enmeshed in many other struggles.

Donald Trump and Anti-Immigrant Sociopolitics

Among these struggles is the shifting nature of US and global political discourse which was in high relief during the 2016–2017 research year. For many Americans, the election and administration of Donald Trump was

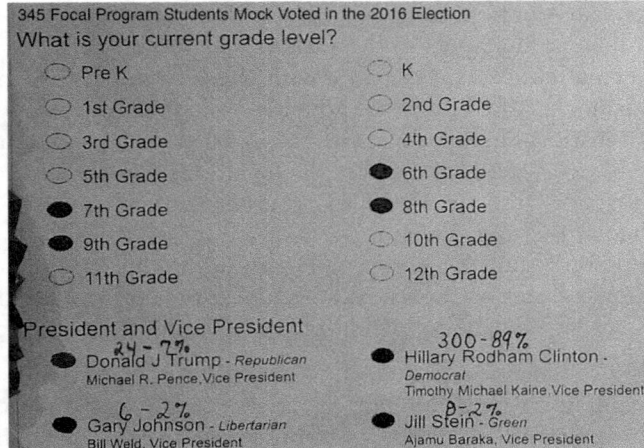

Figure C.1 Image from YES's mock 2016 election

a rude reintroduction to the politics of overt racism and White resentment. Although the voting patterns of all the program actors are not clear, the program held a mock election and the results profiled in Figure C.1 show the students' perspective quite clearly, with 89% voting for Hillary Clinton. Moreover, most conversations I had with other teachers, administrators, bilingual assistants or students tended to reflect this political alignment. Of course, the actual Ohio results put Trump over Clinton by ~8 percentage points, highlighting that, while the program, the focal city and the other major Ohio cities have many liberal elements, the rest of Ohio is considerably more conservative. As a response to this reality, Ms Cabot put up the sign shown in Figure C.2 outside her door immediately after the election.

Figure C.2 Sign Ms Cabot put up outside her classroom following the 2016 presidential election

Talk about Trump's victory within the school followed an arc similar to that in the broader society and media. At the beginning, many students and staff expressed their surprise but also hoped that Trump would pivot to the center and expressed a 'Let's wait and see' attitude. However, as the year went on and the first immigration ban was attempted, people's trust rapidly started to give way to frustration and fear. For example, Mr Barre, a Somali refugee who is now an American citizen with American citizen children, said that he was spending a considerable time explaining to them that neither they nor their father were going to be deported or rounded up, or at least not as long as some rule of law remained in the United States. However, many of the students with undocumented status expressed fear at this situation in different ways. One of them said that they regretted coming to the US at all. Moreover, the administration and counselors told me that they were encountering more students expressing stress or asking about legal options, and I often counseled people to visit local refugee support agencies' legal aid teams.

However, in many respects life at the program went on and the students continued to learn and interact. Sometimes these talks would intersect with Trump in ways that, like the *'chicki-chicki'* episode above, illustrate how students were making meaning out of their lives and situations in interesting and even amusing ways. For example, several of the male students enjoyed watching WWE videos on their phones after completing the class activities. Yadu loved Roman Reigns and often he, Jhuma and Mohammed would stage small mock battles between themselves, especially at the end of the school day. During one of these times, Omar came up to me, we started to talk about Trump's election, and he pointed out Trump's animosity towards Syrians and Arabs in general. Then, noticing Yadu's phone, he commented that Trump had been involved in professional wrestling earlier in his career and said, in Arabic, 'If only he had stayed with that.' I laughed and agreed.

Despite the legal challenges to Trump's travel bans, he, his advisors and his administration made slowing or even stopping immigration to the US a significant priority. They directly or indirectly questioned the legitimacy of most migration categories, including students, laborers, spouses, family reunification and refugees, in addition to their strong opposition to unauthorized migration or amnesty. Refugee resettlement, which impacts YES considerably, was officially reduced to admitting 40,000 refugees per year in 2018 and, as of writing, less than 20,000. This is down from the Obama-era high of 100,000 and far below the peak of over 200,000 that Ronald Reagan set. However, even this low number masks the indirect ways in which the administration impacted the process by closing resettlement offices worldwide, instituting wait periods and creating additional administrative hassles (Amos, 2018; Rosenberg, 2018; Weinstein & Ferwerda, 2018). As a result, actual refugee resettlement often did not even reach the assigned threshold.

These shifts, if they become long-term trends, would certainly impact YES, possibly causing it to close and merge students in 'mainstream' schools or to forego the new program trajectories that Mr Smith envisioned. Alternatively, these trends might have a positive impact on the program in that, given a reduction in the overall numbers, the program actors might be able to pause and critically reassess the program's approaches. Some of these changes have indeed happened – enrollment during Fall 2019 at YES was a little lower at 600 and the proportion is about 50% students from Mexico, Central and South America due to the reduction in refugee resettlement and the 'Muslim' ban. In addition, a potentially positive move is that the international high school has been co-located with YES, opening up opportunities for multilingual learning and peer interaction.

As of writing, the 2020 election of Joe Biden and Kamala Harris perhaps restores some hope for refugee resettlement and support of migrants more generally. However, it must be stressed that Ohio, again, voted for Trump by a significant margin. These realities underline the complex politics that surround YES in its quest to provide equitable educations to its students.

Coming Full Circle

In the Introduction, I emphasized that this book is meant to contribute to two central issues and goals. The first is the promotion of a global society where people can not only move freely but also be welcomed and assisted in their adaptation to new societal contexts and languages. Interwoven here is a two-sided goal: on the one hand, to support learners acquiring the dominant societal languages; and, on the other hand, to challenge the hegemony of these languages to support bi/multilingual societies and citizens. This book's engagement with an adolescent newcomer program in Central Ohio speaks to these issues in, I believe, profound ways. The creation of the program itself, despite the potentially discriminatory segregation of students, responds to the superdiverse changes in the region and points to a commitment of the public school district to welcome and support these global learners. On the other hand, despite an awareness of translanguaging and the imperative to support students' languacultural backgrounds, it is clear that the English-centricity of the state, district and program is limiting and reductive, masking or muting many exciting bi/multilingual approaches that could promote more equitable program designs and improve student outcomes.

My goal throughout this book has been to carefully document and acknowledge the broad challenges that this program is designed to address. I have a great deal of respect for all the program actors' experiences, reflective stances and goals for the future. In addition, it is important to celebrate the successes: at the time of writing, many of the focal students I am still in contact with have now graduated from high school, having shared pictures from their Covid-19 modified celebrations on social media. On the other hand, some of the other students such as Salah have long since dropped out and, while their lives are progressing in their own ways, I wonder what impact a more sustained and positive schooling experience might have brought.

I close with a final reflection on this book's calligraphic metaphor which strives to encapsulate so many of the book's issues: English-centricity, White mainstream schooling, academic language, superdiversity, translanguaging, culturally relevant and sustaining educations and so on. Throughout, I have tried to highlight that many parts of this work are difficult to discern or disappointing while, in contrast, much is admirable and even beautiful, pointing towards new and more equitable futures. Moreover, I am aware that the specific struggles and successes at YES are part of the broader narrative of US education described in Chapter 1. The current moment which is wrestling with Covid-19, the 2020 election aftermath, the Black Lives Matter movement, #MeToo and many other challenges underlines the ongoing imperative to enact 'difficult loving care' from 'both sides of the line' (García, 2020), and recalls similar yet distinct reflections from more than a century ago by W.E.B. Du Bois (1994 [1903]):

> The history of the American Negro is the history of this strife – this longing to attain self-conscious manhood, to merge his double self into a better and truer self. In this merging, he wishes neither of the older selves to be lost. He would not Africanize America, for America has too much to teach the world and Africa. He would not bleach his Negro soul in a flood of white Americanism, for he knows that Negro blood has a message for the world. He simply wishes to make it possible for a man to be both a Negro and an American, without being cursed and spit upon by his fellows, without having the doors of Opportunity closed roughly in his face. This, then, is the end of his striving, to be a co-worker in the kingdom of culture, to escape both death and isolation, to husband and use his best powers and his latent genius. (Du Bois, 1994 [1903]: 3)

These words, certainly written for a different time and context, remind us that, despite the centuries-long oppression inherent in America and its educational practices, including the English-centricity of YES and all the inequities embedded in mainstream education, 'academic' language, proficiency tests and so on, America does have much to offer YES's students and the world. On the other hand, this cannot be accomplished through assimilation, without challenging educational systems and actors to respect, engage and adapt to new students and communities. It is unachievable without a radical and consistent focus on understanding students' home languages, prior educations, current circumstances and future aspirations. However, if this can be achieved, a new picture of America and even of the world can and will emerge from this palimpsest, radiating, like our calligraphic metaphor, with dazzling and unexpected beauty.

Methodological Appendix

> To write an ethnography requires at a minimum some understanding of the language, concepts, categories, practices, rules, beliefs, and so forth, used by members of the written-about group.
>
> van Maanen, 2011: 13

Foundations for Research Questions: Before Method, Theory

Theory guides research. The Greek verb θεωρέω 'I look at/see' combines two other words, θέα 'a view' and ὁράω 'I see'. From this, theory involves seeing a phenomenon from a certain perspective or perspectives. This is especially important when considering human social research in contrast to behavioral and social science (Agar, 2013). The latter seeks to create a priori hypotheses, devise and conduct experiments to test them, and then report the results as clearly and objectively as possible. In contrast, the former approaches situations without specific hypotheses or categories and is often deeply invested in deconstructing these named categories, resulting in new, more finely tuned categories that could themselves be investigated or interrogated (e.g. Lee, 1994, on the category of 'Asian-American'). Most importantly, human social research is open to multiple variables drawing on different theories and conducted in the ecology of real life rather than a laboratory (Agar, 2013: 12–15; see also Bronfenbrenner, 1976, 1994). This requires an acknowledgement of, openness to and respect for the multiple voices that exist in human experience and, although one can develop this position from multiple sources, Bakhtin's (1982) writings about polyphony and dialogue are positive contributions in the analysis of, for example, how Dosteyvsky's characters were written to their fullest logical and emotional potential.

Thus, if human social research is something distinct growing from an essential respect for individuals, their lives and their voices, the next step is considering human relationships and the networks that create connections and meaning throughout life. These have been explored by multiple writers, with perhaps some of the most elaborate theories naming these connections as systems, actor-networks, webs of meaning or rhizomes (Bronfenbrenner, 1976, 1994; Deleuze & Guattari, 1987; Geertz, 1977; Latour, 2005). These approaches require the researcher to look widely for influences, to follow people and things closely, to document carefully and to be open to ideas and connections that may seem extraneous but that are nevertheless crucial to understanding. Sometimes this is quite random and difficult to imagine, but writers such as Larsen-Freeman (1997) in the field of language learning help one navigate the implications of chaos/complexity and how these manifest in dynamic systems that are changeable yet patterned and reactive to context (see also Blommaert, 2013a). The context of migration connects here, with Portes and Rumbaut (2001) suggesting that the outcomes for migrants are non-linear and segmented, forming new networks and possibilities through the processes of moving across borders, mixing and living within them or challenging their very existence, which writers such as Anzaldúa (2012) express so creatively and eloquently.

In sum, these broad perspectives insist on (1) valuing each human life and seeking to understand it as complexly as possible, (2) considering the importance of how humans create and use connections to other people, things and ideas as they make meaning of the world, and (3) being sensitive to the fact that small changes in individuals or their connections can have profound impacts at the individual, community or societal level. These fundamentals underpin much educational research and certainly this project. In contrast, with such a foundation, educational research involving, for example, classroom surveys or analyses of existing quantitative data seeking to understand the relationship between, for example, gender, race and final GPA become difficult to sustain. Although some answers to these questions would certainly be found, the remaining variance is usually quite high and therefore the explanatory power less convincing. This is not to say that these approaches are not useful, but what remains is a desire to have long-term engagement with people in a certain context while using methods that allow for robust recording and analysis of their activities. These allow for more nuanced understandings of how people understand themselves, their connections and their activities over time. In other words, this type of theoretical perspective is something different and has been described as 'mid-level' theory, which

> hovers just over the particularity of events, seeking to explain human social life as situated, contextualized, and indeterminate. As such, mid-level theory eschews the universal and instead theorizes a bounded series of social events as complexly and multi-leveled structured meanings. Rather than being inductive, an emphasis is placed on abductive reasoning and inferencing. (Newell *et al.*, 2015: 6–7)

This theoretical perspective informs this research project and has important implications for the methods I employ, combining institutional ethnography and classroom discourse analysis, in order to document, analyze and explain the interconnections among contexts and how these manifest in settings such as schools or regular events such as classrooms. However, another criterion remains important, the significance of the researched issue in context.

Research Rationale: Why the US? Why a Newcomer Program? Why Lab Students?

As mentioned in the Introduction, I came to The Ohio State University without a specific idea about what my focal research would be. In truth, I had been eager to spend a few years doing coursework in Ohio and then do fieldwork abroad, ideally in Morocco and/or perhaps other countries in the Middle East and North Africa, Europe or Sub-Saharan Africa where my languacultural abilities would be useful. I imagined researching a topic such as service-learning or civic education in the region, most likely focused on high school or higher education.

However, after arriving in Central Ohio and discovering the manifold issues around refugees and other migrants, I started to consider staying in the local region. This had obvious practical and financial advantages (I have a wife and young son whom I was not eager to uproot again for overseas research). Moreover, schools such as the newcomer program almost immediately became known to me in my first semester, and I started to adopt a position that I could do global research here in the Midwestern United States, a region that, due to superdiverse migratory flows, has been called 'The Middle of Everywhere' (Pipher, 2002). This perspective was reinforced in talks with my advisor who spoke about the enhanced research possibilities when staying in a region for several years versus spending a year (typical for Fulbright funding, for example) abroad and then 'coming home' to write up the research results.

Beyond these practicalities and an interest in supporting refugees and migrants, I was highly influenced by the classic piece by Laura Nader (1972) which encouraged students, especially anthropologists, to 'study up,' by which she meant that rather than sending students with dubious languacultural knowledge to learn about other societies, they might better profit by staying home and studying their own cultural and social institutions using similar anthropological tools. Moreover, these studies might help uncover many of the power structures and patterns at play, which would be scientifically interesting and also contribute to the functioning of democratic societies. This sentiment is closely connected to the field of institutional ethnography, in which researchers locate themselves in various businesses, groups, corporations, etc. and collect data using participant observation, interviews and artifact collection to explore not only 'What is happening here?' but also the perspectives of societally marginalized people (Forsythe, 1999a, 1999b; Gebhard, 2012; Harklau, 2007; Ó Riain, 2009; Olsen, 2008; Smith, 2006). This is quite important, not only because these organizations are large and complex, but moreover because they wield enormous power through their money and often multinational characters. Educational institutions are no exception, and my decision to pursue this research project is in part an attempt to follow Nader's advice while having my proverbial cake as well by researching in such a superdiverse environment. In addition, I felt that researching a particular group of students and their shared experiences, particularly through regular audio-video recording and participant observation of their classroom experiences, would allow for warranted claims about the interconnectedness of the institution and regular classroom activities (Bloome et al., 2005).

My focus on an adolescent newcomer program in Central Ohio is conscious because it is a public (i.e. taxpayer funded) response to a significant issue. In contrast, although I might have enjoyed, for example, researching private weekend *dugsi* classes with Somali or Arabic-speaking families, Nepali heritage language courses or the like, I felt that it was important to do research on the public education system for several reasons. The first is that, for most migrants and refugees, the public system is the one available to them (although public charters are also prominent locally and throughout Ohio, often attracting migrant or refugee students). Thus, the quality of the public spaces where they go to school must be high. Connected to this point, there is a narrative about public education in the US that has not always been positive. Indeed, public schools, especially since the 1980s, have consistently been positioned as 'at risk' (US National Commission on Excellence in Education, 1983), with myriad accusations, explanations or solutions being made for this, from blaming teachers and teacher unions (Kumashiro, 2012) to declines in funding for schools (Strauss, 2012) or lack of appropriate choices for parents, with responses such as magnet schools, charters or private school vouchers offered (Carey, 2017). Although the reality of these claims is often dubious in that measured learning has been improving in the US for several decades (Institute of Education Sciences, 2012), other well-publicized tests such as the PISA or TIMSS show that students in other nations now consistently outperform their US counterparts (e.g. Sparks, 2016). This contributes, among other factors, to a perception and discourse about failing public schools which has been used for decades for political purposes such as reducing/expanding school funding, teachers' unions or private or charter schools (Schneider, 2017). Although these trends are clearly part of the broader picture, this research was an attempt to consider how a specific public response, newcomer programs, to a pressing concern, rapid demographic change, was working in the Ohio context.

Initial Research Questions and Methodology: What Did I Want to Know? Why is Ethnography Well Suited for the Inquiry? What Kinds of Ethnography? How Does it All Fit Together?

In this section I describe both the guiding research questions and methods and the interplay between these questions and methods. In general, this research is commensurate with ecological approaches to educational research, with Bronfenbrenner (1976, 1994) being a key figure elaborating a research agenda focused on the connections and interactions between various 'systems' from the macro to the micro. This work has been extended to the multifaceted nature of language learning in that the macro level structure of various beliefs and value systems impacts the meso level structure of various sociocultural institutions and communities. These in turn impact the micro level of regular social activity between individuals which is in part moderated by neurobiological and cognitive activity. Most importantly, this is not a strictly hierarchical relationship with the macro determining the other levels; indeed, changes in individual cognitive understandings of phenomena or new social arrangements have the power to impact the entire system (The Douglas Fir Group, 2016: 25).

Connected to this final point is the role of time, or Bronfenbrenner's 'chronosystem' which represents 'change or consistency across time' within or across the contexts (Bronfenbrenner, 1994: 40) and is directly related to the notion of chronotope mentioned earlier, the combination of time and space linking history and momentary agency (Blommaert, 2015). This aspect underlines that any context and the activities therein are both the product of and reaction to the past, from the individual to the macro level, and these present contexts and activities will shape the future.

Given the weight of the available evidence that linguistically and culturally sustaining environments and pedagogies are best for linguistically and culturally minoritized groups, yet tempered by the fact that adolescent newcomer research is less robust and coherent than K-8 studies, the initial questions guiding the project were:

(1) How do the environment, actors and policies that Lab students encounter reveal ideologies about language and content learning for adolescent newcomers?
    (a) What national, state or district policies frame the program's goals and pedagogies?
    (b) How has the program evolved over time?
    (c) Who are the main actors, their trajectories to the program and their stated beliefs or ideologies about language and learning?
    (d) What does the linguistic landscape look like?
    (e) What policies and practices regulate student behavior?
    (f) What are the main classroom resources, instructional patterns and interventions or specialized programs?
    (g) From all these resources, patterns, policies and interventions/programs, what parts relate directly to the students' languacultural backgrounds?
(2) What outcomes are desired by the teachers and administration for the Lab students?
    (a) What are the broad learning and behavioral outcomes desired?
    (b) What are the specific learning targets?

(3) What outcomes actually manifest?
    (a) Student performance over time.
    (b) Learning gains through various assessments.
    (c) Focused cases of individual students.
(4) What future visions do actors have for a program like this?

Thus, in order to answer these questions, I deployed the traditional ethnographic toolkit of observation, interviews and artifact collection (Wolcott, 2001), linking the aforementioned institutional ethnography with discourse analysis of classroom events by using audio-visual recordings and participant observation of regular classroom activities, participant observation in institutional meetings, interviews with students, teachers, staff and administrators, and artifact collection from the classrooms, meetings and school environment.

Linking institutional ethnography and discourse analysis is important because very little research on newcomer programs has been done combining these approaches and methods. Although the work of Short and Boyson (2004, 2012) was instrumental in mapping out the broader institutional features of newcomer programs, it lacked some of the fine-grained and critical inquiry brought by other scholars looking at similar contexts and institutions (Harklau, 1994, 2000; Olsen, 2008). In addition, discourse analysis studies of newcomers in their contexts have been critical to underlining their challenges and opportunities in multiple contexts that range from difficulties in being seen and heard (L. Bartlett, 2007) to the potential dynamism of environments specifically designed to support newcomers and their multilingualism (García & Sylvan, 2011). Overall, it is critical, particularly in spaces where language and content learning is central, to link documentation and analysis of the broader institution's policies, actors or linguistic landscape to the classroom itself as the primary locus of learning and teaching. This permits a type of discourse analysis to emerge that is layered and complex, allowing for a

> reconceptualization of classroom SLA as an institutional phenomenon shaped by cultures and structures at work in educational systems. Such a reconceptualization is important because studies of classroom SLA, even those grounded in social orientations, have tended to decontextualize classroom discourses as isolated islands of linguistic practice without exploring the ways in which larger institutional practices associated with schooling shape those discourses. (Gebhard, 1999: 545)

This perspective, following broad orientations in sociocultural and cultural-historical theory, reminds researchers that institutions and learners have knowledges rooted in social and cultural practices that are not static, apolitical or ateleological. The issue then often returns to power and how it is distributed and practiced in a system, keeping in mind that while some hierarchical relationships exist here, all actors in a system have some power and various means to deploy it to achieve their ends. In educational spaces, perhaps the goal is that power should be used as 'caring relations' between learners, their teachers and the institution, although this is often not achieved (Bloome et al., 2005: Ch. 4).

With these theories as a foundation, I conducted the research using the following methods:

Method 1: Audio-video recordings of regular classroom activities

Qualitative research can often distinguish between what is actually happening and what people say is happening, otherwise known as the 'attitudinal fallacy' (Jerolmack & Khan, 2014). Participant observation combined with careful fieldnotes is a cornerstone of this work, but the advent of audio-video recording in educational environments allows for review and analysis of these recordings and has certainly revolutionized many aspects of educational research (Derry, 2007). This has been especially useful in discourse analysis or language-in-use research such as language socialization where a researcher relies on (1) a longitudinal study design, (2) field-based collection of naturalistic audio-video data, (3) a broad ethnographic perspective and (4) attention to micro and macro systems and the linkages among them (Garrett, 2008: 189–201).

Thus, a key method for addressing the first question was audio-video recordings of the four focal subject-area classrooms, English, math, science and social studies, where the Lab students spend the majority of their time while in school. In order to record what was happening there, I used one GoPro camera with a wide-angle lens to record video. At different times, I placed the camera in the room for a certain wide-angle shot or carried it close to students while they were working. In addition, I carried a small microphone to record focused conversations when the camera was set at too far a distance to capture useful audio. I recorded each content class at least once per week.

Thus, in terms of the research records, there are three strata. First were the large class activities, often teacher directed and where I could transcribe the discussions easily into English. Second were the focused conversations I had with students that were often in English or in the home language or mediated by another student or a digital assistant like Google Translate. As I would move throughout the room, I would often sit next to a student and record these focused conversations. Third were the student–student conversations that happened throughout the class time. These were often a product of the camera position – one day a predominantly Nepali group might be in the foreground and thus audible, and another day it might be a different group.

In addition to these four classrooms, I audio-video recorded the 'Reading Clinic,' a small-group intervention for students assessed as 'pre-K' on the Dominie assessment. The Reading Clinic was led by the team of instructional assistants, of whom many are bilingual and part of the

Methodological Appendix 171

Table A.1 List of teachers/instructional assistants involved in audio-video recordings

Name	Subject	Gender	Ethnicity	Time in program	Linguistic repertoire
Ms Cabot	English	Female	White American	15 years	English, some learning of Latin, German, French, Spanish
Mr Barre	Math	Male	Somali	16 years	English and Somali with advanced proficiency in Italian
Mr Shahiya	Science	Male	Somali	16 years	English, Somali, Arabic
Ms Popov	Social Studies	Female	Russian	17 years	English, Russian, Spanish
Ms Grey	Reading Clinic	Female	African-American	3 years	English
Ms Son	Reading Clinic	Female	Cambodian	3 years	English, Cambodian
Mr Dahal	Reading Clinic	Male	Bhutanese-Nepali	3 years	English, Nepali, Hindi, Dzongkha
Ms Tucek	English (long-term substitute for Ms Cabot)	Female	White American	2 months	English, some French learning

newcomer program's long-term effort to address the languacultural needs of the student body. Table A.1, a redaction of Table 2.1 above, summarizes the regular teachers and instructional assistants involved in audio-video recordings.

In addition to these regular teachers, there were a number of substitute teachers who were involved in the audio-video recordings for one or two days. These were mainly substituting for Ms Cabot in that she was pregnant during the academic year, had a number of doctor's appointments as a result, and stopped teaching in late March 2017, replaced by Ms Tucek. This group of substitutes was also relatively diverse and mainly composed of either retired teachers seeking to continue working part-time for a few years or new teachers or teachers-in-training working in the system until a permanent position became available.

Method 2: Participant observation with fieldnotes of the classroom, meetings and general environment

In addition to the audio-video recordings, I engaged in participant observation in the classroom, sometimes simply observing and at other times assisting the teachers and students where possible/needed as well as having informal conversations with the students and teachers about their lives in and out of school and seeking to connect this to the coursework. During this time I engaged in a range of activities including: greeting students, complimenting them, explaining activities, checking their work, pointing out relevant instructional material in the room, mediating disputes, giving advice, explaining the school system, explaining educational research, practicing English expressions and conversations, sharing aspects of my life experience and joking with them.

My talk with students, however, was not random or atheoretical, but rather guided by many of the aforementioned principles or commitments. Thus, my talk often would have the following arc:

- Initial engagement with the student, usually connected with asking a socio-emotional question such as 'how are you?' or a pedagogical 'how is this activity going?'. In the latter case, many students requested that I help with an activity or confirm that their answers were correct. In the former case, I would often ask students directly if they felt sick, tired, angry or otherwise disaffected in the class. On occasion, students would ask me to help with some extracurricular problem such as an issue with the school administration or in their home lives, and I would seek a resolution to these issues to the best of my ability. Beyond the basic academic or personal support I offered, my talk with students was based on my conviction that developing conversational ability in a target language is key and that this type of talk can benefit from pedagogical support and direct teaching that, while present in the program, is marginalized in favor of 'academic' topics.
    - From a data/empirical perspective, these talks provided some indication of the students' overall progress in the program as well as insight into the students' feelings and issues happening in their home lives.
- Deeper discussions, usually probing the students' languacultural background or experiences and, to the greatest extent possible, connecting that background to the lesson goals. This move is founded on the conviction that (1) honoring and understanding the students' background is essential to forming a connection to the academic topic, and (2) related to the first point, that using the home language and translanguaging pedagogy are equally essential to helping students make meaning. Wherever possible, I would share my own experiences and try to create talk with other students about these topics. When appropriate, I might affirm, challenge or question the students' responses either to support views that might be felt in the context as nonnormative or to destabilize opinions that could be oppressive to others.
    - From a data/empirical perspective, these talks provided information about the students' home lives and also evidence about how they were making meaning out of this transition time.
- Return to the academic task at hand. Usually, after these moves, I would return the student to the academic topic or activity they were trying to complete. Although in some cases I would have loved to stay in the 'deeper discussion' phase, this move indexes both my and the program's commitment to the students' learning of the academic

topics, preparation for tests and so on. Thus, even if we might criticize these curricula and assessments, the reality is that demonstrating competence on these topics is the key to academic progress, and I wanted my efforts to contribute in part to these outcomes.

Beyond the classroom, I attended and took notes at relevant meetings, especially the weekly Lab Teacher-Based Team and Instructional Assistant meetings, as well as monthly staff meetings and Building Leadership Team meetings. I also attended the Community Council meeting and a few other meetings with district personnel, including the district superintendent. That said, many of these school meetings were postponed or canceled, especially in the Spring 2017 semester when testing, other obligations and a general relaxing of the school culture became more prominent.

I also did general participant observations of the school environment, especially in the cafeteria or gymnasium or outside during lunch periods. As I become close with a few students, I visited them in their homes or at other sites outside of the school, taking mental notes during these interactions and later writing them into fieldnotes.

At the end of the day, I would take my handwritten fieldnotes and make a digital version in Microsoft Word, often with the assistance of the voice-to-text program Dragon Dictation to speed up the fieldnoting process.

Method 3: Interviews

In order to gain insight into the various actors involved in the school, I conducted at least one semi-formal and audio-recorded interview with many of the focal Lab students, all the teachers, most of the instructional assistants, one of the school counselors, one of the main community-based support organization's staff and all the administrators. During these interviews, I asked questions designed to elicit their (1) trajectory to the newcomer program, (2) role and activities in the program and (3) ideas about how it could improve with the existing resources and if more resources were available. All these interviews were later transcribed and, if necessary, translated into English (a few interviews had non-English language content, specifically in Spanish, Portuguese and French).

These interviews form a critical part of the data, but it is important to remember that the 'attitudinal fallacy' is a significant methodological issue in social sciences due to the fact that 'what people say is often a poor predictor of what they do' (Jerolmack & Khan, 2014: 178). Thus, most researchers consider and (re)design their interviewing techniques with care in addition to collecting a variety of other information that can either confirm or challenge any insights that emerge from the interviews. However, it is unlikely that there is any set of techniques that can resolve these issues due to the other fact that the interview itself is an experience of metacommunication that operates partly within but also outside the regular rules of interpersonal communication (Briggs, 1986). More specifically, Alvesson (2010) points out at least eight problems that, from the interviewee's perspective, exist within interviews:

- The social problem of coping with an interpersonal relation and complex interaction in a non-routine situation.
- The cognitive problem of finding out what it is all about (beyond the level of the espoused).
- The identity problem of adapting a self-position which is contextually relevant (and/or comfortable for the interviewee).
- The institutional problem of adapting to normative pressure and cognitive uncertainty through mimicking standard forms of expression.
- The problem (or option) of maintaining and increasing self-esteem that emerges in any situation involving examination and calling for a performance (or allowing esteem-enhancement to flourish in the situation).
- The motivation problem of developing an interest or rationale for active participation in the interview.
- The representation-construction problem of how to account for complex phenomena through language.
- The autonomy-determinism problem of a powerful macro-discourse operating behind and on the interview subject. (Alvesson, 2010: 78)

In the context of schools, these issues are in high relief. Teachers are often asked or even required to be observed or interviewed as part of their professional development, and in the context of a research project they may have relatively little investment in the overall outcome or a lurking fear that their participation might undermine their professional status, or simply find the whole thing a waste of their time. Administrators may feel similarly or have a stronger desire to present their programs in a positive light. Students, in turn, may perceive a researcher as another teacher or assistant. Throughout, interviewees often feel a standard sociocultural push towards convivial relations with the researchers simply 'to feel good and to give others similar feelings' (Blommaert, 2013a). Thus, the research methods linked interviews with careful recording and examination of what is actually happening in day-to-day activities.

Method 4: Artifact collection

Finally, throughout the research project, I collected artifacts from the classroom, meetings and general environment. For the classroom, these included student work, lesson plans, handouts and assessment data. In the meetings, these included written agendas and other handouts. Throughout the school, these included pictures of signs, posters, displayed student work and other non-human semiotic artifacts.

Permission, Access and Consent/Assent

My initial informal engagement with YES began in the Fall of 2014 and then extended in a number of ways including my work at the refugee support agency and, most notably, through the research partnership with Derek Braun. The process of gaining permission to conduct research both from The Ohio State University's Institutional Research Board and the school district began formally in the summer of 2015 and, after a number of revisions to the protocol, was approved mid-Fall 2015. With that approval, Derek and I were able to approach Mr Smith, present the project and gain his permission to conduct research at YES. Official research with Derek started and continued throughout Spring 2016 with the intention of continuing and expanding to focus on a Lab cohort throughout the 2016–2017 academic year. However, Derek was moved to another school site but helped to secure the participation and written consent for research with Ms Cabot and other teachers.

When the school year started, I was present with the Lab cohort from the first day of school but only informally observed. During the first few weeks, I presented the parental consent forms to all students who were under 18 years old. I provided multiple translated documents for these parents and explained the project to the students either personally with my own linguistic repertoire or with the help of a bilingual assistant. On one occasion, a caregiver visited the school to ask directly about the project and the form. Caregivers, with very few exceptions, gave permission. When the forms were returned, I asked the students to provide their verbal assent for the project and, if provided, included them in the research project. Students aged over 18 were given a verbal and written overview of the project and asked to provide their verbal consent to participate in the research. When new students arrived, I repeated this process.

Methodological Strengths Yet Several Issues to Address

Although these research questions and methods are robust and constitute a significant advance in research on newcomer programs, there are gaps. The first is engagement with and documentation of the students' home lives, which would have informed my understanding of how students respond to the classroom or broader program environment. Although I do have some knowledge of this from the interviews and informal conversations with most of the students while in school and informal interaction with them in community or online contexts, I do not have systematic evidence of all students or how they organize and understand their out-of-school lives. Addressing this would have required a change in research questions and methods such as, for example, giving students cameras to take home, riding the bus home with them, making a more concerted effort to spend time in their homes and communities, or a more intentional and intense push into their social media lives. On the other hand, I assume and have partial evidence of their complicated and challenging home lives garnered from the broader contextual data from my work with the refugee agency, reading of the literature and in-class talk with students. For example, the students reported the following activities in their after-school routine: cooking food for family, taking care of siblings, watching TV, doing homework, sleeping, going to the gym, social media (Facebook, WhatsApp) or work. However, these brief reports certainly mask much richer adolescent out-of-school lives.

The second issue is longitudinal. Although one year is a reasonable period for focused qualitative inquiry of school life, a fuller understanding of the experience of the Lab students would extend for several years and explore the long-term experiences and results of their participation in the program. This could be possible with more mixed methods, such as tracking students through the district's student management system and following a certain subset of the students ethnographically. However, the focus on one Lab cohort allowed me to see in detail what factors might attract a student to YES during the critical first year of the program where issues of mobility, placement and appropriate service provision dominate.

The third issue is directly related to superdiversity and the ethnographic challenge and opportunity for researchers to work with highly mobile and multilingual groups. One solution to these issues would have been to focus in on one or two languacultural groups that I have the closest connections to, such as Arabic or French speakers, and then seek to write a deeper ethnography of this group's experience in the newcomer program. However, just like the teachers, staff and administration in the program, I felt that it was important for me to work to the best of my ability to understand the experiences of all of the students. Thus, although I developed some closer connections with certain students due to linguistic, personal or cultural affinities, I made efforts to connect with all students by drawing on a broad understanding of my linguistic repertoire. This is what might be called a *translanguaging methodology* and, as mentioned above, there are three dimensions – individual, social and multimodal. At the individual level, my linguistic repertoire matched relatively well with many students, particularly the Arabic and French speakers; there was also strong overlap with Spanish and Portuguese due to my background in French and Latin, Nepali with my prior work in the Bhutanese refugee community, and even Somali or Swahili with my Arabic ability in addition to the fact that I converted to Islam in 2010. In addition, many students already had strong English abilities. For example, the interviews with Maria, Gloire or Mohammed above were conducted solely by drawing on my and the student's linguistic repertoires. However, in those cases where my linguistic repertoire was not wide enough to cross the languacultural divide (e.g. during an extended

Table A.2 General research schedule

	Monday	Tuesday	Wednesday	Thursday	Friday
Classroom audio-video recording and observation	Reading clinic 2nd period; Mr Isse 3rd period	Mr Shahiya 7th period; Ms Cabot 8th period	Ms Cabot 1st period	Ms Popov 5th period	
Meetings	Staff and Building Leadership Team meeting after school 1st and 3rd weeks of the month			Lab Teacher-Based Team meeting 4th period; Community Council meetings last week of each month	Instructional Assistant meeting 1st period
General environment observation	Daily when on-site	Daily when on-site	Daily when on-site	Daily when on-site	Focus on lunch hour 6th period

interview), I was able to draw on the social environment of other students or school and community members with the requisite linguistic repertoire. For instance, the extended interviews above with Mateo or Beatriz were conducted with the assistance of school or community members with stronger Spanish and Portuguese ability. In addition, I was able to use many digital multimodal tools such as Google Translate to do real-time translation; critically, I also endeavored to expand my linguistic repertoire using Duolingo and other online learning tools. For example, my discussions with Gabriela above were often highly mediated by Google Translate even as she and I endeavored to deploy our emerging Portuguese and English abilities to communicate. Thus, in general I was able to gain insight into many aspects of the students' lives. Throughout the project, I was somewhat lucky in that no students arrived with whom I would have had little in common in terms of their linguistic repertoire (e.g. a speaker of Mandarin Chinese) or where digital tools would have been limited (e.g. Zomi or Chin speakers).

In summary, the research questions and methods were designed to explore the experience of Lab students and their environment. In order to be at the school as much as possible, I followed the general weekly research schedule shown in Table A.2. Naturally, there was some variation due to school and personal circumstances; however, I strove to be in the school on a daily basis, to see each class on a weekly basis and to attend all weekly and monthly meetings relevant to the Lab students and the general functioning of the school.

Corpus of Data

Through these methods, I was able to collect the data shown in Table A.3.

Table A.3 Corpus of data

Type of data	Quantity of data
Classroom recordings	
Audio-video recordings	142 hours, 6 minutes, 48 seconds
Audio only	2 hours, 28 minutes, 58 seconds
Fieldnotes	*187 total files*
Classroom focused	123 files
Meetings	74 files
General environment	46 files
Professional development days	3 files
Fieldtrips	1 file
Out-of-school student meetings	6 files
Semi-formal interviews	*28 total*
Students	10
Teachers	6
Instructional assistants	5
Support staff	2
Administration	6
Artifacts	
Classroom	~1300 pictures, handouts, student work, etc.
General environment	~300 pictures, handouts, meeting agendas, etc.

Analysis: Or, How to Make Meaning

Having a relatively large data corpus is certainly a positive thing, but organizing and making meaning of the data is a significant task that requires technical skill and support as well as relevant theoretical frameworks.

Transcription and conventions

An essential aspect of qualitative research is the creation of transcripts based on audio-video recordings. With the nature of the large corpus of data, this aspect of the research was a significant task. In order to work efficiently and effectively, I used Transana Professional 3.21 (Woods, 2017), which is a qualitative research software with the capacity not only to create multiple and layered transcripts of audio-video data but also to organize that data for analytical purposes. In this process, it is important to recall that transcripts themselves are not neutral documents but are rather guided by the transcriber's theoretical understanding, awareness and interests (Ochs, 1979). These transcripts may therefore reveal subtle linguistic features such as breathing or gesture, hierarchical relationships between the actors, or the like.

For this project, interviews were transcribed marking standardized spellings of the spoken language and, when the talk was not in English, a translation in '' followed. For the classroom video, I adapted and simplified Jefferson's (1978, 2004) transcription conventions, generally rendering the standardized spellings of the spoken language and marking any gestures, laughs or other relevant paralinguistic information in double parentheses. The exception to the standardized spellings came with the Arabic discourse, for which I used a transliteration and transcription system based on the Peace Corps Morocco (2011) textbook.

Technical aspects: Maintaining safe, backed up and organized data

At the end of each day, I would move the audio-video recordings from the camera and microphone to my password-protected and hard drive encrypted computer. In order to maintain backups of the data, I kept multiple copies – one on the main computer, one on password-protected and encrypted external hard drives and one in The Ohio State University's cloud storage system, BuckeyeBox. As mentioned above, I made daily fieldnotes of all research activities and paired them when appropriate with the audio-video recordings. Any interviews or artifacts were saved on my computer's hard drive as well as backed up in multiple locations.

Because the research was occurring daily, it was difficult to engage in deep analysis of the material throughout the year. Although the fieldnotes helped to isolate certain important elements throughout the year, the more rigorous and systematic organization of the data began after the active fieldwork ended.

In order to organize and analyze the data, I also used Transana Professional to work effectively with the entire corpus of data. The organization of the data included these steps:

- Creating a 'library' of the raw data and indices/transcripts of audio-video recordings, interviews and fieldnotes. Figure A.1 shows how the following information is organized in Transana Professional.
    - Audio-video recordings: After loading the videos into Transana and syncing the audio and video files (where possible), I created:
        - An initial transcript of the general classroom activities (e.g. teacher-fronted instruction, group work, testing, etc.) with as much specificity as possible. This transcript was then coded by activity type in Transana for quick reference and deeper analysis over time.
        - Transcripts of student-focused conversations.
    - Interviews:
        - The interviews were first transcribed and then loaded into Transana.

Figure A.1 Library image from Transana

- Then, the interview transcripts were read and the content organized into various broad areas (e.g. background/trajectory to school, ideas about program improvement, etc.) and/or important or illustrative quotes.
• Creating 'collections' from the raw data. These collections consist of quotes or clips from the audio-video indices, interview transcripts or fieldnotes. These serve as an organizing tool as well as initial meaning-making processes. Figure A.2 demonstrates this process in Transana Professional.

Figure A.2 Collections image from Transana

- Creating 'keywords' relevant to the collections. These keywords were used as codes to apply meaning(s) to the various collection elements. Figure A.3 demonstrates this process.

Figure A.3 Keywords image from Transana

Caveats

Through this technical organizing and analyzing process, the various themes and patterns in the research can be identified, retrieved and scrutinized with greater facility. However, despite this large corpus of data and the use of Transana, these do not reveal essential truths or insights by themselves. They are records and tools of the research process, useful for making meaning when informed by relevant theory. This research project and its data are not framed by one dominant theory but are aligned closely with detailed approaches to the study of language and culture, translanguaging, superdiversity and the critical study of institutions. Arnaut *et al.* (2016: 11) articulate this intersection well: 'if superdiversity sometimes tempts us to foreground Bakhtin, heterglossic translanguaging, and creativity in public culture, securitization and surveillance emphasize the relevance of Foucault's ideas about control, normativity, and subjectification.' This relationship with Foucault is enhanced by more 'critical' scholarship interrogating the multiple dimensions of power with education such as through language (Alim, 2010), gender (Lather, 1992) and so on.

This intersection of data and theory is essential, and theoretically informed empirical research projects can lead to important insights useful to practitioners. For example, it has been shown that migrant students or students from non-dominant cultures often do not get to talk as much in class because of cultural differences in communication; as a result, they might not be seen as intelligent as their peers (Au, 1980). However, when educators in these spaces become aware of these often unconscious patterns, they can make corrective adjustments that, when taken broadly, become new pedagogies designed to re-center education on these formerly marginalized groups.

This book's discussion of García's translanguaging pedagogy is a prominent and relevant example. My approach to the documentation, analysis and exposition of translanguaging is to focus on the broader policies and teacher pedagogies that support the students' home languages and translanguaging practices. In other words, I take it as a given that the students themselves will be engaged in a multitude of translanguaging practices in their everyday and academic talk. However, the focus throughout the book is how the program's policies and actors have stances, designs and shifts supportive of the students' home languages and backgrounds.

As a final point, theoretical arguments become more salient and convincing when supported by various data points. For example, if a student does something that seemed interesting or unusual in a class that provoked a certain event (e.g. rich discussion, reward or punishment, etc.), that and the talk and other activities can be analyzed by itself. When those events are 'triangulated,' or brought into dialogue with other evidence such as interviews and artifacts, more complex and convincing arguments can emerge. Wherever possible, this book has sought to bring different

On Writing

> To figure out what the native says and does, what the devil he thinks he's up to, the result being an interpretation of the way a people live which is neither imprisoned within their mental horizons, an ethnography of witchcraft written by a witch, nor systematically deaf to the distinct tonalities of their existence, the ethnography of witchcraft written by a geometer ... To grasp concepts which, for another people, are experience-near, and to do so well enough to place them in illuminating connection with those experience-distant concepts that theorists have fashioned to capture the general features of social life is clearly a task at least as delicate, if a bit less magical, as putting oneself into someone else's skin. (Geertz, 1974: 29)

The final aspect to elaborate on is the critical but sometimes overlooked aspect of research – the process of writing. This project allowed me to spend many hours in a relatively unique site, with and among vastly diverse students, teachers, administrators and staff at a specific and even difficult time in this program's development, and at a contentious time in US and world history. How I write about myself and this experience is an important question: Will I disappear entirely, appear at certain moments or be ubiquitous? Am I a benevolent and wise figure or a naïve nuisance? Do I acknowledge that the writing process is directly linked to the thinking and analyzing process? All of these considerations underline what Denzin (1999) means when he states 'Writing is not an innocent practice' but rather demands a new ethic in which personal experience joins directly and explicitly with the political, as 'tools for critique and political action' (Denzin, 1999: 568).

van Maanen (2011) identifies three broad types of ethnographic writing or 'tales' – realist, confessional and impressionist. 'Realist' accounts generally use a third-person voice and seek to describe in detail the 'comings and goings of members of the culture, theoretical coverage of certain features of the culture, and usually a hesitant account of why the work was undertaken in the first place' (van Maanen, 2011: 45). These types of tales are relatively common and are akin to documentaries of certain cultures where the camera is portrayed as simply a window on the world of the culture. Here, no-one breaks the fourth wall to acknowledge that a cameraperson or even an entire film crew has been following, for example, a certain group of nomads across the desert. 'Confessional' narratives are characterized by 'their highly personalized styles and their self-absorbed mandates' (van Maanen, 2011: 73). Extending the documentary analogy further, these tales certainly break the fourth wall and, in some sense, turn the camera around entirely, documenting and commenting more on the process of the research. Rabinow's (1977) discussion of his fieldwork in Morocco is a clear example of this type. 'Impressionist' tales strive to bridge these two while evoking 'an open, participatory sense in the viewer and as with all revisionist forms of art, to startle complacent views accustomed to and comfortable with older forms' (van Maanen, 2011: 101). Most importantly, these tales focus on especially notable moments in the fieldwork that somehow cut through, explain or give greater meaning to the day-to-day regular activities of fieldwork. Writing impressionist tales requires taking on a certain 'textual identity,' using 'fragmented knowledge' carefully, allowing the researched people to be 'characterized,' and exhibiting 'dramatic control' (van Maanen, 2011: 101–104). Using the documentary metaphor again, these tales show the camera, the documentarian and the documented group somehow in dialogue with one another. The documentary itself describes the context well enough that certain important moments, either by themselves or in succession, can be understood as powerful and meaningful by the viewer.

In this book, these three styles blend together in different ways. Some of the description of the school and the context appear much more 'realist.' However, the student case studies have an 'impressionist' style where I have sought to distill and explain the journeys of students through this newcomer program. Finally, I have endeavored to provide some elements of a 'confessional' account by pointing out that I exist in this research project and have foregrounded certain strengths and limitations. That said, my goal in this book is not to lose sight of the bigger picture – those key events and outcomes evoked by the 'impressionist' or even 'realist' versions – of ethnography. In this case, it is YES's ability to attract, retain and excite learners and support their journeys to self-sustaining lives of dignity.

References

Agar, M.H. (1990) Text and fieldwork: Exploring the excluded middle. *Journal of Contemporary Ethnography* 19 (1), 73–88.
Agar, M.H. (1994) The intercultural frame. *International Journal of Intercultural Relations* 18 (2), 221–237.
Agar, M.H. (1996) *Language Shock: Understanding the Culture of Conversation.* New York: Harper Paperbacks.
Agar, M.H. (2013) *The Lively Science: Remodeling Human Social Research.* Maitland, FL: Mill City Press.
Agha, A. (1999) Register. *Journal of Linguistic Anthropology* 9 (1/2), 216–219.
Alim, H.S. (2006) *Roc the Mic Right: The Language of Hip Hop Culture.* New York: Routledge.
Alim, H.S. (2010) Critical language awareness. In N.H. Hornberger and S.L. McKay (eds) *Sociolinguistics and Language Education* (pp. 205–231). Bristol: Multilingual Matters.
Alim, H.S., Rickford, J.R. and Ball, A.F. (eds) (2016) *Raciolinguistics: How Language Shapes our Ideas about Race.* Oxford: Oxford University Press.
Allard, E.C. (2015) Undocumented status and schooling for newcomer teens. *Harvard Educational Review* 85 (3), 478–501. doi:10.17763/0017-8055.85.3.478
Allard, E.C. and Mortimer, K. (2008) Telling and retelling the story: Positioning Mexican immigrant students as English language learners in community and school. *Working Papers in Educational Linguistics* 23 (2), 23.
Allen, D. (2007) Just who do you think I am? The name-calling and name-claiming of newcomer youth. *Canadian Journal of Applied Linguistics* 10 (2), 165–175.
Alvesson, M. (2010) *Interpreting Interviews.* Thousand Oaks, CA: Sage.
Amos, D. (2018) *The Year the U.S. Refugee Resettlement Program Unraveled.* NPR.org, 1 January. See https://www.npr.org/sections/parallels/2018/01/01/574658008/the-year-the-u-s-refugee-resettlement-program-unraveled.
Ancess, J. (2003) *Beating the Odds: High Schools as Communities of Commitment.* New York: Teachers College Press.
Anderson, J.D. (2006) A tale of two Browns: Constitutional equality and unequal education. *Yearbook of the National Society for the Study of Education* 105 (2), 14–35.
Anzaldúa, G. (2012) *Borderlands/la Frontera: The New Mestiza* (4th edn). San Francisco, CA: Aunt Lute Books.
Arias, M.B. and Faltis, C.J. (eds) (2013) *Academic Language in Second Language Learning.* Charlotte, NC: Information Age Publishing.
Arnaut, K. (2016) Superdiversity: Elements of an emerging perspective. In K. Arnaut, J. Blommaert, B. Rampton and M. Spotti (eds) *Language and Superdiversity* (pp. 49–70). New York: Routledge.
Arnaut, K., Blommaert, J., Rampton, B. and Spotti, M. (eds) (2016) *Language and Superdiversity.* New York: Routledge.
Au, K.H.-P. (1980) Participation structures in a reading lesson with Hawaiian children: Analysis of a culturally appropriate instructional event. *Anthropology & Education Quarterly* 11 (2), 91–115.

Auer, P. (1984) *Bilingual Conversation*. Amsterdam and Philadelphia, PA: John Benjamins.

Auerbach, E.R. (1993) Reexamining English only in the ESL classroom. *TESOL Quarterly* 27 (1), 9–32.

August, D. (2002) *Transitional Programs for English Language Learners: Contextual Factors and Effective Programming*. Baltimore, MD: Johns Hopkins University, CRESPAR Publications Department. See https://www.govinfo.gov/content/pkg/ERIC-ED466889/pdf/ERIC-ED466889.pdf.

August, D. and Shanahan, T. (2006) *Developing Literacy in Second-language Learners: Report of the National Literacy Panel on Language-minority Children and Youth*. Mahwah, NJ: Lawrence Erlbaum.

Backhaus, P. (2006) *Linguistic Landscapes: A Comparative Study of Urban Multilingualism in Tokyo*. Clevedon: Multilingual Matters.

Bajaj, M. and Bartlett, L. (2017) Critical transnational curriculum for immigrant and refugee students. *Curriculum Inquiry* 47 (1), 25–35. doi:10.1080/03626784.2016.1254499

Baker, C. (2011) *Foundations of Bilingual Education and Bilingualism* (5th edn). Bristol: Multilingual Matters.

Bakhtin, M.M. (1982) *The Dialogic Imagination: Four Essays* (M. Holquist, ed.; C. Emerson, trans.). Austin, TX: University of Texas Press.

Bal, A. (2014) Becoming in/competent learners in the United States: Refugee students' academic identities in the figured world of difference. *International Multilingual Research Journal* 8 (4), 271–290. doi:10.1080/19313152.2014.952056

Bales, B.L. (2007) Making it personal: The policy micropolitics of stakeholders in the standards-based teacher education reform effort. *Journal of Ethnographic & Qualitative Research* 2 (1), 6–14.

Ball, S.J. (1987) *The Micro-politics of the School: Towards a Theory of School Organization*. London: Methuen.

Bang, H.J. (2011) Newcomer immigrant students' perspectives on what affects their homework experiences. *Journal of Educational Research* 104 (6), 408–419. doi:10.1080/00220671.2010.499139

Barnard, A., Saad, H. and Hubbard, B. (2016) Aleppo evacuation halted amid confusion and concerns about killings. *The New York Times*, 16 December. See https://www.nytimes.com/2016/12/16/world/middleeast/aleppo-evacuation-assad-syria.html.

Bartlett, L. (2007) Bilingual literacies, social identification, and educational trajectories. *Linguistics and Education* 18 (3–4), 215–231. doi:10.1016/j.linged.2007.07.005

Bartlett, L. and Vavrus, F. (2016) *Rethinking Case Study Research: A Comparative Approach* (1st edn). New York: Routledge.

Bartlett, T. (2009) Towards intervention in positive discourse analysis. In C. Coffin, T. Lillis and K. O'Halloran (eds) *Applied Linguistics Methods: A Reader* (pp. 133–147). Abingdon: Routledge.

Bear, D.R., Invernizzi, M.R., Templeton, S.R. and Johnston, F. (2011) *Words Their Way: Word Study for Phonics, Vocabulary, and Spelling Instruction* (5th edn). Boston, MA: Pearson.

Ben-Rafael, E., Shohamy, E., Hasan Amara, M. and Trumper-Hecht, N. (2006) Linguistic landscape as symbolic construction of the public space: The case of Israel. *International Journal of Multilingualism* 3 (1), 7–30. doi:10.1080/14790710608668383

Bialystok, E. (2009) Bilingualism: The good, the bad, and the indifferent. *Bilingualism: Language and Cognition* 12 (1), 3. doi:10.1017/S1366728908003477

Birman, D. and Tran, N. (2015) *The Academic Engagement of Newly Arriving Somali Bantu Students in a U.S. Elementary School*. Washington, DC: Migration Policy Institute.

Blackburn, M.V. (2002) Disrupting the (hetero) normative: Exploring literacy performances and identity work with queer youth. *Journal of Adolescent & Adult Literacy* 46 (4), 312–324.

Blase, J. (1993) The micropolitics of effective school-based leadership: Teachers' perspectives. *Educational Administration Quarterly* 29 (2), 142–163. doi:10.1177/0013161X93029002003

Bloch, M. and Gebeloff, R. (2009) Remade in America: Immigration explorer. *The New York Times*, 10 March. See https://archive.nytimes.com/www.nytimes.com/interactive/2009/03/10/us/20090310-immigration-explorer.html?_r=.

Blommaert, J. (2013a) *Ethnography, Superdiversity and Linguistic Landscapes: Chronicles of Complexity*. Bristol: Multilingual Matters.

Blommaert, J. (2013b) Complexity, accent, and conviviality: Concluding comments. *Applied Linguistics* 34 (5), 613–622. doi:10.1093/applin/amt028

Blommaert, J. (2015) Chronotopes, scales, and complexity in the study of language in society. *Annual Review of Anthropology* 44 (1), 105–116. doi:10.1146/annurev-anthro-102214-014035

Blommaert, J. (2016a) Superdiversity and the neoliberal conspiracy. *Ctrl+Alt+Dem*, 3 March. See https://alternative-democracy-research.org/2016/03/03/superdiversity-and-the-neoliberal-conspiracy/.

Blommaert, J. (2016b) Teaching the language that makes one happy. *Tilburg Papers in Culture Studies* 154.

Blommaert, J. (2016c) The conservative turn in linguistic landscape studies. *Tilburg Papers in Culture Studies* 156.

Blommaert, J. (2017) 'Home language': Some questions. *Tilburg Papers in Culture Studies* 183.

Blommaert, J. and Bulcaen, C. (2000) Critical discourse analysis. *Annual Review of Anthropology* 29, 447–466.

Bloome, D. (1989) Beyond access: An ethnographic study of reading and writing in a seventh grade classroom. In D. Bloome (ed.) *Classrooms and Literacy* (pp. 53–106). New York: Praeger.

Bloome, D. and Enciso, P. (2006) Looking out across Columbus: What we mean by 'multiple literacies'. *Theory into Practice* 45 (4), 296–303.

Bloome, D., Puro, P. and Theodorou, E. (1989) Procedural display and classroom lessons. *Curriculum Inquiry* 19 (3), 265. doi:10.2307/1179417

Bloome, D., Carter, S.P., Christian, B.M., Otto, S. and Shuart-Faris, N. (2005) *Discourse Analysis and the Study of Classroom Language and Literacy Events: A Microethnographic Perspective*. New York: Routledge.

Bomer, R., Dworin, J., May, L. and Semingson, P. (2008) Miseducating teachers about the poor: A critical analysis of Ruby Payne's claims about poverty. *Teachers College Record* 110 (12), 2497–2531.

Bourdieu, P. (1986) The forms of capital. In J. Richardson (ed.) *Handbook of Theory and Research for the Sociology of Education* (pp. 241–258). Westport, CT: Greenwood.

Bourdieu, P. and Passeron, J.C. (1990) *Reproduction in Education, Society and Culture*. Thousand Oaks, CA: Sage.

Bourne, J. (2001) Doing 'what comes naturally': How the discourses and routines of teachers' practice constrain opportunities for bilingual support in UK primary schools. *Language and Education* 15 (4), 250–268. doi:10.1080/09500780108666813

Boyson, B.A., Coltrane, B. and Short, D.J. (eds) (2002) *Proceedings of the First National Conference for Educators of Newcomer Students*. Washington, DC: Center for Applied Linguistics.

Bregman, R. (2016) *Utopia for Realists: The Case for a Universal Basic Income, Open Borders, and a 15-hour Workweek* (E. Manton, trans.). Amsterdam: The Correspondent.

Briggs, C.L. (1986) *Learning How to Ask: A Sociolinguistic Appraisal of the Role of the Interview in Social Science Research*. Cambridge: Cambridge University Press.

Bronfenbrenner, U. (1976) The experimental ecology of education. *Educational Researcher* 5 (9), 5. doi:10.2307/1174755

Bronfenbrenner, U. (1994) Ecological models of human development. In *International Encyclopedia of Education, Vol. 3* (2nd edn) (pp. 1643–1647). Oxford: Elsevier.

Brown, K.D. (2012) The linguistic landscape of educational spaces: Language revitalization and schools in southeastern Estonia. In D. Gorter, H.F. Marten and L.V. Mensel (eds) *Minority Languages in the Linguistic Landscape* (pp. 281–298). Houndmills: Palgrave MacMillan.

Budach, G. and de Saint-Georges, I. (2017) Superdiversity and language. In S. Canagarajah (ed.) *The Routledge Handbook of Migration and Language*. Routledge Handbooks Online. doi:10.4324/9781315754512.ch3

Busch, B. (2012) The linguistic repertoire revisited. *Applied Linguistics* 33 (5), 503–523. doi:10.1093/applin/ams056

Busch, B. (2017) Expanding the notion of the linguistic repertoire: On the concept of Spracherleben – the lived experience of language. *Applied Linguistics* 38 (3), 340–358. doi:10.1093/applin/amv030

Cable, C. (2004) 'I'm going to bring my sense of identity to this': The role and contribution of bilingual teaching assistants. *Westminster Studies in Education* 27 (2), 207–222. doi:10.1080/0140672042000277134

CAL (2013) *Heritage Language Programs Database*. Washington, DC: Center for Applied Linguistics. See http://webapp.cal.org/Heritage/Default.aspx.

CAL (2014) *Secondary Newcomer Programs in the U.S.* Washington, DC: Center for Applied Linguistics. See http://webapp.cal.org/Newcomer/.

CAL (2016) *Dual Language Program Directory*. Washington, DC: Center for Applied Linguistics. See http://webapp.cal.org/DualLanguage/ProgramSearch.aspx.

Canagarajah, S. (2011) Translanguaging in the classroom: Emerging issues for research and pedagogy. *Applied Linguistics Review* 2, 1–28.

Capote, T. (1966) *In Cold Blood*. New York: Random House.

Carey, K. (2017) Dismal voucher results surprise researchers as DeVos era vegins. *The New York Times*, 23 February. See https://www.nytimes.com/2017/02/23/upshot/dismal-results-from-vouchers-surprise-researchers-as-devos-era-begins.html.

Cenoz, J., Genesee, F. and Gorter, D. (2014) Critical analysis of CLIL: Taking stock and looking forward. *Applied Linguistics* 35 (3), 243–262. doi:10.1093/applin/amt011

Center for School and District Improvement (2004) *English Language Learner (ELL) Programs at the Secondary Level in Relation to Student Performance*. Portland, OR: Northwest Regional Educational Laboratory.

Chang, H.N.-L. (1990) *Newcomer Programs: Innovative Efforts to Meet the Educational Challenges of Immigrant Students*. San Francisco, CA: California Tomorrow Immigrant Students Project.

Chappell, S.V. and Faltis, C.J. (eds) (2013) *The Arts and Emergent Bilingual Youth: Building Culturally Responsive, Critical and Creative Education in School and Community Contexts*. New York: Routledge.

Cherng, H.-Y.S. and Halpin, P.F. (2016) The importance of minority teachers: Student perceptions of minority versus White teachers. *Educational Researcher* 45 (7), 407–420. doi:10.3102/0013189X16671718

Choi, J. and Yi, Y. (2016) Teachers' integration of multimodality into classroom practices for English language learners. *TESOL Journal* 7 (2), 304–327. doi:10.1002/tesj.204

Choi, Y. (2013) Teaching social studies for newcomer English language learners: Toward culturally relevant pedagogy. *Multicultural Perspectives* 15 (1), 12–18. doi:10.1080/15210960.2013.754640

Clark, U. (2013) *Language and Identity in Englishes*. New York: Routledge.

Cohen, J. (1988) *Statistical Power Analysis for the Behavioral Sciences* (2nd edn). New York: Routledge.

Collier, V.P. and Thomas, W.P. (2004) The astounding effectiveness of dual language education for all. *NABE Journal of Research and Practice* 2 (1), 1–20.

Collier, V.P. and Thomas, W.P. (2009) *Educating English Learners for a Transformed World*. Albuquerque, NM: Dual Language Education of New Mexico.
Collier, V.P. and Thomas, W.P. (2014) *Creating Dual Language Schools for a Transformed World: Administrators Speak* (1st edn). Albuquerque, NM: Fuente Press.
Common Core (2018) *Students who are College and Career Ready in Reading, Writing, Speaking, Listening and Language*. Common Core State Standards Initiative. See http://www.corestandards.org/ELA-Literacy/introduction/students-who-are-college-and-career-ready-in-reading-writing-speaking-listening-language/.
Constantino, R. and Lavadenz, M. (1993) Newcomer schools: First impressions. *Peabody Journal of Education* 69 (1), 82–101.
Cox, D., Dionne, Jr., E.J., Galston, W.A. and Jones, R.P. (2011) What it means to be an American: Attitudes in an increasingly diverse America ten years after 9/11. *Brookings*, 6 September. See https://www.brookings.edu/research/what-it-means-to-be-an-american-attitudes-in-an-increasingly-diverse-america-ten-years-after-911/.
Crawford, J. (2004) *Educating English Learners: Language Diversity in the Classroom* (5th edn). Los Angeles, CA: Bilingual Education Services.
Creese, A. and Blackledge, A. (2010) Translanguaging in the bilingual classroom: A pedagogy for learning and teaching? *The Modern Language Journal* 94 (1), 103–115.
Cumming, G. (2011) *Understanding the New Statistics: Effect Sizes, Confidence Intervals, and Meta-analysis*. New York: Routledge.
Cummins, J. (1979) Linguistic interdependence and the educational development of bilingual children. *Review of Educational Research* 49 (2), 222–251.
Cummins, J. (2000) *Language, Power and Pedagogy: Bilingual Children in the Crossfire*. Clevedon: Multilingual Matters.
Cummins, J. (2005) Teaching for cross-language transfer in dual language education: Possibilities and pitfalls. *TESOL Symposium on Dual Language Education: Teaching and Learning Two Languages in the EFL Setting* (pp. 1–18). Alexandria, VA: Teachers of English to Speakers of Other Languages. See http://www.tesol.org/docs/default-source/new-resource-library/symposium-on-dual-language-education-3.pdf.
Cummins, J. (2007) Rethinking monolingual instructional strategies in multilingual classrooms. *Canadian Journal of Applied Linguistics* 10 (2), 221–240.
Cummins, J. (2009) Multilingualism in the English-language classroom: Pedagogical considerations. *TESOL Quarterly* 43 (2), 317–321.
Custodio, B. (2010) *How to Design and Implement a Newcomer Program*. Boston, MA: Pearson Education.
Custodio, B. and O'Loughlin, J.B. (2017) *Students with Interrupted Formal Education: Bridging Where They Are and What They Need*. Thousand Oaks, CA: Corwin.
Davidson, C.N. (2012) *Now You See It: How Technology and Brain Science Will Transform Schools and Business for the 21st Century*. New York: Penguin.
Davidson, C.N. (2017) *The New Education: How to Revolutionize the University to Prepare Students for a World in Flux*. New York: Basic Books.
Davidson, C.N., Goldberg, D.T. and Jones, Z.M. (2009) *The Future of Learning Institutions in a Digital Age*. Cambridge, MA: MIT Press.
de Costa, P.I. (2016) *The Power of Identity and Ideology in Language Learning: Designer Immigrants Learning English in Singapore*. Dordrecht: Springer.
de Jong, E.J. (2011) *Foundations for Multilingualism in Education: From Principles to Practice*. Philadelphia, PA: Caslon.
Degler, C. (1986) *Neither Black nor White: Slavery and Race Relations in Brazil and the United States* (1st edn). Madison, WI: University of Wisconsin Press.
del Carmen Salazar, M. (2008) English or nothing: The impact of rigid language policies on the inclusion of humanizing practices in a high school ESL program. *Equity & Excellence in Education* 41 (3), 341–356. doi:10.1080/10665680802174783

Deleuze, G. and Guattari, F. (1987) *A Thousand Plateaus: Capitalism and Schizophrenia* (B. Massumi, trans.). Minneapolis, MN: University of Minnesota Press.

Denzin, N.K. (1999) Two-stepping in the '90s. *Qualitative Inquiry* 5 (4), 568–572.

Derry, S. (ed.) (2007) *Guidelines for Video Research in Education*. Chicago, IL: Data Research and Development Center.

DeVillar, R.A. and Faltis, C.J. (1991) *Computers and Cultural Diversity: Restructuring for School Success*. Albany, NY: State University of New York Press.

Dissard, J.-M. and Peng, G. (Dir.) (2013) *I Learn America*. Brooklyn, NY: I Learn America.

Dolch, E.W. (1936) A basic sight vocabulary. *The Elementary School Journal* 36, 456–460. See https://doi.org/10.1086/457353.

Drake, B. and Poushter, J. (2016) In views of diversity, many Europeans are less positive than Americans. *Pew Research Center*, 12 July. See http://www.pewresearch.org/fact-tank/2016/07/12/in-views-of-diversity-many-europeans-are-less-positive-than-americans/.

du Bois, W.E.B. (1994 [1903]) *The Souls of Black Folk* (Dover Thrift edn). New York: Dover Publications.

Duff, P.A. (2008) Language socialization, participation and identity: Ethnographic approaches. In N.H. Hornberger (ed.) *Encyclopedia of Language and Education* (pp. 860–872). Boston, MA: Springer. See http://link.springer.com/10.1007/978-0-387-30424-3_65.

Duff, P.A. and Anderson, T. (2015) Academic language and literacy socialization for second language students. In N. Markee (ed.) *The Handbook of Classroom Discourse and Interaction* (pp. 337–352). Malden, MA: Wiley-Blackwell.

Echevarria, J.J., Vogt, M.J. and Short, D.J. (2017) *Making Content Comprehensible for English Learners: The SIOP Model* (5th edn). Upper Saddle River, NJ: Pearson.

Ernst-Slavit, G. and Wenger, K.J. (2006) Teaching in the margins: The multifaceted work and struggles of bilingual paraeducators. *Anthropology & Education Quarterly* 37 (1), 62–82. doi:10.1525/aeq.2006.37.1.62

Evans, R. (2010) The perils of being a borderland people: On the Lhotshampas of Bhutan. *Contemporary South Asia* 18 (1), 25–42. doi:10.1080/09584930903561598

Fairclough, N. (1992) Intertextuality in critical discourse analysis. *Linguistics and Education* 4 (3), 269–293.

Faltis, C.J. (2010) Immigrant students in U.S. schools: Building pro-immigrant, English plus education counterscript. *Journal of Global Initiatives: Policy, Pedagogy, Perspective* 2 (1), 2.

Faltis, C.J. and Coulter, C.A. (2007) *Teaching English Learners and Immigrant Students in Secondary Schools*. Upper Saddle River, NJ: Pearson Education.

Faltis, C.J. and Hudelson, S.J. (1997) *Bilingual Education in Elementary and Secondary School Communities: Toward Understanding and Caring*. Upper Saddle River, NJ: Pearson Education.

Farr, M. (2011) Urban plurilingualism: Language practices, policies, and ideologies in Chicago. *Journal of Pragmatics* 43 (5), 1161–1172. doi:10.1016/j.pragma.2010.10.008

Farr, M. and Song, J. (2011) Language ideologies and policies: Multilingualism and education. *Language and Linguistics Compass* 5 (9), 650–665. doi:10.1111/j.1749-818X.2011.00298.x

Feinberg, R.C. (2000) Newcomer schools: Salvation or segregated oblivion for immigrant students. *Theory into Practice* 39 (4), 220–227. doi:10.1207/s15430421tip3904_5

Fine, M., Stoudt, B. and Futch, V. (2005) *The Internationals Network for Public Schools: A Quantitative and Qualitative Cohort Analysis of Graduation and Dropout Rates*. New York: Graduate Center, City University of New York. See http://www.internationalsnps.org/pdfs/FineReport.pdf.

Flessa, J. (2009) Educational micropolitics and distributed leadership. *Peabody Journal of Education* 84 (3), 331–349. doi:10.1080/01619560902973522

Fleuret, C., Bangou, F. and Ibrahim, A. (2013) Langues et enjeux interculturels: Une exploration au cœur d'un programme d'appui à l'apprentissage du français de scolarisation pour les nouveaux arrivants. *Canadian Journal of Education* 36 (4), 280–298.

Flores, N. (2014) Let's not forget that translanguaging is a political act. *The Educational Linguist*, 19 July. See https://educationallinguist.wordpress.com/2014/07/19/lets-not-forget-that-translanguaging-is-a-political-act/.

Flores, N. (2019) Do we need a revolution in educational linguistics? *The Educational Linguist*, 27 April. See https://educationallinguist.wordpress.com/2019/04/27/do-we-need-a-revolution-in-educational-linguistics/.

Forsythe, D.E. (1999a) Ethics and politics of studying up in technoscience. *Anthropology of Work Review* 20 (1), 6–11.

Forsythe, D.E. (1999b) 'It's just a matter of common sense': Ethnography as invisible work. *Computer Supported Cooperative Work (CSCW)* 8 (1–2), 127–145.

Francis, D.J., Rivera, M., Lesaux, N., Kieffer, M. and Rivera, H. (2006) Practical guidelines for the education of English language: Research-based recommendations for serving adolescent newcomers. Houston, TX: University of Houston for the Center on Instruction. See http://eric.ed.gov/?id=ED517791.

French, M. and de Courcy, M. (2016) A place for students' multilingual resources in an Australian high school. In S. Nichols and C. Snowden (eds) *Languages and Literacies as Mobile and Placed Resources* (pp. 153–169). Abingdon: Routledge.

Friedlander, M. (1991) *The Newcomer Program: Helping Immigrant Students Succeed in U.S. Schools*. NCBE Program Information Guide Series No. 8. Washington, DC: National Clearinghouse for Bilingual Education.

Fry, E. (1980) The New Instant Word List. *The Reading Teacher* 34 (3), 284–289.

Fry, R. (2005) The higher drop-out rate of foreign-born teens. *Pew Research Center's Hispanic Trends Project*, 1 November. See http://www.pewhispanic.org/2005/11/01/the-higher-drop-out-rate-of-foreign-born-teens/.

Fry, R. (2014) U.S. high school dropout rate reaches record low, driven by improvements among Hispanics, blacks. *Pew Research Center*, 2 October. See http://www.pewresearch.org/fact-tank/2014/10/02/u-s-high-school-dropout-rate-reaches-record-low-driven-by-improvements-among-hispanics-blacks/.

Gaither, M. (2014) The history of North American education, 15,000 BCE to 1491. *History of Education Quarterly* 54 (3), 323–348.

Gándara, P. and Hopkins, M. (eds) (2010) *Forbidden Language: English Learners and Restrictive Language Policies*. New York: Teachers College Press.

Gao, F. and Shum, M.S.K. (2010) Investigating the role of bilingual teaching assistants in Hong Kong: An exploratory study. *Educational Research* 52 (4), 445–456. doi:10.1080/00131881.2010.524753

García, O. (2008a) Multilingual language awareness and teacher education. In N.H. Hornberger (ed.) *Encyclopedia of Language and Education* (pp. 385–400). Boston, MA: Springer. doi:10.1007/978-0-387-30424-3_163

García, O. (2008b) *Bilingual Education in the 21st Century: A Global Perspective*. Chichester: Wiley-Blackwell.

García, O. (2020) The education of Latinx bilingual children in times of isolation: Unlearning and relearning. *MinneTESOL Journal* 36 (1). See http://minnetesoljournal.org/wp-content/uploads/2020/05/Garci%CC%81a_The-education-of-Latinx-bilingual-children-in-times-of-isolation_-Unlearning-and-relearning.pdf.

García, O. and Bartlett, L. (2007) A speech community model of bilingual education: Educating Latino newcomers in the USA. *International Journal of Bilingual Education and Bilingualism* 10 (1), 1–25. doi:10.2167/beb364.0

García, O. and Li Wei (2014) *Translanguaging: Language, Bilingualism, and Education*. Houndmills: Palgrave Pivot.

García, O. and Sylvan, C.E. (2011) Pedagogies and practices in multilingual classrooms: Singularities in pluralities. *The Modern Language Journal* 95 (3), 385–400. doi:10.1111/j.1540-4781.2011.01208.x

García, O., Kleifgen, J.A. and Falchi, L. (2008) *From English Language Learners to Emergent Bilinguals*. Equity Matters Research Review No. 1. New York: Campaign for Educational Equity, Teachers College.

García, O., Johnson, S.I. and Seltzer, K. (2016) *The Translanguaging Classroom: Leveraging Student Bilingualism for Learning*. Philadelphia, PA: Caslon.

Garrett, P.B. (2008) Researching language socialization. In N.H. Hornberger (ed.) *Encyclopedia of Language and Education* (pp. 189–201). Boston, MA: Springer. See http://link.springer.com/10.1007/978-0-387-30424-3_254.

Gebhard, M. (1999) Debates in SLA studies: Redefining classroom SLA as an institutional phenomenon. *TESOL Quarterly* 33 (3), 544–557. doi:10.2307/3587679

Gebhard, M. (2012) Institutional ethnography. In C. Chapelle and L. Harklau (eds) *The Encyclopedia of Applied Linguistics* (pp. 2703–2708). Oxford: Wiley-Blackwell.

Gee, J.P. (2000) Identity as an analytic lens for research in education. *Review of Research in Education* 25, 99–125.

Gee, J.P. (2015) Discourse, small-d, Big D. In K. Tracy, C. Ilie and T. Sandel (eds) *The International Encyclopedia of Language and Social Interaction* (pp. 418–422). Oxford: Wiley-Blackwell.

Gee, J.P., Hull, G. and Lankshear, C. (1996) *The New Work Order*. Boulder, CO: Westview Press.

Geertz, C. (1974) 'From the native's point of view': On the nature of anthropological understanding. *Bullameracadarts Bulletin of the American Academy of Arts and Sciences* 28 (1), 26–45.

Geertz, C. (1977) *The Interpretation of Cultures*. New York: Basic Books.

Goffman, E. (1961) *Asylums: Essays on the Social Situation of Mental Patients and Other Inmates*. New York: Anchor Books/Doubleday.

Gonzales, R.G. (2011) Learning to be illegal: Undocumented youth and shifting legal contexts in the transition to adulthood. *American Sociological Review* 76 (4), 602–619.

Gonzalez, N., Moll, L.C. and Amanti, C. (eds) (2005) *Funds of Knowledge: Theorizing Practices in Households, Communities, and Classrooms*. New York: Routledge.

Gort, M. (2012) Code-switching patterns in the writing-related talk of young emergent bilinguals. *Journal of Literacy Research* 44 (1), 45–75. doi:10.1177/1086296X11431626

Gort, M. (2015) Transforming literacy learning and teaching through translanguaging and other typical practices associated with 'Doing being bilingual'. *International Multilingual Research Journal* 9 (1), 1–6. doi:10.1080/19313152.2014.988030

Gorter, D. (2017) Linguistic landscapes and trends in the study of schoolscapes. *Linguistics and Education* 44, 80–85. doi:10.1016/j.linged.2017.10.001

Greene, J.P. (1998) *A Meta-analysis of the Effectiveness of Bilingual Education*. Claremont, CA: Tomas Rivera Policy Institute. http://www.languagepolicy.net/archives/greene.htm.

Gulla, A.N. (2015) Nobody knows the stories of others: High school English language learners find their poetic voices by responding to works of art. *TESOL Journal* 6 (4), 612–620. doi:10.1002/tesj.227

Gulzar, M.A. (2010) Code-switching: Awareness about its utility in bilingual classrooms. *Bulletin of Education & Research* 32 (2), 23–44.

Gunderson, L. (2002) Reception classes for immigrant students in Vancouver, Canada. *TESOL Quarterly* 36 (1), 93–98.

Gutiérrez, K.D. (2008) Developing a sociocritical literacy in the third space. *Reading Research Quarterly* 43 (2), 148–164. doi:10.1598/RRQ.43.2.3

Gutiérrez, K.D. and Rogoff, B. (2003) Cultural ways of learning: Individual traits or repertoires of practice. *Educational Researcher* 32 (5), 19–25. doi:10.3102/0013189X032005019

Gutmann, A. (1999) *Democratic Education*. Princeton, NJ: Princeton University Press.
Haas, E. and Gort, M. (2009) Demanding more: Legal standards and best practices for English language learners. *Bilingual Research Journal* 32 (2), 115–135. doi:10.1080/15235880903169951
Halliday, M.A. (2003) Written language, standard language, global language. *World Englishes* 22 (4), 405–418.
Harklau, L. (1994) ESL versus mainstream classes: Contrasting L2 learning environments. *TESOL Quarterly* 28 (2), 241–272.
Harklau, L. (2000) From the 'good kids' to the 'worst': Representations of English language learners across educational settings. *TESOL Quarterly* 34 (1), 35–67.
Harklau, L. (2007) The adolescent English language learner. In J. Cummins and C. Davison (eds) *International Handbook of English Language Teaching* (pp. 639–653). Boston, MA: Springer. See http://link.springer.com/chapter/10.1007/978-0-387-46301-8_41.
Hauser, B. (2012) *The New Kids: Big Dreams and Brave Journeys at a High School for Immigrant Teens*. New York: Atria Books.
Haymes, S.N. (2001) 'Us ain't hogs, us is human flesh': Slave pedagogy and the problem of ontology in African American slave culture. *Educational Studies* 32 (2), 129–176.
Hayter, T. (2004) *Open Borders: The Case Against Immigration Controls* (2nd edn). London: Pluto Press.
Herczog, M.M., Kidwell, F.L. and Croddy, M. (2011) *Preparing Students for College, Career, and Citizenship: A California Guide to Align Civic Education and the Common Core State Standards for English Language Arts and Literacy in History/Social Studies, Science and Technical Subjects*. Los Angeles, CA: Los Angeles County Office of Education.
Hersi, A.A. and Watkinson, J.S. (2012) Supporting immigrant students in a newcomer high school: A case study. *Bilingual Research Journal* 35 (1), 98–111. doi:10.1080/15235882.2012.668869
Hertzberg, M. (1998) Having arrived: Dimensions of educational success in a transitional newcomer school. *Anthropology & Education Quarterly* 29 (4), 391–418. doi:10.1525/aeq.1998.29.4.391
Higby, E., Kim, J. and Obler, L.K. (2013) Multilingualism and the brain. *Annual Review of Applied Linguistics* 33, 68–101. doi:10.1017/S0267190513000081
Hones, D.F. (2007) 'A meeting place for us': Milpera, a newcomer high school. *Multicultural Education* 14 (4), 8–15.
Hornberger, N.H. (2005) Opening and filling up implementational and ideological spaces in heritage language education. *The Modern Language Journal* 89, 605–609.
Howard, E.R., Lindholm-Leary, K.J., Rogers, D., Olague, N., Medina, J., Kennedy, B., Sugarman, J. and Christian, D. (2018) *Guiding Principles for Dual Language Education* (3rd edn). Washington, DC: Center for Applied Linguistics.
Howard, K.M. and Lipinoga, S. (2010) Closing down openings: Pretextuality and misunderstanding in parent–teacher conferences with Mexican immigrant families. *Language & Communication* 30 (1), 33–47. doi:10.1016/j.langcom.2009.10.004
Huseman, J. (2016) Welcome to America. Pack a parka. *Slate Magazine*, 5 June. See http://www.slate.com/articles/life/tomorrows_test/2016/06/the_newcomers_center_has_made_anchorage_alaska_one_of_the_best_school_districts.html.
Institute of Education Sciences (2012) *NAEP 2012: Trends in Academic Progress, Reading 1971–2012, Mathematics 1973–2012*. Washington, DC: US Department of Education.
Internationals Network for Public Schools (n.d.) *School Map*. See http://internationals-nps.org/international-high-schools/school-map/ (accessed 21 December 2016).
Jane-Francis, A.A. and Foncha, J.W. (2014) Language ideologies in the linguistic landscape of one university in South Africa. *Mediterranean Journal of Social Sciences* 5 (7), 623–630. doi:10.5901/mjss.2014.v5n7p623

Jefferson, G. (1978) Sequential aspects of storytelling in conversation. In J. Schenkein (ed.) *Studies in the Organization of Conversational Interaction* (pp. 219–248). New York: Academic Press.

Jefferson, G. (2004) Glossary of transcript symbols with an introduction. In G.H. Lerner (ed.) *Conversation Analysis: Studies from the First Generation* (pp. 13–31). Amsterdam and Philadelphia, PA: John Benjamins.

Jerolmack, C. and Khan, S. (2014) Talk is cheap: Ethnography and the attitudinal fallacy. *Sociological Methods & Research* 43 (2), 178–209. doi:10.1177/0049124114523396

Jewitt, C. (2013) Multimodal methods for researching digital technologies. In S. Price, C. Jewitt and B. Brown (eds) *The SAGE Handbook of Digital Technology Research* (pp. 250–265). Thousand Oaks, CA: Sage.

Johnson, D.C. and Freeman, R. (2010) Appropriating language policy on the local level: Working the spaces for bilingual education. In K. Menken and O. García (eds) *Negotiating Language Policies in Schools: Educators as Policymakers* (pp. 12–31). New York: Routledge.

Kachru, B.B. (1982) The bilingual's linguistic repertoire. In B.S. Hartford, A. Valdman and C.R. Foster (eds) *Issues in International Bilingual Education: The Role of the Vernacular* (pp. 25–52). New York: Plenum Press.

Kachru, B.B. (1990) World Englishes and applied linguistics. In M.A.K. Halliday, J. Gibbons and H. Nicholas (eds) *Learning, Keeping and Using Language* (pp. 178–205). Amsterdam and Philadelphia, PA: John Benjamins. doi:10.1075/z.lkul2.19kac

Kanno, Y. and Kangas, S.E.N. (2014) 'I'm not going to be, like, for the AP': English language learners' limited access to advanced college-preparatory courses in high school. *American Educational Research Journal* 51 (5), 848–878. doi:10.3102/0002831214544716

Kanno, Y. and Norton, B. (2003) Imagined communities and educational possibilities: Introduction. *Journal of Language, Identity, and Education* 2 (4), 241–249.

Keating, D. and Karklis, L. (2016) The increasingly diverse United States of America. *Washington Post*, 25 November. See https://www.washingtonpost.com/graphics/national/how-diverse-is-america/.

Keating, E. (2015) Discourse, space, and place. In D. Tannen, H.E. Hamilton and D. Schiffrin (eds) *The Handbook of Discourse Analysis* (pp. 244–261). New York: John Wiley.

Kennedy, E. (2007) School for change: Establishing an ELL newcomer program. *ESL Magazine* 60, 9–14.

King, L. and Carson, L. (eds) (2016) *The Multilingual City: Vitality, Conflict and Change*. Bristol: Multilingual Matters.

Kingston, L.N. and Stam, K.R. (2015) Recovering from statelessness: Resettled Bhutanese-Nepali and Karen refugees reflect on lack of legal nationality. *Journal of Human Rights* 11, 1–18. doi:10.1080/14754835.2015.1132156

Knoster, T. and Drogan, R. (2016) *The Teacher's Pocket Guide for Positive Behavior Support: Targeted Classroom Solutions*. Baltimore, MD: Paul H. Brookes Publishing.

Kolodner, M. (2017) Will high school segregation for refugees lead to better integration? *The Hechinger Report*, 4 May. See http://hechingerreport.org/refugees-can-choose-separate-high-school-kentucky-town/.

Kovelman, I., Baker, S.A. and Petitto, L.-A. (2008) Bilingual and monolingual brains compared: A functional magnetic resonance imaging investigation of syntactic processing and a possible 'neural signature' of bilingualism. *Journal of Cognitive Neuroscience* 20 (1), 153–169. doi:10.1162/jocn.2008.20011

Krashen, S.D. (1985) *The Input Hypothesis: Issues and Implications*. New York: Addison-Wesley Longman.

Kreck, C. (2014) *Learning English in Rural America*. Denver, CO: Education Commission of the States.

Kruk, R. (1987) Pregnancy and its social consequences in mediaeval and traditional Arab society. *Quaderni Di Studi Arabi* 5/6, 418–430.

Kumashiro, K.K. (2012) *Bad Teacher! How Blaming Teachers Distorts the Bigger Picture*. New York: Teachers College Press.

Ladson-Billings, G. (1995) Toward a theory of culturally relevant pedagogy. *American Educational Research Journal* 32 (3), 465–491.

Ladson-Billings, G. (2009) *The Dreamkeepers: Successful Teachers of African American Children*. San Francisco, CA: Jossey-Bass.

Larsen-Freeman, D. (1997) Chaos/complexity science and second language acquisition. *Applied Linguistics* 18 (2), 141–165.

Lather, P. (1992) Critical frames in educational research: Feminist and post-structural perspectives. *Theory Into Practice* 31 (2), 87–99. doi:10.1080/00405849209543529

Latour, B. (2005) *Reassembling the Social*. Oxford: Oxford University Press.

Lee, S.J. (1994) Behind the model-minority stereotype: Voices of high- and low-achieving Asian American students. *Anthropology & Education Quarterly* 25 (4), 413–429.

Leonet, O., Cenoz, J. and Gorter, D. (2017) Challenging minority language isolation: Translanguaging in a trilingual school in the Basque country. *Journal of Language, Identity & Education* 16 (4), 216–227. doi:10.1080/15348458.2017.1328281

Lesko, N. (2012) *Act your Age! A Cultural Construction of Adolescence* (2nd edn). New York: Routledge, Taylor & Francis.

Lewis, L. and Gray, L. (2016) *Programs and Services for High School English Learners in Public School Districts: 2015–16*. Washington, DC: NCES, IES, U.S. Department of Education.

Lippi-Green, R. (2011) *English with an Accent: Language, Ideology and Discrimination in the United States* (2nd edn). New York: Routledge.

Macedo, D. and Bartolomé, L.I. (2014) Multiculturalism permitted in English only. *International Multilingual Research Journal* 8 (1), 24–37. doi:10.1080/19313152.2014.852426

Macgilchrist, F. (2016) Positive discourse analysis: Contesting dominant discourses by reframing the issues. *Critical Approaches to Discourse Analysis Across Disciplines* 1 (1), 74–94.

Macías, A.H., Fontes, A.A.D.L., Kephart, K. and Blume, M. (2013) Sheltered instruction for English language learners: Insights and challenges. *TESOL Journal* 4 (1), 83–105. doi:10.1002/tesj.50

MacSwan, J. (2017) A multilingual perspective on translanguaging. *American Educational Research Journal* 54 (1), 167–201. doi:10.3102/0002831216683935

Makoni, S. and Pennycook, A. (eds) (2006) *Disinventing and Reconstituting Languages*. Clevedon: Multilingual Matters.

Malen, B. (1994) The micropolitics of education: Mapping the multiple dimensions of power relations in school polities. *Journal of Education Policy* 9 (5), 147–167. doi:10.1080/0268093940090513

Malen, B. and Cochran, M.V. (2014) Beyond pluralistic patterns of power: Research on the micropolitics of schools. In B.S. Cooper, J.G. Cibulka and L.D. Fusarelli (eds) *Handbook of Education Politics and Policy* (2nd edn) (pp. 3–36). New York: Routledge.

Martin, J.R. (2004) Positive discourse analysis: Solidarity and change. *Revista Canaria de Estudios Ingleses* 49, 179–202.

Matas, A.K. (2012) Analyzing best practices in the schooling of secondary-level Latino newcomer immigrant youth: A comparison study of two yearlong specialized programs. DPhil dissertation, Faculty of Claremont Graduate University and San Diego State University. See https://scholarship.claremont.edu/cgi/viewcontent.cgi?article=1069&context=cgu_etd. doi:10.5642/cguetd/68.

Matthews, J. (2008) Schooling and settlement: Refugee education in Australia. *International Studies in Sociology of Education* 18 (1), 31–45. doi:10.1080/09620210802195947

May, S. and Sleeter, C.E. (eds) (2010) *Critical Multiculturalism: Theory and Praxis*. New York: Routledge.

McBrien, J.L. (2005) Educational needs and barriers for refugee students in the United States: A review of the literature. *Review of Educational Research* 75 (3), 329–364.
McCarty, T.L. (2007) Revitalizing indigenous languages in homogenising times. In O. García and C. Baker (eds) *Bilingual Education: An Introductory Reader* (pp. 33–49). Clevedon: Multilingual Matters.
McDermott, R. (1999) Culture is not an environment of the mind. *Journal of the Learning Sciences* 8 (1), 157–169.
McDermott, R., Goldman, S. and Varenne, H. (2006) The cultural work of learning disabilities. *Educational Researcher* 35 (6), 12–17.
McDonnell, L.M. and Hill, P.T. (n.d.) *Newcomers in American schools: Meeting the Educational Needs of Immigrant Youth*. Santa Monica, CA: Rand Corporation.
McHugh, M. and Sugarman, J. (2015) *Transatlantic Symposium Report: Improving Instruction for Immigrant and Refugee Students in Secondary Schools*. Washington, DC: Migration Policy Institute.
McHugh, M., Herzog-Punzenberger, B., Sugarman, J., von Dewitz, N. and Wong, C. (2015) *Serving Newcomer Immigrant and Refugee Students in Secondary Schools: Comparing U.S. and European Practices* (Webinar, 22 October). Washington, DC: Migration Policy Institute.
McKay, S.L. (2010) English as an international language. In N.H. Hornberger and S.L. McKay (eds) *Sociolinguistics and Language Education* (pp. 89–115). Bristol: Multilingual Matters.
Mehan, H. (1985) The structure of classroom discourse. In T.A. van Dijk (ed.) *Handbook of Discourse Analysis, Vol. 3* (pp. 120–131). New York: Academic Press.
Meissner, F. and Vertovec, S. (2015) Comparing super-diversity. *Ethnic and Racial Studies* 38 (4), 541–555. doi:10.1080/01419870.2015.980295
Mendenhall, M., Bartlett, L. and Ghaffar-Kucher, A. (2017) 'If you need help, they are always there for us': Education for refugees in an International High School in NYC. *The Urban Review* 49, 1–25. doi:10.1007/s11256-016-0379-4
Menken, K. (2005) When the test is what counts: How high-stakes testing affects language policy and the education of English language learners in high school. Doctoral dissertation, Teachers College, Columbia University.
Menken, K. (2008) *English Learners Left Behind: Standardized Testing as Language Policy*. Clevedon: Multilingual Matters.
Mijares, L. and Relaño Pastor, A.M. (2011) Language programs at Villababel High: Rethinking ideologies of social inclusion. *International Journal of Bilingual Education and Bilingualism* 14 (4), 427–442. doi:10.1080/13670050.2011.573066
Mitchell, J.C. (1984) Typicality and the case study. In R.F. Ellen (ed.) *Ethnographic Research: A Guide to General Conduct* (pp. 238–241). New York: Academic Press.
Moll, L.C. (1992) Funds of knowledge for teaching: Using a qualitative approach to connect homes and classrooms. *Theory into Practice* 31 (2), 132–141.
Montanaro, D. (2016) How the browning of America is upending both political parties. NPR.org, 12 October. See https://www.npr.org/2016/10/12/497529936/how-the-browning-of-america-is-upending-both-political-parties.
Moore, L.C. (2006) Learning by heart in Qur'anic and public schools in northern Cameroon. *Social Analysis* 50 (3), 109–126.
Moriarty, M. (2012) Language ideological debates in the linguistic landscape of an Irish tourist town. In D. Gorter, H.F. Marten and L.V. Mensel (eds) *Minority Languages in the Linguistic Landscape* (pp. 74–88). Houndmills: Palgrave MacMillan. doi:10.1057/9780230360235_5
Muller, A. and Beardsmore, H.B. (2004) Multilingual interaction in plurilingual classes: European school practice. *International Journal of Bilingual Education and Bilingualism* 7 (1), 24–42. doi:10.1080/13670050408667799
Munoz, M.A. and Clavijo, C. (2000) *Working with Limited English Proficient Students: Input from the Field on High School Newcomer Programs*. Louisville, KY: JCPS.

Murray, K.E. and Marx, D.M. (2013) Attitudes toward unauthorized immigrants, authorized immigrants, and refugees. *Cultural Diversity and Ethnic Minority Psychology* 19 (3), 332–341. doi:10.1037/a0030812

Nader, L. (1974) Up the anthropologist: Perspectives gained from studying up. In D.H. Hymes (ed.) *Reinventing Anthropology* (pp. 285–311). New York: Vintage Books. See http://eric.ed.gov/?id=ED065375.

Nakamura, P. (2014) *Facilitating Reading Acquisition in Multilingual Environments in India*. Washington, DC: American Institutes for Research.

National Academies of Sciences, Engineering, and Medicine (2017) *Promoting the Educational Success of Children and Youth Learning English: Promising Futures*. Washington, DC: National Academies Press. doi:10.17226/24677

National Council for the Social Studies (2013) *College, Career, and Civic Life (C3) Framework for Social Studies State Standards*. Silver Spring, MD: National Council for the Social Studies. See http://www.socialstudies.org/c3.

NCES (National Center for Educational Statistics) (2016). English language learners in public schools. *IES > NCES*, May. See http://nces.ed.gov/programs/coe/indicator_cgf.asp.

Neuroskeptic (2015) Do bilingual people have a cognitive advantage? *Discover Magazine*, 4 December. See https://www.discovermagazine.com/mind/do-bilingual-people-have-a-cognitive-advantage.

Newell, G.E., Bloome, D. and Hirvela, A. (2015) *Teaching and Learning Argumentative Writing in High School English Language Arts Classrooms*. New York: Routledge.

Nichols, S. and Snowden, C. (2016) *Languages and Literacies as Mobile and Placed Resources*. New York: Routledge.

Nicoladis, E. and Montanari, S. (2016) *Bilingualism Across the Lifespan: Factors Moderating Language Proficiency*. Berlin: Walter de Gruyter.

Norton, B. (2013) *Identity and Language Learning: Extending the Conversation* (2nd edn). Bristol: Multilingual Matters.

Norton, B. and McKinney, C. (2011) An identity approach to second language acquisition. In D. Atkinson (ed.) *Alternative Approaches to Second Language Acquisition* (1st edn) (pp. 73–94). Abingdon: Routledge.

Norton Peirce, B. (1995) Social identity, investment, and language learning. *TESOL Quarterly* 29 (1), 9. doi:10.2307/3587803

Ó Riain, S. (2009) Extending the ethnographic case study. In D. Byrne and C.C. Ragin (eds) *The SAGE Handbook of Case-Based Methods* (pp. 289–306). London: Sage. See http://srmo.sagepub.com/view/the-sage-handbook-of-case-based-methods/SAGE.xml.

Ochs, E. (1979) Transcription as theory. In E. Ochs (ed.) *Developmental Pragmatics* (pp. 43–72). New York: Academic Press.

OECD (2015) *Immigrant Students at School*. Paris: Organisation for Economic Co-operation and Development. See http://www.keepeek.com/Digital-Asset-Management/oecd/education/immigrant-students-at-school_9789264249509-en.

Ohio Department of Education (2014) *Characteristics of Programs Serving LEP Students in Ohio*. Columbus, OH: Ohio Department of Education.

Ohio Department of Education (2018) *Guidelines for Identification and Assessment of English Learners*. Columbus, OH: Ohio Department of Education.

Oliver, M.L. and Shapiro, T.M. (2006) *Black Wealth, White Wealth: A New Perspective on Racial Inequality*. New York: Taylor & Francis.

Olsen, L. (2008) *Made in America: Immigrant Students in Our Public Schools* (10th edn). New York: New Press.

Orellana, M.F. (2016) *Immigrant Children in Transcultural Spaces: Language, Learning, and Love*. New York: Taylor & Francis.

Ortega, L. (2008) *Understanding Second Language Acquisition*. Abingdon: Routledge.

Osumare, H. (2008) *The Africanist Aesthetic in Global Hip-Hop: Power Moves* (1st edn). Houndmills: Palgrave Macmillan.

Otheguy, R., García, O. and Reid, W. (2015) Clarifying translanguaging and deconstructing named languages: A perspective from linguistics. *Applied Linguistics Review* 6 (3), 281–307. doi:10.1515/applirev-2015-0014

Otheguy, R., García, O. and Reid, W. (2018) A translanguaging view of the linguistic system of bilinguals. *Applied Linguistics Review* 10 (4). doi:10.1515/applirev-2018-0020

Overberg, P. (2014) The changing face of America: Mapping diversity interactive. *USA Today*. See http://www.gannett-cdn.com/GDContent/2014/diversity-map/index.html.

Paap, K.R., Johnson, H.A. and Sawi, O. (2015) Bilingual advantages in executive functioning either do not exist or are restricted to very specific and undetermined circumstances. *Cortex* 69, 265–278. doi:10.1016/j.cortex.2015.04.014

Pacheco, M.B. (2016) *Translanguaging in the English-centric Classroom: A Communities of Practice Perspective*. Nashville, TN: Vanderbilt University.

Páez, M.M., Tabors, P.O. and López, L.M. (2007) Dual language and literacy development of Spanish-speaking preschool children. *Journal of Applied Developmental Psychology* 28 (2), 85–102. doi:10.1016/j.appdev.2006.12.007

Paris, D. (2012) Culturally sustaining pedagogy: A needed change in stance, terminology, and practice. *Educational Researcher* 41 (3), 93–97. doi:10.3102/0013189X12441244

Pascopella, A. (2011) Successful strategies for English language learners. *District Administration* 47 (2), 29–44.

Payne, R.K. (2005) *A Framework for Understanding Poverty* (4th edn). Highlands, TX: aha! Process.

Peace Corps Morocco (2011) *Moroccan Arabic*. Peace Corps Morocco. See https://friendsofmorocco.org/Docs/Darija/Moroccan%20Arabic%20textbook%202011.pdf.

Pennycook, A. (2006) The myth of English as an international language. In S. Makoni and A. Pennycook (eds) *Disinventing and Reconstituting Languages* (pp. 90–115). Clevedon: Multilingual Matters.

Pennycook, A. and Otsuji, E. (2015a) Making scents of the landscape. *Linguistic Landscape* 1 (3), 191–212. doi:10.1075/ll.1.3.01pen

Pennycook, A. and Otsuji, E. (2015b) *Metrolingualism: Language in the City*. New York: Routledge.

Piketty, T. (2014) *Capital in the Twenty-first Century* (1st edn). Cambridge, MA: Belknap Press.

Piot, L. and Kelchtermans, G. (2016) The micropolitics of distributed leadership. *Educational Management Administration & Leadership* 44 (4), 632–649. doi:10.1177/1741143214559224

Pipher, M. (2002) *The Middle of Everywhere: The World's Refugees Come to our Town*. Boston, MA: Houghton Mifflin Harcourt.

Plonsky, L. and Oswald, F.L. (2014) How big is 'big'? Interpreting effect sizes in L2 research. *Language Learning* 64, 878–912. doi:10.1111/lang.12079

Porter, R.P. (1996) *Forked Tongue: The Politics of Bilingual Education* (2nd edn). Piscataway, NJ: Transaction Publishers.

Porter, R.P. (1998) The case against bilingual education. *The Atlantic*, May. See http://www.theatlantic.com/magazine/archive/1998/05/the-case-against-bilingual-education/305426/.

Portes, A. (2007) Migration, development, and segmented assimilation: A conceptual review of the evidence. *ANNALS of the American Academy of Political and Social Science* 610 (1), 73–97. doi:10.1177/0002716206296779

Portes, A. and Rumbaut, R.G. (2001) *Legacies: The Story of the Immigrant Second Generation* (1st edn). Berkeley, CA: University of California Press.

Rabinow, P. (1977) *Reflections on Fieldwork in Morocco*. Berkeley, CA: University of California Press.

Razfar, A. and Rumenapp, J.C. (2012) Language ideologies in English learner classrooms: Critical reflections and the role of explicit awareness. *Language Awareness* 21 (4), 347–368. doi:10.1080/09658416.2011.616591

Riley, J.L. (2008) *Let Them In: The Case for Open Borders*. New York: Gotham.
Rivera, C.I. (2009) The impact of an immersion program for newcomers on the transitional period. EdD dissertation, Northcentral University. See http://www.proquest.com/en-US/products/dissertations/individuals.shtml.
Rogers, R. (ed.) (2011) *An Introduction to Critical Discourse Analysis in Education* (2nd edn). New York: Routledge, Taylor & Francis.
Rolstad, K. (2005) The big picture: A meta-analysis of program effectiveness research on English language learners. *Educational Policy* 19 (4), 572–594. doi:10.1177/0895904805278067
Rosenberg, M. (2018) Exclusive: Dozens of refugee resettlement offices to close as Trump downsizes program. *Reuters*, 14 February. See https://www.reuters.com/article/us-usa-immigration-refugees-exclusive/exclusive-dozens-of-refugee-resettlement-offices-to-close-as-trump-downsizes-program-idUSKCN1FY1EJ.
Rossell, C.H. and Baker, K. (1996) The educational effectiveness of bilingual education. *Research in the Teaching of English* 20, 7–74.
Roxas, K. (2011) Creating communities: Working with refugee students in classrooms. *Democracy & Education* 19 (2), 1–8.
Roy, L.A. and Roxas, K.C. (2011) Whose deficit is this anyhow? Exploring counterstories of Somali Bantu refugees' experiences in 'doing school'. *Harvard Educational Review* 81 (3), 521–542.
Rymes, B. (2010) Classroom discourse analysis: A focus on communicative repertoires. In N.H. Hornberger and S.L. McKay (eds) *Sociolinguistics and Language Education* (pp. 528–546). Bristol: Multilingual Matters.
Rymes, B. (2014) Communicative repertoire. In C. Leung and B.V. Street (eds) *The Routledge Companion to English Studies* (pp. 287–302). Abingdon: Routledge.
Salerno, A.S. and Kibler, A.K. (2015) Vocational training for adolescent English language learners in newcomer programs: Opportunities or isolation? *TESOL Journal* 6 (2), 201–224.
Salomone, R.C. (2010) *True American: Language, Identity, and the Education of Immigrant Children*. Cambridge, MA: Harvard University Press.
Sayer, P. (2014) *Ambiguities and Tensions in English Language Teaching: Portraits of EFL Teachers as Legitimate Speakers*. Abingdon: Routledge.
Schneider, J. (2017) Why Americans think so poorly of the country's schools. *The Atlantic*, 17 July. See https://www.theatlantic.com/education/archive/2017/07/the-education-perception-gap/533898/.
Schnur, B. (1999) A newcomer's high school. *Educational Leadership* 56 (7), 50.
Schultz, R. and Vana, C. (2008) Coming to America: Minneapolis's newcomer program. *School Administrator* 65 (10), 18–19.
Scollon, R. (2013) Geographies of discourse. In *Multilingualism and Multimodality* (pp. 183–198). New York: Springer. See http://link.springer.com/chapter/10.1007/978-94-6209-266-2_10.
Scollon, R. and Scollon, S.W. (2003) *Discourses in Place: Language in the Material World*. New York: Taylor & Francis.
Scully, J.E. (2016) Going to school in the United States: Voices of adolescent newcomers. *TESOL Journal* 7 (3), 591–620. doi:10.1002/tesj.226
Segura, G. (2012) The browning of America. *Democracy*, 25. See https://democracyjournal.org/magazine/25/the-browning-of-america/.
Seilstad, B. (2012) Using tailor-made YouTube videos as a preteaching strategy for English language learners in Morocco: Towards a hybrid language learning course. *Teaching English with Technology* 4, 31–47.
Seilstad, B. (2014a) Designing, implementing, and evaluating a department-wide service-learning program for English language learners in Morocco. *Journal of Higher Education Outreach and Engagement* 18 (1), 229–263.

Seilstad, B. (2014b) Towards a broad-based understanding of effective CALL practice: Reactions and recommendations of university-level Moroccan English language learners. *Teaching English with Technology* 2, 27–50.

Seilstad, B. (2015) Hip hop culture in a small Moroccan city. *Journal of Hip Hop Studies* 2 (1), 65–98.

Seilstad, B. (2017) Citizenship classes for Bhutanese-Nepali elders: From cognitive deficits to cultural-historical understandings. *International Journal of Society, Culture & Language* 5 (2), 73–90.

Seilstad, B. (2018) Partially shared objects and the (elusive) potential of expansive learning: The case of 'jury' in community-based citizenship classes for Nepali-speaking Bhutanese refugee elders. *Mind, Culture, and Activity* 25 (4), 308–323.

Seilstad, B. and Kim, S. (2020) 'Colibrí' 'Hummingbird' as translanguaging metaphor. In Z. Tian, L. Aghai, P. Sayer and J.L. Schissel (eds) *Envisioning TESOL Through a Translanguaging Lens: Global Perspectives* (pp. 253–273). Springer International. doi:10.1007/978-3-030-47031-9

Seilstad, B. and Meftah, S. (2016) Service learning dans les etudes supérieurs marocaines. In M. Behnassi, H. Ouamouch and D. Bouzaffour (eds) *Université publique et dynamiques sociétales au Maroc: De nouveaux enjeux, des référentiels émergents* (pp. 126–138). Agadir: CERES Publishing.

Seilstad, B., Braun, D., Kim, S. and Choi, M.-S. (2019) Bilingual biomes: Revising and redoing monolingual instructional practices for multilingual students (10th grade). In M.A. Stewart and H. Hansen-Thomas (eds) *Engaging Research: Transforming Practices for the High School* (pp. 111–126). Alexandria, VA: TESOL Press.

Sensoy, O. and DiAngelo, R. (2011) *Is Everyone Really Equal? An Introduction to Key Concepts in Social Justice Education*. New York: Teachers College Press.

Short, D.J. (2002) Newcomer programs: An educational alternative for secondary immigrant students. *Education and Urban Society* 34 (2), 173–198. doi:10.1177/0013124502034002004

Short, D.J. (2016) *Helping Newly Arrived Students Succeed: Research on Newcomer Programs and Practices*. Washington, DC: Regional Educational Laboratory Southwest.

Short, D.J. and Boyson, B.A. (2004) *Creating Access: Language and Academic Programs for Secondary School Newcomers*. McHenry, IL: Delta Systems.

Short, D.J. and Boyson, B.A. (2012) *Helping Newcomer Students Succeed in Secondary Schools and Beyond*. Washington, DC: Center for Applied Linguistics.

Short, D.J. and Fitzsimmons, S. (2007) *Double the Work: Challenges and Solutions to Acquiring Language and Academic Literacy for Adolescent English Language Learners*. New York: Carnegie Corporation of New York.

Short, D.J., Vogt, M.J. and Echevarria, J.J. (2010) *The SIOP Model for Teaching Science to English Learners*. Boston, MA: Pearson.

Sierens, S. and van Avermaet, P. (2013) Language diversity in education: Evolving from multilingual education to functional multilingual learning. In D. Little, C. Leung and P.V. Avermaet (eds) *Managing Diversity in Education: Languages, Policies, Pedagogies* (pp. 204–222). Bristol: Multilingual Matters.

Silver, N. (2015) *The Signal and the Noise: Why So Many Predictions Fail – But Some Don't*. Harmondsworth: New York: Penguin.

Silver, N. (2017) The media has a probability problem. *FiveThirtyEight*, 21 September. See https://fivethirtyeight.com/features/the-media-has-a-probability-problem/.

Silverstein, M. (1972) Chinook jargon: Language contact and the problem of multi-level generative systems, I. *Language* 48 (2), 378–406. doi:10.2307/412141

Silverstein, M. (1996) Monoglot 'standard' in America: Standardization and metaphors of linguistic hegemony. In D. Brenneis and R.K.S. Macaulay (eds) *The Matrix of Language: Contemporary Linguistic Anthropology* (pp. 284–306). Boulder, CO: Westview Press.

Silverstein, M. (2014) How language communities intersect: Is 'superdiversity' an incremental or transformative condition? *Language & Communication* 44, 7–18. doi:10.1016/j.langcom.2014.10.015

Slavin, R.E., Madden, N., Calderón, M., Chamberlain, A. and Hennessy, M. (2011) Reading and language outcomes of a multiyear randomized evaluation of transitional bilingual education. *Educational Evaluation and Policy Analysis* 33 (1), 47–58.

Smith, D.E. (ed.) (2006) *Institutional Ethnography as Practice*. Lanham, MD: Rowman & Littlefield.

Smyth, E., Darmody, M., McGinnity, F. and Byrne, D. (2009) *Adapting to Diversity: Irish Schools and Newcomer Students*. Dublin: ESRI.

Song, S. and Kellogg, D. (2011) Word meaning as a palimpsest: A defense of sociocultural theory. *The Modern Language Journal* 95 (4), 589–604. doi:10.1111/j.1540-4781.2011.01236.x

Sparks, S.D. (2016) Summing up results from TIMSS, PISA. *Education Week*, 14 December. See http://www.edweek.org/ew/section/multimedia/summing-up-results-from-timss-pisa.html.

Sparrow, W., Butvilofsky, S., Escamilla, K., Hopewell, S. and Tolento, T. (2014) Examining the longitudinal biliterate trajectory of emerging bilingual learners in a paired literacy instructional model. *Bilingual Research Journal* 37 (1), 24–42. doi:10.1080/15235882.2014.893271

Spotti, M. (2011) Modernist language ideologies, indexicalities and identities: Looking at the multilingual classroom through a post-Fishmanian lens. *Applied Linguistics Review* 2, 29–50.

Steinbach, M. (2010) Quand je sors d'accueil: Linguistic integration of immigrant adolescents in Quebec secondary schools. *Language, Culture and Curriculum* 23 (2), 95–107. doi:10.1080/07908311003786711

Stewart, M.A. (2014) Social networking, workplace, and entertainment literacies: The out-of-school literate lives of newcomer Latina/o adolescents. *Reading Research Quarterly* 49 (4), 365–369.

Stone, D. (2011) *Policy Paradox: The Art of Political Decision Making* (3rd edn). New York: W.W. Norton.

Straubhaar, R. (2014) Student use of aspirational and linguistic social capital in an urban immigrant-centered English immersion high school. *High School Journal* 97 (2), 92–106.

Strauss, V. (2012) How grossly underfunded are public schools? *Washington Post*, 25 November. See https://www.washingtonpost.com/news/answer-sheet/wp/2012/11/25/how-grossly-underfunded-are-public-schools/.

Street, B.V. (1993) Culture is a verb: Anthropological aspect of language and cultural process. In D. Graddol (ed.) *Language and Culture: Papers from the Annual Meeting of the British Association of Applied Linguistics Held at Trevelyan College, University of Durham, September 1991* (pp. 23–43). Clevedon: Multilingual Matters.

Suárez-Orozco, C., Suárez-Orozco, M.M. and Todorova, I. (2008) *Learning a New Land: Immigrant Students in American Society*. Cambridge, MA: Belknap Press of Harvard University Press.

Suárez-Orozco, C., Gaytán, F.X., Bang, H.J., Pakes, J., O'Connor, E. and Rhodes, J. (2010) Academic trajectories of newcomer immigrant youth. *Developmental Psychology* 46 (3), 602–618. doi:10.1037/a0018201

Suárez-Orozco, C., Yoshikawa, H., Teranishi, R.T. and Suárez-Orozco, M.M. (2011) Growing up in the shadows: The developmental implications of unauthorized status. *Harvard Educational Review* 81 (3), 438–473.

Subedi, B. (2013) Photographic images of refugee spatial encounters: Pedagogy of displacement. *Qualitative Research in Education* 2 (3), 277–301.

Sylvan, C.E. (2013) Newcomer high school students as an asset: The Internationals Approach. *Voices in Urban Education* 37, 19–24.

Taylor, A.M. (2013) Pedagogy for Latino/a newcomer students: A study of four secondary social studies teachers in New York City urban newcomer schools. PhD thesis, Columbia University. See http://www.proquest.com/en-US/products/dissertations/individuals.shtml.

Teaford, J. (1970) The transformation of Massachusetts education, 1670–1780. *History of Education Quarterly* 10 (3), 287–307.

The Douglas Fir Group (2016) A transdisciplinary framework for SLA in a multilingual world. *The Modern Language Journal* 100 (S1), 19–47. See https://doi.org/10.1111/modl.12301.

Thomas, W.P. and Collier, V.P. (2012) *Dual Language Education for a Transformed World*. Albuquerque, NM: Fuente Press.

Thorstensson Dávila, L. (2018) The pivotal and peripheral roles of bilingual classroom assistants at a Swedish elementary school. *International Journal of Bilingual Education and Bilingualism* 21 (8), 956–967. doi:10.1080/13670050.2016.1224224

Trueba, H.T. (1988) English literacy acquisition: From cultural trauma to learning disabilities in minority students. *Linguistics and Education* 1, 125–152.

Tse, L. (2001) *Why Don't They Learn English? Separating Fact from Fallacy in the U.S. Language Debate*. New York: Teachers College Press.

Umansky, I.M. and Reardon, S.F. (2014) Reclassification patterns among Latino English learner students in bilingual, dual immersion, and English immersion classrooms. *American Educational Research Journal* 51 (5), 879–912. doi:10.3102/0002831214545110

US Department of Justice and US Department of Education (n.d.) *Ensuring English Learner Students Can Participate Meaningfully and Equally in Educational Programs*. See https://www2.ed.gov/about/offices/list/ocr/docs/dcl-factsheet-el-students-201501.pdf.

US National Commission on Excellence in Education (1983) *A Nation at Risk*. See https://www2.ed.gov/pubs/NatAtRisk/risk.html.

Valentino, R.A. and Reardon, S.F. (2015) Effectiveness of four instructional programs designed to serve English learners: Variation by ethnicity and initial English proficiency. *Educational Evaluation and Policy Analysis* 37 (4), 612–637.

van Maanen, J. (2011) *Tales of the Field: On Writing Ethnography* (2nd edn). Chicago, IL: University Of Chicago Press.

Vazquez, D. (2013) Educación bilingüe a nivel de escuela secundaria/Dual-language education at the high school level. *Voices in Urban Education* 37, 14–18.

Vertovec, S. (2007) Super-diversity and its implications. *Ethnic and Racial Studies* 30 (6), 1024–1054. doi:10.1080/01419870701599465

Vertovec, S. (2009) *Transnationalism*. New York: Routledge.

Vertovec, S. (2016) *Super-diversity*. New York: Routledge.

Vogt, M.J. and Echevarria, J.J. (2007) *99 Ideas and Activities for Teaching English Learners with the SIOP Model*. Boston, MA: Pearson.

Waggoner, D. (1999) Who are secondary newcomer and linguistically different youth? In C.J. Faltis and P.M. Wolfe (eds) *So Much to Say: Adolescents, Bilingualism, and ESL in the Secondary School* (pp. 13–41). New York: Teachers College Press.

Wagner, D.A. (1994) *Literacy, Culture and Development: Becoming Literate in Morocco*. Cambridge: Cambridge University Press.

Wagner, D.A. (2017) *Learning as Development: Rethinking International Education in a Changing World*. Abingdon: Routledge.

Waninge, F., Dörnyei, Z. and de Bot, K. (2014) Motivational dynamics in language learning: Change, stability, and context. *The Modern Language Journal* 98 (3), 704–723. doi:10.1111/j.1540-4781.2014.12118.x

Warren, D. (2014) American Indian histories as education history. *History of Education Quarterly* 54 (3), 255–285.

Waters, M.C., Tran, V.C., Kasinitz, P. and Mollenkopf, J.H. (2010) Segmented assimilation revisited: Types of acculturation and socioeconomic mobility in young adulthood. *Ethnic and Racial Studies* 33 (7), 1168–1193. doi:10.1080/01419871003624076

Weinstein, J. and Ferwerda, J. (2018) Trump has undercut U.S. refugee resettlement. Here's one way to restore it. *Foreign Policy*, 12 February. See https://foreignpolicy.com/2018/02/12/trump-has-undercut-u-s-refugee-resettlement-heres-one-way-to-restore-it/.

Wenger, K.J., Lubbes, T., Lazo, M., Azcarraga, I., Sharp, S. and Ernst-Slavit, G. (2004) Hidden teachers, invisible students: Lessons learned from exemplary bilingual paraprofessionals in secondary schools. *Teacher Education Quarterly* 31 (2), 89–111.

Wiley, T.G. (2007) Accessing language rights in education: A brief history of the U.S. context. In O. García and C. Baker (eds) *Bilingual Education: An Introductory Reader* (pp. 89–107). Clevedon: Multilingual Matters.

Williams, A. and Emamdjomeh, A. (2018) America is more diverse than ever – but still segregated. *Washington Post*, 2 May. See https://www.washingtonpost.com/graphics/2018/national/segregation-us-cities/.

Williams, C.P. (2015) Investing in immigrants in Minnesota & the Midwest. *New America*, 19 March. See https://www.newamerica.org/education-policy/edcentral/midwesternimmigrants/.

Wolcott, H.F. (2001) *Writing Up Qualitative Research* (2nd edn). Thousand Oaks, CA: Sage.

Woods, D. (2017) *Transana v3.21*. Madison, WI: Spurgeon Woods. See https://www.transana.com.

Woolard, K.A. and Schieffelin, B.B. (1994) Language ideology. *Annual Review of Anthropology* 23, 55–82.

Wortham, S. (2001) Language ideology and educational research. *Linguistics and Education* 12 (3), 253–259.

Wortham, S. and Reyes, A. (2015) *Discourse Analysis Beyond the Speech Event*. Abingdon: Routledge.

Yi, Y. and Angay-Crowder, T. (2016) Multimodal pedagogies for teacher education in TESOL. *TESOL Quarterly* 50 (4), 988–998. doi:10.1002/tesq.326

Yip, J. (2013) The challenge of graduating on time for newcomer immigrant youth in New York City high schools. *Theory, Research, and Action in Urban Education* II (1). See http://traue.commons.gc.cuny.edu/issue-2-fall-2013/yip/.

Yosso, T.J. (2005) Whose culture has capital? A critical race theory discussion of community cultural wealth. *Race Ethnicity and Education* 8 (1), 69–91. doi:10.1080/1361332052000341006

Index

Assessments
  American Institution of Research (AIR) 89, 145
  Dominie 7, 88–89, 105, 109, 118, 136–139, 146, 150, 170
  Home Language 79, 89–90, 122, 136, 150–151
  Measures of Academic Progress (MAP) 87, 89, 118, 135–137, 139, 145,
  Ohio English Language Proficiency Assessment (OELPA) 87, 89, 136–137, 145
  Ohio Graduation Test (OGT) 51, 89

Dimensions of linguistic repertoire
  Individual, social, multimodal 21, 77–78, 176–177
Donald Trump 8, 17, 99–100, 141, 159–162

Immigration in popular media
  New York Times 16
  USA Today 15
  Washington Post 16

Key curricula and learning websites:
  BrainPOP 86–87, 106
  Flowcabulary 84–85
  Raz-kids 84–86, 105–107
  SIOP Model 65
  ST Math 84–85, 105
  Words Their Way 65, 85–86, 105, 108, 120
Key scholars and institutions
  Agar 1, 14, 103, 120, 164
  Blommaert 15, 18, 21, 26, 45, 57, 96, 168, 174
  Bourdieu 25–26, 34
  Fine *et al*. and Internationals Network for Public Schools 42–43

Flores 57, 158
Fry and Pew Research Center 5, 31, 36, 38
García 4, 11–13, 19–21, 28, 30, 42–43, 45, 93, 163, 169, 182
Lewis and Gray 28
Orellana 8, 14, 21, 21–22, 84, 86
Piketty 22, 38
Plonsky and Oswald 139–140
Sensoy and DiAngelo 26
Short, Boyson and Center for Applied Linguistics 6, 31–32, 36–37, 39–41, 65, 101–102, 149, 169
Sierens and van Avermaet 7
Silver 39, 141
Suárez-Orozco *et al*. 36–37, 44, 134
Vertovec 3, 12, 14–18, 21, 35
Key theoretical framings
  Bi/multilingualism 19–20, 22, 24, 28, 30, 55
  Capital 34, 41
  Comprehensible input 65, 109
  Cultural-historical 22
  Effect size 139
  English-centricity 3–4, 9, 24, 46, 52, 62, 63, 67, 78, 84, 86, 90–92, 110, 125, 121, 133–135, 146, 149, 151, 156, 158–159, 162–163
  Languaculture 1, 3–5, 9, 14, 17, 28–29, 43, 45–46, 48, 53–56, 58, 60, 63–65, 67, 71–71, 74, 76–78, 80, 84–86, 91–92, 97–98, 101, 104, 120, 125, 134, 143, 146, 148, 150, 152–153, 158, 162, 166, 168, 171–172, 176
  Limited English Proficient and pre-functional as deficit approach to learners 3, 33, 45, 87, 108, 133, 146, 148, 155–156
  Mainstream 18, 23–27, 30–34, 38, 41, 43, 45–47, 51, 64, 131, 143–145, 154, 158, 162–163

Probability 38–39, 87, 141
Segmented assimilation 34, 44
Sexuality 97, 112, 120
Students with Limited or Interrupted Formal Education (SLIFE) 31, 33, 37–38, 135, 146–149, 151
Superdiversity 7, 9, 14–18, 22–23, 27, 31, 43, 45, 55–56, 92–93, 98, 101, 103, 118, 133, 151, 157–159, 162, 166, 176, 182
  mobility, complexity, and unpredictability 15, 18, 22, 96
Symbolic violence 23, 26–27, 45
Trajectories 3, 9, 34–37, 47, 63–64, 91, 108–110, 118, 125, 140, 142–144, 162, 168, 173, 180
Translanguaging 8, 18, 20–23, 27, 29–30, 35, 42–43, 45, 55, 64, 67, 118–120, 133, 151, 158–159, 162–163, 176, 182
  Translanguaging methodology 176
  Translanguaging pedagogy 30, 151, 158–159, 182
Whiteness and White privilege 25

Metaphors
  Calligraphic 3, 92, 142, 163
  Fish 25, 32
Micropolitics 89, 153

National educational policy
  No Child Left Behind 40, 45, 87
  Every Student Succeeds Act 50, 87

Ohio Department of Education 29, 45–46, 50, 133
Other US States
  Texas 15, 29
  Florida 15–16, 29
  New York 15, 29
  Minnesota 29, 42, 157
  California 12, 15, 29, 39–40, 53
  Arizona 29, 40
  Massachusetts 12, 29, 40

Profiles of administrators
  Mr Smith 5, 36, 38–39, 47, 49–53, 56, 87, 103–104, 108, 123, 135, 139–140, 144–145, 148, 154–156, 162, 175
  Ms Johnston 47, 49–50, 52, 62–64, 84, 134–135, 139, 143, 153
  Ms Lincoln 47, 49, 51–52, 103, 124–127, 132, 135, 145–146, 151, 153–154
  Ms Sharp 16–17, 47–49, 53, 55, 88, 90, 101, 156
Profiles of bilingual assistants
  Mr Adisa 49, 62
  Mr Dahal 49, 108, 131, 144, 171
  Ms Abadi 49, 123–125, 135, 151, 154
  Ms Grey 49, 69–71, 74–78, 85, 146, 171
  Ms Ilich 49, 54–55
  Ms Lee 49, 88, 146–147
  Ms Som 115–116, 118
Profiles of counselors
  Mr Samuelson 17, 49, 56
  Ms Fey 153
Profiles of students
  Abdullah 94, 99–101, 117, 119, 122, 137, 142, 150–151
  Amal 78, 94, 137
  Beatriz 94, 101–111–112, 114–118, 124, 127, 130, 134, 136–137, 141, 150, 177
  Belvie 95, 119–120, 132–133, 138, 152
  Dhan 82–83, 94, 99–101, 120, 122, 128, 137, 150
  Fatima 81–82, 94, 137
  Gabriela 82, 94, 97, 101, 111–118, 124, 127, 134, 137, 150, 177
  Gloire 95, 11, 138, 152, 176
  Hajar 95, 87, 121, 127, 131–133, 138, 151
  Hayat 94, 120, 132–133, 138, 150
  Jhuma 95, 97–98, 111, 120, 128, 138, 161
  Maria 76–79, 82, 94–95, 111–115, 127, 129, 137, 139, 142, 145, 150, 176
  Mateo 68–69, 72, 95, 103, 121, 127–132, 138, 142, 145, 177
  Mohammed 81–82, 90, 97–98, 104, 111–117, 161, 176
  Omar 73–74, 83, 86, 94, 103–110, 115–120, 124, 132, 137, 150, 161
  Puspa 82, 86, 94, 97–98, 120, 137, 150

Profiles of students (*Continued*)
  Salah 73, 78, 90, 94, 121–127, 131–132, 134–135, 137, 142, 144, 150
  Tara 77–78, 83, 94, 137, 150
  Yadu 95, 136, 138, 161
  Zahra 95, 133, 138, 142
Profiles of teachers
  Mr Barre 7, 47, 49, 53, 67–68, 72, 74, 85, 104–105, 107, 110, 114, 116, 119–120, 128, 131, 153, 161, 171
  Mr Shahiya 7 47, 49, 61, 67, 72–74, 85–86, 107, 116, 119, 122, 153, 171, 177
  Ms Cabot 5–7, 23, 47–50, 53, 56, 65, 67, 71, 77, 85–86, 97, 99, 101, 103–108, 113–114, 120, 122, 125, 132, 136–137, 140, 142, 145–148, 151, 160, 171, 175, 177
  Ms Popov 7, 47, 49, 53, 67–69, 72, 74, 78–85, 88–89, 106–107, 113, 128, 130, 136–137, 141, 145, 153, 171, 177

Reading clinic 7, 48–49, 53, 64, 67, 69, 75, 88–89, 105–106, 108, 115, 117–118, 124, 131, 139, 142, 145–146, 150, 170–171, 177
Reading lists
  Fry 75, 85, 106
  Dolch 85
Refugee resettlement 5, 34, 77, 149, 161–162

Seal of biliteracy 27
Supreme Court decisions:
  Lau v Nichols 12, 46
  Castañeda v Pickard 13
Suspensions 123–127, 132–133, 159

Teacher talk
  Curtailing 67–68, 71, 84
  Supportive 64–65, 67–68, 71–72, 84–85, 91

Undocumented or unauthorized status 35, 98, 112, 161

For Product Safety Concerns and Information please contact our EU Authorised Representative:

Easy Access System Europe

Mustamäe tee 50

10621 Tallinn

Estonia

gpsr.requests@easproject.com